CW00663966

WELSH SOLDIERS, CIVILIANS AND EISTEDDFODAU IN WW1

To: Mike,

Your daughter-in-law Hillary thought of you and asked me to sign this book.

Robert H. Griffiths.

December 2016.

Welsh Soldiers, Civilians and Eisteddfodau in WW1

Robert H. Griffiths

First published in 2015

© Robert H. Griffiths

© Llygad Gwalch 2015

All rights reserved. No part of this publication
may be reproduced, stored in a retrieval system,
or transmitted in any form or by any means, electronic,
electrostatic, magnetic tape, mechanical, photocopying,
recording, or otherwise, without prior permission
of the authors of the works herein.

ISBN: 978-1-84524-239-8

Cover design: Eleri Owen

Published by Gwasg Carreg Gwalch,
12 Iard yr Orsaf, Llanrwst, Wales LL26 0EH
tel: 01492 642031
fax: 01492 641502
email: books@carreg-gwalch.com
website: www.carreg-gwalch.com

To my wonderful sister-in-law, Mair Eluned Morris of Penygroes, near Caernarfon, who sadly passed away on Sunday, 28th September 2014, aged sixty. She was a great inspiration to all who had the privilege to have known her. Mair who was born in Henllan, near Denbigh, is greatly missed by her loving family and many friends, and she shall truly be in our hearts forever.

AND

To my late, dear mother-in-law, Margaret Eluned Jones, known as Eluned, whom I called 'Mam', of Henllan, near Denbigh, Denbighshire. She died on 25th February 1995, aged sixty-five. She was born Margaret Eluned Owen at Llansannan, then in Denbighshire, and she will never be forgotten. Eluned loved to attend Welsh National Eisteddfodau and enjoyed the Welsh art of the writing of *englynion* (classical Welsh strict meter verses).

Contents

Introduction

This book is about Wales in the First World War, with the emphasis on the northern part of the country. North Wales may not have suffered from Zeppelin raids or from the shells and explosions of trench warfare, but in all other aspects of the war, it was as involved and as deeply affected as the rest of Europe.

Throughout the country, unremitting weekly lists in the newspapers of the dead, the wounded or the missing in action on the Western Front (France & Flanders), the Dardanelles and beyond had to be contended with. Men were lost forever in the war, from so many small close-knit communities. If they were not actually related, they were the local postman, policeman, shopkeeper, farm labourer, or co-workers, co-worshippers in the same chapel, or co-players in the same football or rugby team.

North Wales had combatants and victims in all of the First World War's major battlefield conflagrations, and the losses at sea.

There were a number of munitions-making factories in the region, with ones at Queensferry and Wrexham being major concerns.

Kinmel Park, Bodelwyddan (near Rhyl) was the largest military training camp in Wales, and indeed one of the biggest in the whole of Britain. It was built from scratch on former lush parkland, having its own specially constructed railway that ran into and through the camp – the Kinmel Camp Railway (the KCR).

North Wales had a German Officer, and a number of German other ranks, prisoner of war camps.

'Aliens', mainly Germans and Austrians living in Wales, many with British spouses and some having British born children, found themselves in First World War Britain to be perceived as 'the enemy within'. Racist hatred was encouraged by the war propaganda machines of all of the belligerent nations including Britain, through newspapers, poster campaigns and the issue of postcards. One such 'alien', a German born hairdresser, his Welsh born wife and their two young children, were the targets of a serious anti-German riot that took place at Rhyl, in late May, 1915.

The Welsh National Eisteddfod, the great Welsh cultural festival struggled during the war years. The 1914 National Eisteddfod was cancelled and in the following year the National Eisteddfod did take place at Bangor, but under great difficulties and required herculean efforts from all concerned to ensure that it was held at all. Then there was the 'Hedd Wyn, Black Chair Eisteddfod' as it was called – the 1917 Birkenhead National Eisteddfod.

Many sets of brothers fought in the First World War, included in this book are three such sets – the Jones-Bateman brothers of Ruthin, the Skillicorn brothers from Llanrwst and the Valentine brothers from Llanddulas. No family's experience of the First World War was exactly the same.

But not everyone during the war was pulling in the same direction – one Henry Alexander Chamberlain was testament to that, for he took advantage of the turmoil of wartime to exploit others for his own benefit.

You also sadly did not have to be at the front or in a military establishment to be blown up by a shell, as two families at the Moss, near Wrexham, found to their terrible cost in 1916.

North Wales also provided something else, or rather someone else, to greatly aid the 'British War Effort'. A man I proffer who was as important to Britain in the First World

War as Winston Churchill was in the Second, but receives today little or no credit for it – David Lloyd George, born on 17 January 1863, at Chorlton-on-Medlock, Manchester, to two Welsh born and Welsh speaking parents, William and Elizabeth George. On the death of William George in June of 1864, his widow Elizabeth went to live with her children, including one year old David, back in her native Llanystumdwy, near Cricieth, North Wales. Here they all lived at Tŷ Newydd, Llanystumdwy, with her brother Richard Lloyd, a shoemaker and Baptist minister. David Lloyd George was raised as a Welsh-speaker and was mentored by his uncle, Richard Lloyd. David Lloyd George came from the Welsh radical non-conformist tradition and became a solicitor, but his true forte was that he was a brilliant, forceful, captivating, mesmerising orator in both the Welsh and English languages.

Whilst Winston Churchill became Prime Minister in May of 1940, replacing Neville Chamberlain, who was no wartime leader, twenty-four years earlier, Lloyd George had at a most critical time of the First World War, early December 1916, become Prime Minister replacing Herbert Asquith, who was also no wartime leader.

Lloyd George and Churchill, very able and shrewd politicians, led wartime coalition governments, both being able to do so when others would have failed miserably in the task, for they were also pragmatists and realists.

Winston Churchill was a great student of history, particularly military history and benefitted greatly I believe from having the template of Lloyd George's term as a British wartime Prime Minister in the previous world war. Also, he had seen how Lloyd George 'manoeuvred' through the unfolding events of the First World War the powerful United States, to firstly 'quietly and unofficially' assist Britain against Germany, and then finally on 6 April 1917, abandon their 'phoney neutrality' by formally declaring war on Germany, and to come out fighting for Britain and its Allies – thereby tipping the balance in the war that had previously been a continuous, murderous stalemate.

Lloyd George in his endeavours as a wartime Prime Minister was not aided as Winston Churchill was by two great communications innovations that only arrived in the late 1920's – radio (wireless) broadcasts and newsreels with sound. These during the Second World War enabled Churchill to truly 'get his message across', time after time to the British nation and beyond, rather than what Lloyd George had to rely upon, namely his speeches to live audiences and the newspapers then reporting upon these speeches.

My own maternal side grandparents – Leonard Price of Broughton, near Wrexham, Denbighshire, was for a long period on active service on the Western Front during the First World War with 4th (Denbighshire) Battalion, the Royal Welch Fusiliers, a Pioneer Territorial Battalion, Regimental Number 201152, and, Margaret Alice Price (nee Ellis), also Broughton, near Wrexham born, in her late teens was a member of Queen Mary's Army Auxiliary Corps (QMAAC) in France, in 1918.

It is my intention in writing this book to honour their memory, and also to show the depth of involvement that Wales, and the northern region in particular, had in this first global, highly industrialised, and mechanised slaughter that was the First World War.

Robert H. Griffiths
Denbigh, October 2015

1

The Jones-Bateman Family – controversial, heroic and ultimately tragic

This is the story of the Jones-Bateman family of Eyarth, Llanfair Dyffryn Clwyd, near Ruthin and of Pentre Mawr, Abergele. Through one of their sons they became very closely linked to Robert Graves the renowned WW1 poet and author, and through another son to 'Coch Bach y Bala', a rogue who was in constant trouble with the law and whose real name was John Jones.

The privileged Jones-Bateman family between the years of 1913 and 1918, can certainly said to be three things – controversial, heroic and ultimately tragic. This Jones-Bateman family gained great notoriety between the years of 1913 and 1918, with them being closely linked with allegations of murder, suspicious deaths and military controversy.

Herbert Burleton Jones-Bateman was born on 4 May 1853 at Solihull, Warwickshire. He was from a minor landed gentry family, and on 11 October 1887, at Henllan Church, Henllan, near Denbigh, Denbighshire, he married Evelyn Heaton, born in 1864, who was also from a similar background of affluence, and whose father was Reverend Hugh Edward Heaton of Plas Heaton, Henllan (some records have it as Trefnant), near Denbigh. Herbert, the son of a well regarded clergyman was educated at Marlborough College and entered the civil service. It was from 16 October 1876, that he took up his first civil service post in India. By 1891, he is described as being a joint magistrate in the Bengal Civil Service. Then in 1892, he had reached the level of a District and Sessions Judge. His wife Evelyn was with him the majority of his service in India, and all four of their children were born in India. In 1904, he retired and moved back with his family to Britain, first settling on the Welsh-English border.

The 1911 Census shows Herbert now aged fifty-seven, being a Pensioner – Indian Civil Service, residing with wife Evelyn and daughter Beatrice at the large property known as Broadway House, Broadway, Churchstoke, Montgomeryshire (now Powys). Broadway House then was described as being a 'Regency Style Gentleman's Residence' with about twenty-six acres of gardens and woodlands. Through wealth creation, astute marriages and the deaths of prosperous relatives, this branch of the Jones-Bateman family found themselves the owners of properties and land at Eyarth House, Llanfair Dyffryn Clwyd, near Ruthin, and Pentre Mawr, Abergele. Their three sons, Llewelyn, known by the family as 'Ll', was born at Azamgarh, India, on 28 January 1889; Reginald, known as 'Rex', was born at Mussoorie, India, on 23 April 1894 (some records show incorrectly 1892), and Francis, known as 'Frank', was born in the North West Provinces, India, in 1896. These three sons all were born and brought up as children in 'British Raj controlled India' and had a true British Colonial upbringing, which may account for some of their later conduct and attitude to life – both good and bad! They were most certainly used to having servants, with the vast majority of the people they came into contact with in India having to be totally subservient to them.

It was known that the Jones-Bateman family at Eyarth House, near Ruthin, as property and landowners were not popular with many of their tenants. Then again, that was and still is I suggest, not an unusual occurrence. However, great controversy and notoriety hit the family in 1913. A local character known as 'Coch Bach y Bala' who was also

Coch Bach y Bala (John Jones) police photos taken in his latter years

The burial of 'Coch Bach y Bala' following the funeral service

The grave at Llanelidan of 'Coch Bach y Bala'

known as 'Little Turpin' and as 'The Little Welsh Terror' was something of a Robin Hood type folk hero to many local people, despite him in reality being an habitual criminal – thieving and poaching high on his long criminal record, though burglary being one of his favoured crimes. 'Coch Bach y Bala' (in English: 'Little Redhead of Bala') was born in 1852, at Llanor, near Bala, so he really should have been called 'Coch Bach y Llanor', which he was back in the 1880's and 1890's, when he first attracted notoriety for his criminal behaviour and his ability to escape from prison cells.

'Coch Bach y Bala', John Jones, was by 1913, now aged sixty-one, and for some time had been living when not in prison rather like a tramp. In his younger days to escape recapture he had quite ably passed himself off as a well-to-do citizen, but those days had gone. Always a great self-publicist, he often let himself down by publicly bragging of his criminal exploits, some of which he had actually made up and ended up in prison as a result. He had spent much of his life in prison, but he had one other specialty, the ability to escape from police and prison custody, which earned him a further nickname, that of 'The Welsh Houdini.' He had served time in a number of prisons including Caernarfon, Chester and the especially bleak, Dartmoor Prison.

On Tuesday, 30 September 1913, 'Coch Bach y Bala', John Jones, had effected his escape from Ruthin Gaol (today it is the site of The Ruthin Gaol Visitor Centre and The Denbighshire Records and Archives Office) in what *The North Wales Times* newspaper edition of later that week described as being in *'a sensational manner'*. He was there only temporarily, waiting to be taken to Stafford Gaol to serve his three year sentence for a burglary at the Bala office of the solicitor, Mr Jordan. Reportedly, he had effected his amazing escape from his cell in Ruthin Gaol between 4.00 a.m. and 5.00 a.m., before the warders carried out their morning duties. The prison authorities and the local police were said to have been baffled as to how he had escaped, and amazed how quickly he had managed to disappear. However, after having lived rough for some four days in the Ruthin area, he was found on Saturday, 4 October 1913, on land near Nantclwyd Isaf, by nineteen year old Reginald (Rex) Jones-Bateman, who was said to have been out hunting partridges in the area with a shotgun, accompanying his father. Other accounts given at the time, point to father and son actually being out with shotguns searching for the escaped convict. There is no doubt that 'Coch Bach y Bala' when found was weary and dishevelled, wearing but underpants, a stolen black coat and some sacking as his only clothing. He allegedly reeked of methylated spirits, colloquially called meths, and was apparently so hungry that he was reduced to eating three tallow (sheep fat) candles. Reginald Jones-Bateman proceeded to shoot 'Coch Bach y Bala' in the leg, just below the knee, with the double-barrelled shotgun he was out 'hunting partridges' with. 'Coch Bach y Bala', John Jones, died shortly afterwards, rapidly bleeding to death from the double gunshot wound he had received.

'Coch Bach y Bala', John Jones, having been shot and killed on Saturday, 4 October 1913, his body was formally identified later the same day, whilst lying in the mortuary at the Ruthin Workhouse, by the Governor of Ruthin Gaol. The Coroner's Inquest with a Jury took place two days later, on Monday, 6 October 1913, at the Ruthin Workhouse, Ruthin, Denbighshire. The Coroner was Mr Robert Davies, the Coroner for West Denbighshire. The *Manchester Courier* edition of Tuesday, 7 October 1913, covered the Inquest that had taken place the previous day:

CONVICT SHOT
INQUEST VERDICT OF MANSLAUGHTER
('FIRED IN FRIGHT')
After a protracted enquiry which did not conclude until ten minutes past eleven last night, a Coroner's Jury at Ruthin returned a verdict of Manslaughter against Reginald Jones-Bateman, a young man of Eyarth Hall, in connection with the death of John Jones, alias Little Turpin of Bala, who escaped from Ruthin Gaol on September 30th, and was fatally shot on Saturday.

The prison governor said he considered Jones a very dangerous criminal. He was sentenced last July to three years' penal servitude for breaking into a solicitor's office at Bala, and had served many terms of penal servitude. Witness added that search parties were not authorised to fire at an escaped convict unless life was in danger, or to prevent him getting away. An officer would be justified in shooting as a last resort.

Mrs Mary Elizabeth Jones said she saw the deceased walking along the railway line on Saturday morning. He shouted an offensive remark to her. Later she saw him again, when he pulled out a screw wrench and said, 'I will kill you'.

Replacing the screw wrench, he advanced towards her with a stick.

A young man, Mr Jones-Bateman of Eyarth Hall, came up, and the convict struck him in the mouth with the stick. Then he took out the screw wrench and attempted to hit Jones-Bateman on the head. In witness' opinion, he had the impression that the convict was handling a revolver. The young man stepped back, holding his gun downwards, and then fired in fright, without taking aim. Jones was shot in the knee, witness said she was certain it was an accident, and that Jones-Bateman fired while in a terrified state.

The *Western Gazette* of Friday, 10 October 1913, like many other newspapers also reported upon this Inquest and included some different details:

MANSLAUGHTER VERDICT AGAINST OXFORD UNDERGRADUATE

Jones escaped last Tuesday from Ruthin Prison, Denbighshire, where he was undergoing a sentence of three years' penal servitude for burglary at Bala. He had cut his way through a wall 30 inches thick, and by means of a rope made of his bedclothes, managed to drop 24 feet into the yard beneath, where he scaled the wall and got clean away. On Friday afternoon the runaway was reported in a wood on the estate of Edward Naylor-Leyland, and a cordon was drawn around the place. In spite of the search, Jones the same evening broke into a dairy of an adjoining farm and was discovered by the farmer Mr Edward Jones, taking refreshment. The convict got away, and all Friday night the police kept watch on the wood.

On Saturday the search was vigorously renewed. Towards eleven o'clock a boy reported that the convict was at Graigadwywynt, near Eyarth, and later he was encountered by Mr R. J.-Bateman who was going out shooting partridges. The convict's legs were wrapped in some sacking, and he was wearing a boys cap. The sportsman called on him to stop and surrender, but he refused, and as the convict assumed a threatening attitude Mr Bateman fired, wounding the man below the knee, and he died from loss of blood before the police had been informed of his whereabouts and could reach the scene.

The body on which was found a chisel, a pound of lump sugar, a bottle of methylated spirits, some candles, and socks, was removed to Ruthin mortuary to await the Inquest.

THE CORONER'S ENQUIRY
A VERDICT OF MANSLAUGHTER AGAINST MR BATEMAN

This report went on to state that young Reginald Jones-Bateman had been out shooting with his father, when they were told that the convict had just passed, and the father went off to inform the police of this. Reginald who 'was accompanying his father as a beater' spotted the escaped convict Jones and then a stand off ensued. The convict John Jones it would appear, even from the evidence of Reginald Jones-Bateman himself at this Inquest, was trying to leave the scene and make off into the nearby wood. Reginald

Jones-Bateman said he fired out of fear, and not to try to prevent the convict's escape, and had spent over half-an-hour before trying to prevent his escape.

A number of things do not add up here. Reginald Jones-Bateman may have been but nineteen, but he was carrying and pointing a double barrelled shotgun at the old, dishevelled John Jones, who despite wearing 'next to nothing' was allegedly able to conceal all sorts of weapons about his person. Reginald Jones-Bateman would appear to have thought himself as 'the law' and was not under any circumstances going to let John Jones escape 'his custody'.

The article continued:

In his summing-up, the Coroner pointed out that every person was in duty, bound to arrest a felon, and should use every justifiable means to do so. The point was whether there was any necessity to resort to shooting, either to effect the apprehension of the man, or to prevent his escape, or otherwise to prevent the destruction of the person firing the shot. If they said there was no necessity to fire, then that would be a verdict of manslaughter.

The Jury's verdict was received with loud cheers by a large crowd outside the court.

Bateman was afterwards brought before the Ruthin Magistrates and remanded to the usual Petty Sessions next Monday. Bail was allowed, his father, who is a well known county resident, being accepted as his surety.

The 'large crowd outside the court' at Ruthin (the Ruthin Workhouse), who had cheered the Inquest Jury's verdict of manslaughter were jubilant. These people would have been local, working class men and women, who with what they had learnt from a combination of the newspapers and gossip, were not prepared to accept that the shooting and killing of John Jones, 'Coch Bach y Bala' was accidental, nor even manslaughter, but cold blooded murder! Dead men cannot of course give evidence in any Inquest or in any Court, so the only versions of events ever presented were highly prejudiced ones due to the class, wealth, and influence of the Jones-Bateman family.

The Inquest Jury had deliberated long, over seventy minutes, and had decided that there was a case to answer, and that the shooting and killing of the convict was not accidental, nor was it in their eyes murder, but manslaughter.

The *Flintshire Observer* of Thursday, 9 October 1913, had this on the aftermath of the Inquest:

A CROWD'S DEMONSTRATION
A large crowd of people who had assembled outside the Workhouse greeted the verdict with ringing cheers, and they followed Mr Jones-Bateman and jeered at him as he was proceeding to the police court, where he was charged formally with manslaughter.

He was remanded on bail till next Monday.

The case now became something of a sensation, and newspapers far and wide, including overseas – the United States, Australia and New Zealand reported upon it, especially the court hearing held the following week.

During the days following the Inquest, some demonstrations took place locally demanding that Reginald Jones-Bateman be tried for murder!

The *Flintshire Observer* of 16 October 1913 had this account of the police court hearing:

SHOOTING OF 'LITTLE TURPIN'
HEARING OF MANSLAUGHTER CHARGE AT RUTHIN
ACCUSED ACQUITTED

A sequel to the sensational escape from Ruthin Prison of John Jones, alias 'Coch Bach y Bala', was heard at Ruthin Police Court on Monday, before Mr G. H. Denton, and a full bench, when Reginald Jones-Bateman, 19, the son of Mr Jones-Bateman, of Eyarth House, was brought up on a charge of manslaughter.

Great interest was taken in the proceedings, and the Court was crowded.

It will be remembered that 'Little Turpin' made a sensational escape from Ruthin Gaol on the 30th ult. By boring through a wall 2ft. 6in. thick, and getting to the outer walls of the prison by means of a rope made out of bedclothes. He was at liberty four days, and was shot by young Bateman in the Nantclwyd Woods.

The defendant is the son of an ex-Indian Judge, and a descendant of one of the oldest Welsh families. He recently won a £200 scholarship to Oxford from Rugby, where he was top boy of his year.

Mr Garth Jones appeared for the prosecution and Mr Gamlin for the defence.

A DANGEROUS CRIMINAL

The Governor of the Gaol gave evidence to the effect that the convict was 61 years of age and had spent most of his life in gaol, and was considered a very dangerous criminal. He went on to describe the state of the convict, whom he found shot in Nantclwyd Woods. His feet and legs were covered with sacking, and he wore a black coat which had been stolen.

Cross-examined, witness said Little Turpin had been sentenced altogether to 49 years' imprisonment, including six sentences of penal servitude for housebreaking, burglary, stealing money, wounding with intent, and office breaking. In 1891, he made a violent attack upon the prison warders, and in the same year made two attempts to escape from prison. For the attack on the warders his sentence was increased from five to seven years.

Instructions were given to the officers and police to use the utmost precaution in recapturing the convict owing to his desperate character, and because he would violently resist recapture.

Asked if he would have shot the convict under similar circumstances, witness said he was not prepared to answer. The warders sent out to chase the man were not armed.

CONVICT'S THREAT

Mary Elizabeth Jones, Beehive Cottage, Pwllglas, who first saw the convict coming along the railway line near her cottage, said the convict threatened to kill her and the young gentleman, when they followed him in the direction of the woods. Bateman asked the convict in a responsible manner to go down to the main road, whereupon the convict refused and struck the young man across the mouth with a stick. The convict afterwards tried to give Bateman a blow with a monkey wrench, but just missing, owing to accused ducking. She believed that Bateman shot at the convict in his fright. The convict was in the act of striking Bateman when the shot was fired. She could not say whether Bateman took deliberate aim or not. Mrs Jones continuing her evidence said they did not go to the convict's aid when he was shot, because they were afraid he was shamming.

LEFT TO DIE

Mr Garth Jones: And he was left to die?
Witness: Yes.

But you knew that he was shot?

Witness: Yes.

Mrs Hughes and David Jones, who were present when the convict was shot, gave corroborative evidence, and stated that they were all afraid to go to the convict's assistance after he had been shot.

In cross-examination, David Jones said he was of the opinion that accused deliberately aimed at the convict's feet. The whole incident took no more than half-a-minute.

Superintendent Woollam proved the arrest of the accused on the coroner's warrant, and said he charged him with manslaughter, to which he made no reply.

In cross-examination witness corroborated the prison governor's evidence as to the convict's dangerous character.

Dr J. Medwyn Hughes described the deceased's injuries, and ascribed death to shock, followed by haemorrhage.

ACCUSED ACQUITTED

The Chief Constable said he had communicated with the Public Prosecutor, who after taking the direction of the Attorney General, had intimated that he did not propose to intervene in the case. The Public Prosecutor's communication continued:

'I may add that on the facts at present before me, where I to undertake prosecution of the case, I should only do so as for the purpose of suggesting that this was not a case in which they ought to commit the accused for trial'.

The solicitor for the defence said the accused, under the circumstances, had acted most courageously, and was justified in shooting.

The defendant was not called, and the Bench, after retiring said they had decided in view of the evidence and the letter of the Public Prosecutor, that a prima facie case had not been made out, and the accused would therefore be discharged.

There was an attempt at cheering when the decision was announced, but the outburst was at once suppressed.

How swiftly the wheels of justice can turn, especially if oiled by a chief constable, in this 'case' of the young, well-heeled toff, versus the dead, nasty old convict. I question not so much the outcome, but rather the speed with which it was achieved. Shot and killed on Saturday, 4 October 1913, the Inquest held on Monday, 6 October 1913, and the police court hearing on Monday, 13 October 1913 – all nicely 'done and dusted' in nine days, including two weekends, even with the involvement of the Public Prosecutor, and that of the Attorney General. Indeed, all nicely and conveniently sorted out some three days before 'the victim' was even buried and just in time for Reginald Jones-Bateman to take up his scholarship at Oxford!

So, to the chagrin of many local people, particularly of the working class, Reginald Jones-Bateman had been acquitted on the day of his court hearing, with the prosecution declining to proceed with the case, and Reginald Jones-Bateman himself not being even called to give evidence, as he had done at the Coroner's Inquest seven days earlier.

It was said that the Chief Constable, Edward Jones, had turned up at the court hearing not to give any evidence in the case, but to appear if required as a character witness for Reginald Jones-Bateman. If true, then the fact that the Chief Constable had been the one who had communicated with the Public Prosecutor, the result of which was the acquittal, then the whole thing stank, and natural justice had not prevailed. If however not true, which is perhaps likely, then it only serves to show the feeling of animosity by many local, working class people against Reginald Jones-Bateman, his family, the police and the prevailing judicial system itself. To many, this was a case of the rich, well connected and powerful, literally getting off scot free with murder! This remember was a time when you could still go to prison for trapping or shooting (poaching) a rabbit or the like on the land of a wealthy landowner.

Postcards of John Jones', alias 'Coch Bach y Bala's' well attended funeral held at Llanelidan, near Ruthin, on Thursday, 16 October 1913, and of the exact spot where he was shot and killed, were sold to the public. John Jones was buried in St Elidan's Churchyard, Llanelidan, near Ruthin, and his grave may be seen there today.

An account of the court hearing at Ruthin also appeared in the Tuesday, 14 October 1913 edition of the *Exeter and Plymouth Gazette*. It included most of the same details that other such newspaper reports had, but with one or two additions:

Mr Gamlin, for the defence said, that in the circumstances he would ask the bench to come to the conclusion that there was no prima facie case to be sent for trial. The defendant bore a splendid character as a public schoolboy, and, under the circumstances had acted most courageously, and was justified in shooting. He (the speaker) protested most strongly against the disgraceful conduct of the riff-raff of Ruthin in jeering at the defendant when he was committed on the Coroner's warrant. Instead of that, they should have cheered him for his courageous act.

The witnesses who gave evidence, particularly the Ruthin Gaol Governor, Charles William Hunt and Superintendent

Woollam had painted a picture of John Jones as a monstrous figure, but of course there was no one to speak up for the 'victim'. The extra two years imprisonment John Jones had received back in 1891 was due, according to the Ruthin Gaol Governor: 'that he made a violent attack upon two prison warders', which was not in fact the case. A few prisoners threw some rocks at two warders injuring them, but there was no evidence that John Jones was directly involved, nor was he accused of it at the time – that came later. Even his detractors stated that John Jones was of above average intelligence, and on a number of occasions over the years he had quite ably conducted his own defence in court, though it must be said, with little success.

Reginald Jones-Bateman and the rest of this Jones-Bateman family continued their lives as before, though there was a great deal of ongoing animosity against them by quite a number of the working class people in the Ruthin area and beyond, as John Jones, 'Coch Bach y Bala' was now becoming something of a legendary figure, his turbulent life and violent death surrounded by myth and half-truths – which is still the case today.

The First World War arrived, and the eldest son, **Llewelyn Jones-Bateman** became a Captain in 'A' Battery, the 103rd Brigade of The Royal Field Artillery (the RFA), having started out as a Second Lieutenant in the regular army after he had left Wellington College in January of 1910. Llewelyn had decided to be a career soldier, and his RFA battery was in the retreat from Mons in late August and early September of 1914, and then involved in the battles of the Aisne, Marne and Festubert. He was killed after suffering a shell wound when on one of his regular visits to the men of his battery at the Front. It was said that shortly before his death on

19 March 1916, his name had been submitted for him to be awarded the Military Cross. Llewelyn Jones-Bateman had been at the Front for the majority of the time since the war began in August of 1914. He was buried in Lapugnay Military Cemetery, Pas de Calais, France, Grave I.F.9. The Jones-Bateman family placed a memorial notice in *The Times* newspaper's In Memoriam section and it read: '*Jones-Bateman, Llewelyn; Captain, Royal Field Artillery – In Ever Loving and Proud Memory, Died of Wounds in France, 19th March 1916.*'

The CWGC headstone on the grave of Llewelyn Jones-Bateman

The *Liverpool Daily Post* of Saturday, 25 March 1916, reported upon the death of Captain Llewelyn Jones-Bateman:

DEATH OF CAPTAIN JONES-BATEMAN

The news has been received of the death of Captain Jones-Bateman, RFA, the eldest son of Mr and Mrs Jones-Bateman, of Eyarth and Pentre Mawr, Abergele. The deceased was educated at Lloyd's School, Winchfield, and Wellington College, and entered the Army in January 1910. His battery was at the retreat at Mons, and at the battles of the Aisne, Marne, and Festubert. He was wounded on the 14th, and his General writes as follows: 'I never wish to have a better officer under me, he was so keen, with all his heart in his work, and a very gallant fellow. Only the other day I submitted his name for the Military Cross as a reward for all his good work'. The deceased was well known in North Wales, and was a very capable and popular officer.

Some letters written by, and to, Captain Llewelyn Jones-Bateman during his time at the Front in France are held in The Denbighshire Records and Archives, Ruthin, and make interesting reading. The letters, a number of which he sent to 'Uncle W' – his mother's brother, Wilfred Heaton of Plas Heaton, Henllan, near Denbigh, a former soldier in the British Army himself. The letters are mostly mundane, everyday ones, but one of them is callous. Some extracts taken from these letters:

It was in a letter dated 13 February 1915 Captain Llewelyn Jones-Bateman gave his 'address' as being 39th Battery, 19th Brigade, Royal Field Artillery, 27th Division.

Another to 'Uncle W', dated 25 February 1915. 'Piou Piou' being the name often given to a French soldier at that time:

When they suddenly found a poor 'Piou Piou'. My servant had just gone for some water for me and a something & I saw the skull just in front of us, there are still about 10 to 15 Frenchmen lying out in between the trenches. They have been there for some months now. They say a lot depends on the wind in the front trench!

To 'Uncle W', dated 8 April 1915:

In this letter he thanked his Uncle W (Wilfred) for sending him a grand parcel of baccy & pipe. He also asks about a relative, 'Hugh ap Ernest' and then wrote in relation to brother Francis (Frank) Jones-Bateman: '*I think I should put Frank up to transferring to the Welsh Guards, as soon as I see him. Can you do anything in that line*'?

To 'Uncle W', dated 24 April 1915:

But it's a long way to Berlin yet, though I do believe we shall all be on the Rhine by July, at least some of us will!

This is the letter, another he sent to 'Uncle W' from the Front in France that has rather disturbing connotations, its content a little too candid, even from a serving soldier to an ex-soldier. C.M. being short for court martial:

I told you how they tie what must be deserters, or anyway convicted by C.M. to death, to trees just above their trenches during the night. So that we can waste our cartridges on them & save theirs.

Another trick of course is to send them out individually to cut our wire, if ever they are allowed, through sheer amazement on part of our perhaps recruits to get as far. Some of our battalions & even companies have evidently been similarly court-martialled by being sent out by themselves to do same job. It's not a trick to be copied, perhaps the Germans learnt it from us & thought it a good idea for deserters. We have given up the trick with battalions & companies.

Rather chilling content in the last letter, which seemed very matter of fact to Captain Llewelyn Jones-Bateman, no doubt jaded by the terrible realities of trench warfare. However, the British soldiers from 'some of our battalions &

even companies' he was referring to, were either old regular soldiers, or more likely volunteers, but not conscripts, for conscription did not come into existence until the following year. These soldiers he spoke of were also of course someone's husband, son, brother, etc. This short newspaper obituary of Captain Llewelyn Jones-Bateman appeared in the *North Wales Chronicle* of 31 March 1916:-

> Captain Jones-Bateman had been at the front from the beginning of the war. He was a gallant soldier, who had won the highest opinions of all who knew him, and none more than of the men who had the privilege of serving under him, of whom at all times he took the greatest care.

Without wishing to unfairly impune the apparent good character of a British soldier who lost his life in action, I cannot help but feel that the wording above absolutely conflicts with the content of 'the letter' to his Uncle Wilfred.

Whilst elder brother Llewelyn was dying of his wounds, **Francis Jones-Bateman** was himself lying in a hospital bed, having been there since September 1915, recovering from severe wounds received when rescuing a fallen comrade on I believe 25 September 1915, in the attack on St Elie, which was part of The Battle of Loos (25 September 1915 to 18 October 1915).

Francis was educated at Rugby School, Warwickshire, and then at Caius College, Cambridge. He rose to the rank of Captain in 3rd Battalion, the Royal Welch Fusiliers. The same service battalion in which my own grandfather, Private Leonard Price, had initially served.

When war broke out, Francis joined the Cambridge Officer Training Corps, and was gazetted to 3rd Battalion, the Royal Welch Fusiliers in October 1914. In April 1915, he was attached to 1st Battalion, the Royal Welch Fusiliers, with whom he went out to the Front in France. Whilst near to recovery from his severe wounds he was promoted to the rank of Captain. Upon leaving hospital he was on active service in England, a spell in Ireland and then returned to France, now with 13th Battalion, the Royal Welch Fusiliers. He subsequently returned to 3rd Battalion, the Royal Welch Fusiliers. Francis Jones-Bateman, known to friends and family as Frank was a good friend of the Great

The CWGC headstone on the grave of Francis (Frank) Jones-Bateman

War poet and writer, Robert (von Ranke) Graves who mentions Francis Jones-Bateman, whom he calls Frank by name on nine separate occasions in his iconic and somewhat controversial autobiographical book on the First World War – *Goodbye To All That.*

Extracts taken from *Goodbye To All That,* by Robert Graves:-

> ... The roadside cottages were now showing more and more signs of dilapidation. A German shell came over and then whoo-oo-oooooooOOO-bump-CRASH! Landed twenty yards short of us. We threw ourselves flat on our faces. Presently we heard a curious singing noise in the air, and then flop! flop! little pieces of shell casing

came buzzing down all around. 'They calls them the musical instruments', said the sergeant. 'Damn them', said my friend Frank Jones-Bateman, cut across the hand by a jagged little piece, 'the devils have started on me early'. 'Aye, they'll have a lot of fun with you before they're done, sir,' grinned the sergeant. Another shell came over. Everyone threw himself down again, but it burst two hundred yards behind us. Only Sergeant Jones had remained on his feet. 'You're wasting your strength, lads,' he said to the draft. 'Listen by the noise they make where they're going to burst.'

Page 93:

... Frank Jones-Bateman, a quiet boy of nineteen, came to visit me from the company on our right. He mentioned with a false ease that he had shot a German just before breakfast. 'Sights at four hundred', he said. He had just left Rugby with a scholarship waiting for him at Clare, Cambridge. His nickname was 'Silent Night'.

Page 95:

... May 23rd. We did company drill in the morning. Afterwards, Jones-Bateman and I lay on the warm grass and watched aeroplanes flying above the trenches pursued by a trail of white shrapnel puffs.

Page 108:

... At the end of July, Robertson, one of the other Royal Welch officers attached to the Welsh, and myself had orders to proceed to the Laventie sector. We were to report to the Second Battalion of the Royal Welch

Fusiliers. Frank Jones-Bateman and Hanmer Jones, two more of us, went to the First Battalion.

Page 108 into Page 109 – On chance encounters in France with the Prince of Wales:

… No other train ran until the next day; so we stopped the night at the Hotel de La France, in which the Prince of Wales, then a Lieutenant in the Fortieth Siege Battery, was billeted sometimes. We did not find him in. I had spoken to him once – in the public bath at Bethune, where he and I were the only bathers one morning.

Dressed in nothing at all, he graciously remarked how bloody cold the water was and I loyally assented that he was too bloody right. We were very pink and white and did exercises on the horizontal bar afterwards. I joked to Frank Jones-Bateman about it: 'I have just met our future King in a bath'. Frank said: 'I can trump that: two days ago I had a friendly talk with him in the ASC latrines.'

Page 146 – October 1915, looking back to The Battle of Loos:

… On October 3rd we were relieved by a composite battalion consisting of about a hundred men of the Second Warwickshire Regiment and about seventy Royal Welch Fusiliers – all that was left of our own First Battalion. Hanmer Jones and Frank Jones-Bateman had both been wounded. Frank had his thigh broken with a rifle bullet while stripping the equipment off a wounded man in No Man's Land; the cartridges in the man's pouches had been set on fire by a shot and were exploding.

He was recommended for a Victoria Cross, but got

nothing because no officer evidence, which is a condition of award, was available.

Page 179:

> ... I rejoined the Third Battalion at Litherland, near Liverpool, where it had been shifted from Wrexham as part of the Mersey defence force. The senior officers generously put no more work on me than I wished to undertake, and I met again three of my Wrexham contemporaries who had been severely wounded (all of them, by coincidence, in the left thigh) and seemed to be out of it for the rest of the war – Frank Jones-Bateman, and 'Father' Watkin, who had been in the Welsh Regiment with me, and Aubrey Attwater, the assistant adjutant, who had gone to the Second Battalion early in 1915, and had been badly hit when out on patrol.

As Captain and second in command of 13th Battalion, the Royal Welch Fusiliers, in late Autumn of 1918, Francis Jones-Bateman was in action at the Second Battle of Sambre –Oise Canal, the last Allied victory of the First World War. In the attack on the German trenches at Englefontaine, Captain Francis Jones-Bateman was killed in action on 4 November 1918, aged but twenty-two – just seven days before the Armistice on 11 November 1918. He was buried in the Cross Roads Cemetery, Fontaine-au-Bois, France, Grave Reference 111.D.22.

In *Goodbye To All That*, by Robert Graves, this appears on Page 246:

> ... In November came the Armistice. I heard at the same time of the deaths of Frank Jones-Bateman, who had

gone back again just before the end, and Wilfred Owen, who often used to send me poems from France.

Robert Graves in uniform

Robert Graves was still stationed at Kinmel Park Military Training Camp, North Wales, post-Armistice, when he sent a letter to 'My Dear Eddie', dated 28 November 1918, headed No. 16, O.C. Btn, Kinmel Park, Rhyl. In this letter to 'Eddie' who was Edward Howard Marsh (later to become Sir Edward Howard Marsh), a classical scholar, patron of the arts, translator and civil servant. As a civil servant he had worked as private secretary to a number of leading politicians including Winston Churchill. But more importantly for Robert Graves, Edward Marsh encouraged and edited poetry submitted to him that he regarded as worthy. Robert Graves wrote thanking 'Eddie' for his own pertinent criticisms of his work and also stated: '*I have never had but 3 good critics, you, Nancy & a certain young Captain named Jones Bateman, who after many months of warfare & a recommendation for the VC was killed with our 13 btn in the week of the armistice*'. High praise indeed from Robert Graves, for Francis (Frank) Jones-Bateman, who had not only been a great friend of his, but also someone he valued as a critic of his literary work.

In recent times the PBFA (Provincial Booksellers Fairs Association), international antiquarian booksellers, have had for sale by auction, two books inscribed by Robert Graves to

Francis (Frank) Jones-Bateman. One being a first edition of 'Goliath & David', which on the inside front cover Robert Graves had inscribed in ink: '*Silent Night from Robert Graves*'. With Graves' then home address (his parents' home) of '*1, Lauriston Road, Wimbledon*' also hand written added. The other was a second impression of Robert Graves', 'Over The Brazier', which he had again inscribed to Francis (Frank) Jones-Bateman, and had signed: '*Robert Graves*' in ink upon it.

Now to return to **Reginald Jones-Bateman**, the man who in 1913, had shot and killed, some say 'in cold blood,' the folk hero, rogue and habitual criminal, 'Coch Bach y Bala'. Reginald was a cadet in the Officer Training Corps, and was commissioned as a second lieutenant on probation with the Welch (sometimes spelt Welsh) Regiment, his rank being confirmed on 16 May 1915.

The Hungry One, is the title of a book of C. P. Clayton's diaries of his First World War experiences, when he served with the Welch Regiment on the Western Front. Many years later, these fascinating diaries were edited by his son, Michael Clayton, into a book, which was first published in 1978. Charles Pritchard Clayton, M.C., M.A., to give his full name, was born in Garthmyl, a small village, then in Montgomeryshire (now Powys), situated on the A483 road mid-way between Newtown and Welshpool. He had Reginald (Rex) Jones-Bateman serve with him during part of the war on the Western Front, when both were serving in 2nd Battalion, the Welch Regiment. C. P. Clayton later became the acting colonel of 2nd Battalion at the Front. These are extracts from the book which relate to Reginald Jones-Bateman. Lieutenant C. P. Clayton had already seen active service on the Western Front as a Second Lieutenant with 1st Battalion, the Welch Regiment, but had been wounded and hospitalised for a time, thereby missing The Battle of Loos.

So, in October 1915, Lieutenant C. P. Clayton as his rank was then, arrived back in France with three other similarly returning officers, and also Reginald Jones-Bateman, a young and inexperienced second lieutenant, as they made their way to join 2nd Battalion, the Welch Regiment at the Front:

Chapter 11 – Page 92:

> ... and soon I find myself with Tommy, Whitfield, Bagallay, and Jones-Bateman stumbling out of a dirty French railway carriage in the little colliery town of Noeux-les-Mines. We are on our way to join the Second Battalion. Outside the station we find a groom waiting with horses and a limber for our kits. We look the horses over and consult the grooms. Strongest is Nobby, a powerful beast with arched neck, and apparently restive. Betsy is said to be lively but not vicious. The others are uninteresting. Nobody seems keen to take Nobby so he falls to me ...

Their 2nd Battalion, the Welch Regiment was now up in the salient close to Loos, in some former German reserve trenches, now occupied by the British Army's own reserve line. The Battalion at this time just after The Battle of Loos in September 1915 had sustained heavy casualties and was very short of officers. The five, including C. P. Clayton and Reginald (Rex) Jones-Bateman, all on horseback, were en-route to join up with their battalion. They had travelled through Mazingarbe along the road to Philosophe, located between Bethune and Lens:

Chapter 11 – Page 93:

> ... As far as Philosophe the road is quite good. Philosophe seems to have been a typical mining village in

a mining district. The inhabitants have been evacuated. The houses have suffered from the shelling. Few of the windows have any glass left in them and most are now covered with sacking. It is very quiet as we pass through, although we can hear a good deal of gunning to the east and south. As we leave Philosophe behind the country changes. Injured houses give place to ruins, broken trees to skeleton trees and finally to splintered trunks. To left and right the ground is a gloomy stretch of shell holes so far as we can see in the half light.

'We are now crossing our old front line', says the Quartermaster, and we can see rough traces of a trench on either side, much blown about. In a few minutes we are crossing the old German front line. And now I notice a familiar smell that takes me back to 'The Salient', the smell of dead horses. The Quartermaster explains, 'The Hun caught the transport of the 48th Division here. They followed up their attacking troops too gaily, and they were trapped just as they came over this rise.

We are in sight of the new front lines here in daylight'. This unlucky transport must have had a bad time. Strung along the roadside for about fifty yards are masses of dead horses and broken limbers.

Only one company commander, Dunn of 'C' Company had survived Loos in the battalion, and Lloyd, the former Adjutant had now taken over the battalion, and when the five officers including Clayton and Reginald (Rex) Jones-Bateman arrived at the Front, Lloyd got down promptly to military matters with them:-

Chapter 11 – Page 94:

... Lloyd quickly gets to business, giving the command of

A Company to Tommy, of B to me, and of D to Whitfield. So now all four of us, who started as very junior subalterns at the Castle in 1914, are within the year, commanding companies. Three of us have been wounded with the Firsts, while the other Dunn, has borne a charmed life with the seconds ever since February.

Jones-Bateman comes with me to B Company. B Company lost all its officers in the action and was afterwards led by the Company Sergeant Major Flavin, who now becomes my Company Sergeant Major. He is a tall, thin, rather taciturn Irishman, smart, soldierly, and keen.

Chapter 15 – Page 135:

… I now have four trusty subalterns, Jones-Bateman, Dart, Ianto Price and Campion.

Chapter 15 – Page 138. C. P. Clayton has now taken over as second in command of 2nd Battalion, the Welch Regiment, and it is early July 1916:

… My new job keeps me busy and July slips by very quickly. We spend a great deal of time in bombing practice. The throwing of the Mills hand grenade is a much less dangerous operation than that of throwing the percussion type which we previously used. Yet accidents happen and one day Jones-Bateman, who is now the Battalion Bombing Officer and responsible for the instruction, together with Seth Owen, a junior officer who assists are rather badly wounded and Sergeant Tracey is killed. When not Bombing Officer, Jones-Bateman has been my senior subaltern in B Company and I shall miss him badly.

This serious 'Bomb Throwing Practice' accident took place on 3 July 1916. Sergeant L. Tracey, Regimental Number 10534, who was killed in the accident was buried at Bully-Grenay Communal Cemetery, British Extension, Grave Reference 11.A.11. Bully-Grenay Cemetery, some 20 kms north of Arras, France, was named after the local railway station. Reginald Jones-Bateman was severely wounded in the accident, but like Seth Owen, survived the injuries he had sustained.

Reginald Jones-Bateman was invalided home and spent months recuperating from his injuries. On 1 July 1917, he was promoted to full lieutenant, and later was made a temporary captain (staff captain) with the Welch Regiment, whilst specially attached with them in North Russia. Unlike his two brothers he managed to survive the carnage of the First World War – but only just!

The *London Gazette* edition of 3 October 1919 stated that Reginald Jones-Bateman had passed the examination for acceptance as an Eastern Cadet for the Colonial Office. This was: *After competition under the Reconstruction Scheme.* So he was to follow in his father's footsteps in the colonial civil service. He relinquished his commission in the British Army on 29 November 1920, retaining the rank of captain. He began his new career in Ceylon (now known as Sri Lanka), in the capacity of the rather lowly job titled, 'office assistant to the Superintendent of Census and Director of Statistics'. He rose to higher ranked positions, including to political magistrate and assistant government agent, all within the Ceylon Civil Service. During the inter-war years he travelled on occasions, first class on ocean going liners between Colombo, Ceylon, and Britain, during his spells of annual leave. He had several books published including: *Some New Principles of Auction Bridge*, (published 1929). Bridge said to have been a particular delight to him. Also, *A*

Refuge from Civilization and other Trifles – Experiences in Ceylon, (published 1931).This book is an autobiographical account of his experiences as a political agent in Ceylon. He also wrote, *An Illustrated Guide to the Buried Treasures of Ceylon*, (published in 1957). He returned to Britain on his retirement from the Ceylon Civil Service and resided for many years at a house in the hamlet of Inner Ting Tong, near Budleigh Salterton, Devon.

Reginald (Rex) Jones-Bateman, died on 16 September 1965, at the Nuffield Nursing Home, Wonford Road, Exeter, aged seventy-one.

The 'myths' surrounding this Jones-Bateman family do not end there. For Herbert Burleton Jones-Bateman, of Eyarth House, Llanfair Dyffryn Clwyd, near Ruthin and of Pentre Mawr, Abergele, father of Llewelyn, Francis and Reginald, himself died before the end of the First World War, and in somewhat strange circumstances, on 19 July 1918. This death notice for him appeared in *The Times* newspaper, 24 July 1918 edition: *Jones-Bateman, On the 19th July, accidentally while fishing. Herbert Burleton Jones-Bateman, late of Pentre Mawr, Abergele and Eyarth, Ruthin, North Wales. Aged 65. No flowers.*

The *Cambrian News and Merionethshire Standard* had this in their edition of Friday, 2 August 1918:

CORWEN
On Friday, Mr Herbert B. Jones-Bateman, Eyarth Hall, Ruthin, was found dead on the river bank, near Carrog. He had been fishing for salmon and when found his left hand was gripping a large fishing rod, and in the right hand was a salmon gaff, with a hook in a salmon weighing eighteen pounds. Deceased appeared to have fallen backwards and struck his head on a boulder. Mr Guthrie

Jones held an inquest on Monday when a verdict of 'Accidental death' was returned.

Herbert Burleton Jones-Bateman had been salmon fishing alone in the river Dee at Carrog, near Corwen, then in Merionethshire, when as he attempted to land a fish, fell backwards striking his head on a large stone and fracturing his skull. Other local newspapers of the following week gave brief accounts of his death. One stated that Herbert Burleton Jones-Bateman had been a judge in India for thirty years, and that he had succeeded to the Pentre Mawr Estate, Abergele, upon the death of his father, eight years earlier. That he had married in 1887, Evelyn, the second daughter of the late Reverend H. Heaton and that three of his sons had 'joined the colours' at the outbreak of war. One had fallen in France and that the other two sons had been wounded. Of course less than four months after his sudden death at Carrog, another of his sons, Francis (Frank) was killed at the Front in France. Probate was granted to the widow, Evelyn Jones-Bateman. Herbert Burleton Jones-Bateman leaving Effects of £35,166 8s 7d.

Evelyn Jones-Bateman the matriarch of the family died on 22 September 1933, aged sixty-nine.

During the First World War and in subsequent years, particularly in the Ruthin area, stories have circulated that Reginald Jones-Bateman was actually 'blown-up' by his own men, for the killing of John Jones, 'Coch Bach y Bala', and that his two brothers, Llewelyn and Francis were also both 'done by their own men' at the Front for being hated martinets. Whilst these stories could be easily dismissed, two things should be borne in mind – firstly that many men from the Ruthin and Bala areas fought, many sadly dying in the First World War, certainly in the battalions in which Reginald and Francis Jones-Bateman were officers. These men would have 'known all about' the Jones-Bateman's of Eyarth Hall, Ruthin, and no doubt that whilst they may have been brave and highly efficient officers, there are serious reservations as to how fairly and decently they would have dealt with the soldiers who served under them.

There was nothing soldiers hated more than being led by a martinet officer, or by overly keen ones, who often in order to gain promotion in rank, or to earn themselves gallantry medals, 'volunteered themselves and their men' to lead attacks or to take unnecessary risks with their own lives, but far worse, with the lives of the men who served under them!

Even today the shooting and killing of John Jones, 'Coch Bach y Bala' and the subsequent rather contrived and speedy acquittal of Reginald Jones-Bateman remains the subject of debate.

2

Munitions Factories and Munitions Workers in North Wales

Quite early in the First World War visits were made to many factories and workshops in North Wales, with the avowed intention of 'rounding-up' all machinery deemed suitable for the manufacture of munitions and concentrating them in specific key locations. It was stated publicly that: *The manufacturers of North Wales have displayed a true patriotic spirit and no obstacles were raised in connection with the proposed removals, which of course involved the crippling of the industries concerned.* In the vast majority of cases consent was readily given to take the required machinery away to other locations, despite the practical difficulties that then ensued for the manufactures stripped of their machinery.

The next step was to acquire suitable sites and premises for these new, key munitions factories. Suggestions were made to the quite recently formed Ministry of Munitions, and it was decided to establish in North Wales three main shell making establishments within premises already going concerns that pre-war produced non-military products or provided non-military services.

1. National Shell Factory (NSF), Caernarfon, at the Vulcan Foundry. Known when an NSF as the Vulcan Factory. Pre-First World War the Vulcan Foundry belonged to Humphrey Owen & Sons, and late in 1915 it became a National Shell Factory managed by a Local Board of Management. It primarily made 18 pounder and 13 pounder high explosive shells. Here the munitions workers, many of them women worked around the clock, twenty-four

'Munitionettes' at the Boston Lodge Works, National Shell Factory, Porthmadog, c. 1915

hours a day, in three shifts of eight hours, ensuring continuous production.

2. National Shell Factory (NSF), Porthmadog, at the Boston Lodge Works. These works were and indeed still are located at Penrhyn Isa, Minffordd, about one mile south east of Porthmadog. Pre-First World War they were the workshops of the now world famous Ffestiniog (Narrow Gauge) Railway. After some improvements had been made, especially safety ones, the Boston Lodge Works NSF opened on 17 September 1915, and was managed by the North Wales Munitions Committee. Many of its workers travelled to and from the establishment using the Ffestiniog Railway. The mainly female staff primarily made 18 pounder and 13 pounder high explosive shells.

3. National Shell Factory (NSF), Wrexham, at the Wrexham Electrical Works. This was the Wrexham Corporation's Electricity Works and Electricity Generation Station, until after alterations it was opened in the spring of 1916, as an NSF. It was managed by a Local Board of Management and primarily also made 18 pounder and 13 pounder high explosive shells.

A board of management was set up in North Wales, under the auspices of the Ministry of Munitions to oversee these new ventures. This Board consisted of Messrs W. Buckley, R. M. Greaves, E. S. Taylor, Evan R. Davies, T. Sauvage and W. G. Pickvance.

Now came the next problem to overcome – a large labour force was needed for the three establishments, many being required to possess engineering skills. But there was a real dearth of such skilled 'men' as they were in the military in the likes of the Royal Engineers building railways, roads and tunnels, or in the Royal Army Ordnance Corps. So, large numbers of workers were taken on, the majority of whom were women and once given the necessary training these women workers soon proved themselves adept at using precision engineering equipment such as gauges. Once up and running, overall, over 80% of the workforce in these three newly created National Shell Factories were women, and their output figures were excellent. So much so that the Ministry of Munitions soon expressed their satisfaction with the output of the very much needed munitions from North Wales for the war effort. After a time the three North Wales establishments not only

*Recruiting poster for women munitions workers
from north Wales*

manufactured high explosive shells, but also 9.2 inch proof-shot cast iron bomb stems, adaptors, plugs, burster containers and parts for aeroplanes.

In North Wales, two HMEF's, His Majesty's Explosives Factories were brought into being. A vast one at Queensferry, Flintshire, in north-east Wales which had to be created virtually from scratch, and a much smaller one at Penrhyndeudraeth, near Porthmadog, north-west Wales, which was already a commercial establishment that produced explosives, albeit on a relatively small scale.

1. HMEF (His Majesty's Explosive Factory), Queensferry, Flintshire.

HMEF Queensferry, at that time often spelt 'Queen's Ferry', had two former uses before becoming a HMEF during the First World War. The site formerly had upon it the Willans & Robinson Limited engineering works, for the production of water tube boilers and specialist steels, such as vanadium. Vanadium steel was in the chassis of the Ford Model T car, as it was light but had high tensile strength. In about 1910 this works closed and remained a derelict site until early August of 1914. This site at Pentre, Queensferry, then from mid-August 1914, became a temporary German Prisoner of War Camp, for the housing of non-officer German and Austrian soldiers and sailors, and for German and Austrian 'alien civilians' that had been rounded-up, including many from the city of Manchester. The old Willans & Robinson Limited works continued as a temporary POW Camp until May 1915, when the military and civilian POW's/Internees were moved to permanent camps on the Isle of Man.

The site was greatly added to, and by July of 1915 improved to become a large explosives factory conveniently located on the main London and North Western Railway (LNWR) line from Chester to Holyhead, and bordered on its north east side by the river Dee. It was under the management of the Factories Branch of the Explosives Supply Department. In December 1915, HMEF Queensferry was officially opened and began firstly to manufacture guncotton.

The records of the Ministry of Munitions show that the lease of part of the land required was done under a legal agreement, but that the remainder of the land required was taken over (requisitioned) under the Defence of the Realm Act (DORA). This HMEF Queensferry was initially intended only to produce guncotton, together with an acids section to make the factory self-contained. However, more functions for it were added, with it having a TNT section, MNT section, a tetryl section, and also what was called a Grillo Oleum plant for the providing of acid for the factories own requirements and for export. The areas given over to the different production sites included: Guncotton section – 37 acres; TNT, TNT acids and Tetryl sections – 99 acres; Grillo oleum section – 42 acres; MNT section – 120 acres.

Much of this factory was designed by K. B. Quinan, an American chemical engineer, who was from 1915 to 1919, the Director (Head) of the British Factories Explosives Department.

Note: HMEF (His Majesty's Explosive Factory), Sandycroft, Flintshire, was initially during the First World War run as a separate entity and managed by the Asiatic Petroleum Company Limited. In about June of 1918, it was nationalised and became part of the much larger nearby HMEF Queensferry. It then came under the management of the Factories Branch of the Explosives Supply Department. This HMEF was often referred to as being HMEF Sandycroft, Chester, and was located right on the Welsh/English border.

2. HMEF (His Majesty's Explosive Factory) Penrhyndeudraeth, near Porthmadog, then in Merionethshire (now Gwynedd).

An explosives producing factory had existed at this location since around 1860. At the outbreak of the First World War it was being operated as a private company by the Ergite Company Limited. On Thursday, 8 October 1914, with the war now in its third month, Mr David Breese, solicitor of Porthmadog made an application on behalf of the Ergite

Company Limited, for formal assent from the Magistrates at the Local Petty Sessions for the establishment of a new magazine at their Penrhyndeudraeth explosives works. Mr Breese stated that the existing magazine was only capable of storing eleven tons of explosives and that the application was for the new one to be capable of storing fifteen tons of explosives. Dr Silberrad, the managing director of the company by letter stated that the company had found a more suitable and safer site for the new, larger magazine, which would entail great expense to the company, especially in the constructing of a new approach road. That, this application as had been previously directed by the Magistrates, had been duly advertised in the Cambrian News for one month, and that no objections had been received in the matter. Also, that the application had met with the assent of the Home Secretary. Mr Breese was asked by the Magistrates if the company was British and whether Dr Silberrad was also British. Mr Breese replied that Ergite was a British company and that Dr Silberrad and his family were English. It was then explained to the Magistrates that if the existing magazine exploded it would affect (a nice term for it) the whole of Penrhyndeudraeth, whereas, the new magazine would be built in a different location at the site, in a hollow in the form of a cup. This being away from the existing site and an explosion would only affect an area devoid of houses. The Magistrates assented to the application.

It was rather a good idea to have moved the magazine to a new, safer location, as in June of 1915 a serious explosion took place that destroyed some buildings, probably one of them would have been the building that housed the magazine. This explosion was kept secret and as far as can be ascertained, it was 'prevented from becoming public knowledge' for obvious reasons.

As a result of this explosion, the Penrhyndeudraeth Explosives Factory was nationalised and became a HMEF, being put under the management of the Factories Branch of the Explosives Supply Department, who rebuilt it, adding a number of significant new safety features. These were to prevent a chain reaction of explosions spreading between the different buildings laid out over eleven acres, and to ensure there was no repeat of the June 1915 explosion. Reopened in January of 1916, its purpose was mainly the production of TNT.

At HMEF Penrhyndeudraeth, during its First World War operation (and probably for a number of years before), a worker was always on hand to monitor the temperature of the explosives when the mixing process was taking place. This worker was to ensure that the piped-in water from a nearby stream flowed constantly, keeping the dangerous mix cool. To ensure that this worker did not go to sleep carrying out the work, a one legged-stool was provided for them to sit on. So, if they fell asleep it would not have been for long! The use of a one-legged stool for such workers was pioneered many years earlier at an Alfred Nobel explosives factory in Scotland.

In 1998, the last owners/operators at the site of the former HMEF Penrhyndeudraeth were ICI (Imperial Chemical Industries), and after production had ceased there for good, they generously donated it to the North Wales Wildlife Trust, who now manage its twenty–eight hectares as a nature reserve that offers excellent views over the beautiful Dwyryd Estuary.

Other North Wales munitions factories
A number of other munitions factories were established in North Wales to meet the vast amount of munitions of all kinds being required by the military. The most successful of

these being the Wrexham factory of Powell Brothers, who pre-war had been solely involved in the manufacturing of agricultural equipment. Now they went into full scale munitions production. From 100 pre-war employees, by 1916 they were employing 900, the vast majority of whom were women. But not all, as I can attest, as my own paternal grandfather, Thomas Griffiths, who was born in Meifod, then in the old county of Montgomeryshire, (now Powys) but residing by 1914 in Wrexham, Denbighshire, was deemed unfit for the military and was employed at Powell Brothers for much of the war. There is a photograph in existence today of many of the Powell Brothers employees, including my grandfather, Thomas Griffiths, taken at this munitions factory between 1916 and 1918.

The output from Powell Brothers was nothing short of phenomenal as soon they were producing 10,000 shells per week, an incredible figure for such an establishment. A figure said to have represented one fiftieth of all shells produced by Britain for use at the Front. It was also commendable that the head of Powell Brothers introduced a social and welfare scheme for the benefit of its wartime employees.

Other munitions-producing factories also got under way. In Denbighshire, these smaller but still important establishments included a shell making factory with the co-operation of Messrs J. C. Edwards and Messrs Richards of Trevor, near Llangollen, being set up by Sir Watkin Williams Wynn on his Wynnstay Estate. At the estate thousands of shells were manufactured with an almost totally local workforce.

At Acrefair, near Ruabon, Wrexham, Messrs Cudworth & Johnson and Messrs Jenkin Davies & Co. set up a munitions factory.

Whilst Messrs Robert Graesser Ltd., produced solely for military use, considerable quantities of carbolic acid, picric acid and high explosives at their Acrefair, (near Ruabon), Wrexham, works.

In the same area as the above three, the Asiatic Petroleum Company Limited had a factory at Plas Bennion, Cefn, near Wrexham, that produced the shell explosive, picric acid.

Another successful munitions making factory in the North Wales area was at Welshpool, and was named the Powysland Ordnance Works. It was set up in premises formerly a mill which had produced flannel, and more latterly leather products, until it went out of business. This now empty four storey mill was purchased and equipped with the machinery for making munitions by Mr J. H. Petersen, who had been born in Denmark. Without any assistance financial or otherwise from the British Government he installed specialised equipment to be able to manufacture six inch high explosive shells and machines that could make fuse parts. After a few months around 500 were employed at this Powysland Ordnance Works. The employees consisted of a small number of trained male staff who acted as charge-hands and the rest were semi-skilled or unskilled mainly former local agricultural workers from the area.

Some newspaper articles on North Wales munitions works and munitions workers

An extract from an article that appeared in the Flintshire Observer of Thursday, 1 July 1915, concerning the setting up of the National Shell Factory (NSF), Wrexham:

MAKING OF MUNITIONS
Wrexham Electricity Works to be utilised
The Corporation of Wrexham, yesterday, unanimously

resolved to place their electricity works at the disposal of the Local Munitions Committee and to co-opt themselves with the latter body.

The depot includes several spacious rooms not at present utilised and it is proposed to borrow from neighbouring works a number of lathes and drills for the making of shells.

Mr W. G. Pickvance, the Borough Electrical Engineer was further authorised to render to the committee such services as may be required and which he may be in a position to render.

It is understood that the Wrexham Munitions Committee, in conjunction with the Council will undertake the production of shells....

The Friday, 2 July 1915 edition of the *North Wales Chronicle* had this piece under news from Bethesda (near Caernarfon), though most likely these particular young men would have been going to munitions factories in South Wales or in England.

BETHESDA
MUNITION WORKERS – About 40 young men left here on Thursday morning to work in ammunition factories. Two batches have also left here during the past two weeks.

The *Flintshire Observer* of Thursday, 28 October 1915:

BARONET AS SHELL-MAKER
Sir Watkin Williams Wynn, Bart, C.B., Lord Lieutenant of Montgomeryshire, has established two ammunition factories at saw yards on his estate, and informed a meeting of the Montgomeryshire Recruiting Committee

on Friday that he spent an average of eight to ten hours per day at the lathe. With estate men as voluntary workers he has 30 men at each factory and is turning out 100 shells per day at each factory. Sir Watkin recently toured the villages of Montgomeryshire, giving lantern lectures on the war to stimulate recruiting. During the South African War he raised and equipped four squadrons of Montgomery Yeomanry, which were under his brother, Colonel R. Williams Wynn, D.S.O. His only son has been wounded in the present war.

Sir Watkin Williams Wynn had turned two sawmills on his estate into two separate shell making factories, which his daughter was in charge of. It was said that with just one trained mechanic these two quite small scale factories turned out shells of a particularly high standard, producing a quarter less faulty (dud) shells than the majority of the other makers of similar shells.

A concert was held at Penrhyndeudraeth in aid of a workman injured in 'the local factory'. He may well have been injured in the 'unreported explosion' there in June of 1915. The *Cambrian News and Merionethshire Standard* of 29 October 1915 had this:

PENRHYNDEUDRAETH
Concert. – A concert promoted by the workmen of the local factory was held on Thursday in aid of an injured workman. Mr Mackay presided over a crowded attendance and the programme was sustained by Messrs Richard Jones and W. Jones, Llanfrothen: R. D. Roberts, Church Street; Miss Blodwen Roberts, Adwy-ddu; Mr Charles Jones, Talsarnau; the Council School children (who gave an action song under the leadership of Miss E.

B. Roberts); Private Bell; Deudraeth Ladies' Choir (Mr R. D. Roberts, conductor). Male Choir (Mr John Roberts, conductor), with Meirionwen Deudraeth as accompanist. The vote of thanks was proposed by the concert secretary, Mr Morris J. Lewis. A surplus of £24 was realised.

The *Birmingham Daily Mail* of Thursday, 11 November 1915:

EISTEDDFOD PRIZE – WINNER MAKING SHELLS
Mr Emlyn Davies, of Trevor, Llangollen, the noted Welsh baritone, winner of many Eisteddfod prizes, is now putting in all his spare time at a North Wales munitions factory.

A correspondent was attracted to the works by a powerful voice singing an old Welsh folk song, and found Mr Davies busy at the lathe, the finished products of his industry being stocked beside him.

The *Cambrian News and Merionethshire Standard* had a full account of an Inquest relating to a death in a North Wales munitions factory, in their 3 December 1915 edition:

PENRHYNDEUDRAETH
DEATH FROM THE EFFECTS OF FUMES
THE INQUEST
An inquest was held at Penrhyndeudraeth on Friday before Mr R. O. Jones, the County Coroner, into the death of Mr William Jones, 1, Park Road, Penrhyndeudraeth, aged thirty-seven years, employed at a munitions factory.

Deceased accompanied by three other employees named William R. Jones, Evan Evans and John Owen, were engaged on Tuesday afternoon emptying a pan in a still house at the Factory. The pan had been idle since June 25th, and contained originally a ton of chemicals. The pan is about six feet deep. Admittance is gained into it by a manhole at the top. The four men worked in the pan alternately. The residue of chemicals in the pan had solidified into a hard mass five or six inches thick at the bottom of the pan and had to be removed by a pick and shovel. To guard against the fumes which the solidified mass gave off as it was broken, the four men had been supplied with respirators. Jones was quite conversant with the work, having been engaged on it for two and a half years and recently he was away in Yorkshire perfecting himself in this class of work. The men were engaged on the work from about one o'clock until six. Jones went home unassisted, but at seven o'clock, Dr J. R. Jones was called in and found him in a serious condition.

Death supervened at seven o'clock the next morning. John Owen and Evan Evans were also affected, but apparently not seriously.

Mr Joseph Roberts, was foreman of the jury, and Mr J. Jones Morris appeared on behalf of the deceased's wife.

Mrs Jones, the widow said she was left with two boys. Her husband was in good health before her calamity.

Mr William Reginald Jones said he was foreman and worked with deceased and two other workmen in the pan. They each wore respirators and only one of them worked in the pan at the same time. Mr Anderson who was in charge of the chemical department, superintended the cleaning of the pan and visited the men continually during the afternoon. They saw very little fumes when at work. He (witness) felt a little from the fumes. So did the other three and complained to each other. The fumes affected them by causing them to cough a little. They did not complain to Mr Anderson, nor to anyone when they finished work, and they all walked home unassisted. Replying to Mr J. Jones Morris, witness said that they were instructed not to remain in the pan for more than two minutes at a time.

There was no means of ventilating the pan. The solidified mass was about five or six inches thick and very hard, and they had to use a pick and shovel, and carry the stuff through the manhole in a bucket. They were supplied with respirators, but there were no restoratives immediately at hand. That was the only pan at the factory and he had never seen one emptied before. They made no complaint to Mr Anderson when he visited them. They simply complained to each other in Welsh about a tickling feeling in the throat which caused them to cough. The fumes were colourless.

Replying to Mr R. T. Jones, a juror, witness said Mr Anderson himself was in the pan during the afternoon.

John Owen, another workman in the pan said he did not feel any ill effects whilst at work except the coughing. Mr Anderson visited them pretty often. He began to feel the effects of the fumes at about nine o'clock that night and sent for the doctor next morning. He felt himself getting on all right now. Deceased started work in the pan before witness. Witness did not start until about 3.15, but deceased was there from one until six. That was the first time for the witness to work on that chemical and he did not know that there was danger. He was not prepared to go on to the pan again.

Lennox Anderson said he had been in charge of the chemical department for two years and a half. No heat had been applied to the pan since June 25th. He paid frequent visits to the pan during the afternoon. The men made no complaints to him and he did not think there was anything the matter with them except for a slight coughing. Each man would be in the pan about two minutes or just long enough to fill a bucket then he came out. Besides, when standing on top of the stuff each man could push his head out of the manhole. Deceased was well used to the work, and was not aware, anymore than the witness was aware, that there was any danger in the conditions under which the four men worked.

Replying to Mr Jones Morris, Mr Anderson said had he known that there was any danger he would not have put the men to do the work. The men knew of course that they were not to work too long in the fumes. Each man would be in the pan about two minutes, or just as long as he filled a bucket. The way taken was the only rapid way of clearing the pan. The other way was a lengthy process. The solid matter would have to be liquified and that would take a long time. There were restoratives at hand but these were not provided until a request was made for them, and not one of the four men complained to him. He (witness) did not cough when he was in the pan.

Replying to the jury he said restoratives would have been applied immediately if the men had complained. He had no idea they were affected. There was no carbolic acid gas in the pan. Slight coughing was natural from fumes. The fumes affected the lungs. Three of the men working in the pan were affected.

Dr J. R. Jones said he was called to the deceased's house between seven and eight o'clock. Deceased was sitting by the fire in the kitchen and told him that he had been in some fumes at the works and had a sinking feeling in the stomach. He had much difficulty in breathing and was suffering from a hacking cough and sickness. On examination the witness found he had intense irritation along the air passages, extending to the minute division of the bronchial tubes and even to the substance of the lung itself. In other words he was suffering from acute bronchitis.

He urged the deceased to go to bed and gave him treatment. Witness was again called at about one in the morning and found that the heart was beginning to fade.

Death supervened at seven in the morning. In his opinion death was due to heart failure as the result of inhaling poison fumes. Fumes did not act immediately because deceased was quite a healthy man.

The manager of the Factory did everything possible to safeguard the health of the workmen who were periodically examined by a Government Doctor. Such an examination was proceeding that day.

The jury returned a verdict that the deceased died from heart failure as the result of inhaling poisonous fumes at work at the Factory. Adding that there was no negligence on the part of anyone.

A vote of sympathy with the widow and two children was passed.

These were the days before 'Health and Safety' was given any kind of consideration, and if there had been any such health and safety thoughts in wartime, then they would no doubt have been circumvented anyway.

The *Cambrian News and Merionethshire Standard* of Friday, 7 January 1916, reported upon a serious accident at 'the Factory', Penrhyndeudraeth:

PENRHYNDEUDRAETH
Accident – Mr William Pritchard, Nazareth Terrace, suffered severe injury at the factory on Thursday as a

result of a heavy piece of iron falling on his chest. He was conveyed home by motor car and medically attended to.

William Pritchard was born near Caernarfon in 1858. Prior to the war he had been a rockman in a local slate quarry. He lived with his Penrhyndeudraeth born wife, Sarah, and their children at 3, Nazareth Terrace, Penrhyndeudraeth. On the 1911 Census, William and Sarah stated that they had, had nine children, six of whom were still living at that time.

But you did not have to be serving in the military or working in the Penrhyndeudraeth munitions factory local to your home to lose your life, as this piece from the same edition of the *Cambrian News and Merionethshire Standard* showed:

Colliery Deaths
PENRHYNDEUDRAETH
Killed at the colliery – News came on Thursday, that two men from Penrhyndeudraeth, Mr Lewis Williams, Tremafon and Mr David Jones, Osmond Terrace, had been killed in a colliery at South Wales. Sympathy is extended to the bereaved relatives.

The *North Wales Chronicle* of Friday, 4 February 1916, had a piece on the working of all seven days of the week by munitions workers at munitions factories:

NO SUNDAY LABOUR
MR LLOYD GEORGE'S CIRCULAR ON MUNITIONS WORKERS
In a circular to munitions manufacturers, Mr Lloyd George has made the suggestion, which is practically a command, that all Sunday labour should be abolished in all 'controlled establishments'. The Minister of

Munitions refers to the committee appointed some time ago to study the question of the effect upon the production of munitions of war by continuous labour involving Sunday work.

Mr Lloyd George believing that all munitions workers should receive one day's rest per week, preferably Sunday.

The *North Wales Chronicle* of Friday, 18 August 1916:

BLAENAU FESTINIOG
MINISTERS AS MUNITIONS WORKERS
The Rev Glyn Evans, Congregational Minister, has been granted leave by his church to take up munitions work. The Rev R. J. Williams, Wesleyan Minister, is also spending his holidays as a munitions worker.

The *Pioneer* newspaper or *Merthyr Pioneer*, as it was also known, was a weekly South Wales newspaper that openly espoused the socialist cause, and other causes such as women's suffrage. The newspaper was launched by Keir Hardie (James Keir Hardie, born 15 August 1856 – died 26 September 1915), the Scottish born union leader, MP and for a time the leader of the Independent Labour Party. He appointed a friend and fellow pacifist, Thomas Evan Nicholas (bardic name; Niclas y Glais) as editor. This article appeared in the Saturday, 27 January 1917 edition:

WOMEN WARRIORS
'Women are now part and parcel of our great army', said the Earl of Derby on July 13th, 1916; 'without them it would be impossible for progress to be made, but with them I believe that victory is assured'. Similarly, Mr E. S. Montagu, speaking on August 15th, said 'Women of

every station, with or without previous experience of the difficulties or of the strain and monotony of munitions work, have proved themselves able to undertake work which before the war was regarded as solely the province of men, and often skilled men alone.... There are, I believe some 500 different munitions processes upon which women are now engaged, two-thirds of which have never been performed by a woman previous to twelve months ago'.

According to Board of Trade returns, in July 1915, 362,000 more women were employed in industrial pursuits than in July 1914, the increase of course, mainly due to munitions work. And 263,000 were reported by the employers as replacing men, or in the case of new work, as doing work hitherto only performed by men.

Under the heading of 'Arsenals, Dockyards etc.', the number of women employed was 2,000 in 1914, 71,000 in 1916, all the new workers taking the place of men.

Women constitute 17 per cent of munitions workers.

In September last, the War Office issued an illustrated report on Women's war work. Twenty trades are mentioned in the list of chief trades represented in munitions work. A summary of processes affords most interesting, if rather technical reading. Still more interesting, perhaps, is the list of manufactured articles, parts etc. For instance: Shells – Shrapnel, 3in., all operations; H. E. Shells, all machine operations on all sizes up to and including 9.2 inch. In other cases with assistance of special tackle for lifting 6 inch, 8 inch, and 9.2 inch, in other cases with one labourer to five or ten women to do the lifting. Under explosives: Cordite-mixing and sifting for paste, pressing into cords and strands; blending, reeling, drying and packing. Optical munitions: Glass, slitting; lenses, roughing, smoothing, polishing, edging, shanking, chamfering, cementing and centreing; prisms, blocking, testing, silvering, mirrors.

A recent explosion in a munitions factory in which 26 women were killed and about 30 injured was a reminder how the women are risking their lives. Sir Douglas Haig brought this to the notice of his troops in the following 'Special Order of the Day':

'The Commander-in-Chief desires to bring to the notice of the troops the following incident which is illustrative of the spirit animating British women who are working with us for the common cause. One night recently a shell burst in a shop at a filling factory in which the great majority of workers are women. In spite of the explosion the work was carried on without interruption, though several women were killed and others seriously wounded. The remainder displayed perfect coolness and discipline in dealing with the emergency. As a result of their gallant and patriotic conduct, the output of munitions was not seriously affected.

The Commander-in-Chief feels sure that the Army will appreciate and be inspired by this splendid example of loyalty and determination with which their comrades in the munitions factories are helping towards victory'.

The *Cambrian News and Merionethshire Standard* had this short piece in their Friday, 18 May 1917 edition:-

HARLECH NEWS
Miss Louisa Jones, daughter of Mrs O. Jones of Clogwyn Terrace is home on sick leave having had an accident at a munitions factory, by a shell dropping on her foot.

The *North Wales Chronicle* of Friday, 18 May 1917, covered the visit of the King and Queen, George V and Queen Mary to Flintshire, and the huge munitions factory at Queensferry. Some extracts taken from this long account of the Royal visit:

ROYALTY IN FLINTSHIRE
KING AND QUEEN VISIT MUNITIONS WORKS
For the purpose of inspecting various munitions and others factories, the King and Queen began on Monday a tour through Flintshire, Cheshire and Lancashire, and everywhere they received an enthusiastic welcome from large crowds of people.

Arriving in Flintshire on Monday, the Royal Party were received by Mr Henry Neville Gladstone, Lord Lieutenant of the county and proceeded to inspect the Government factory.

The special train conveying the Royal Party and their suite arrived punctually at 9.55. Their Majesties were met on alighting by Lord Moulton, Colonel Waring, Captain Iremonger and Mr Cripps, junior. The Royal visitors proceeded towards the main entrance of the works. Immediately the Queen accompanied by Lady Ampthill (Lady-in-waiting) and Katherine, Duchess of Westminster, left in the Royal and other motor cars, to pay a visit to the Women's Hostel in the district, while the King proceeded to the inspection of the works ...

... The glorious sunshine was reflected in the welcome given to the King and Queen by 3,000 munitions girls, roughly half the staff. Some in cream costumes, some in brown and many of them wearing red caps and sashes. They swarmed after the Royal visitors, looking like gaily plumaged birds and always, everywhere, they sang 'God save the King' and 'Rule Britannia'.

Many of the girls are Welsh and their nationality is

reflected in their singing. Two hours were spent going over the huge war improvised factory, which occupies nearly two miles of country, that less than three years ago was agricultural land.

Both the King and Queen were delighted with all they saw and chatted freely with men and women everywhere. Most of the girls told the King with pride, the number of brothers they had fighting. One the King asked why she did not wear gloves to protect her hands. 'Oh', she said, 'I do my work better without them'.

On entering the factory the King was asked to give up his cigarette case, matches and to take off his spurs and these were not returned to him until he left the premises. In two departments, the King and Queen had to put on slippers over their boots before they were allowed to enter ...

The visit to a 'Women's Hostel in the district' by Queen Mary referred to above, was a visit to one of the specially built hostels near HMEF Queensferry that catered for some, though not many of the woman munitions workers who had been brought in to work there from outside the locality.

Dr Christopher Addison, MP (later became 1st Viscount Addison), a medical doctor, was from 10 December 1916 to 17 July 1917, the Minister of Munitions in David Lloyd George's wartime coalition government. In this capacity, a statement he made to Parliament was reported upon in the *North Wales Chronicle* of Friday, 6 July 1917:

The romance of munitions related so phlegmatically by Dr Addison in the House of Commons on Thursday was brimful of interest to us all as evidence of British capacity, resource, and will to victory. Of special interest to North

Wales was the Minister's statement concerning Queensferry. 'In the great works erected on the green fields of Gretna, Queensferry, and other places', said Dr Addison, 'from the designs of Mr Quinan, the American engineer, we have factories which will be of great permanent value to peace industries. We are now able to cease making explosives in nearly all those factories which are in the centres of population.'

When the factory was in the course of construction at Queensferry we were all told, one by the other, by way of a secret that no Hun should hear, that the authorities had decided to put up in Flintshire, a 'second Woolwich'. Those who had not seen the works listened sceptically, but those who had the opportunities of realising the scale and character of the building operations were tempted to believe the assertion. If Dr Addison did not altogether confirm it, he made it perfectly clear that the works would not be dismantled. We may yet live to see Flintshire and East Denbighshire entitled to be described as the 'Black Country of North Wales'.

Sadly for the thousands of employees at HMEF Queensferry, and for the businesses that benefitted from its existence, Dr Addison's enthusiastic statement of July 1917, proved to be just hot air one once the war ended. The government could not close production down fast enough at the vast, ultra-modern Queensferry establishment. It was widely regarded that HMEF Queensferry was highly efficient in all that it did, much to the annoyance it was said of the larger private munitions companies. Therefore to appease them and their interests, not the country's or the local areas interests, it was closed down as fast as was practicably possible.

The *Herald of Wales* of Saturday, 4 August 1917, reported upon a factory explosion: *The Minister of Munitions regrets to announce that an explosion took place yesterday afternoon at a munitions factory in South Wales. Considerable damage was done to the factory and it is regretted that at present the following casualties have been reported – six killed and three injured.*

This munitions factory explosion had taken place on Tuesday, 31 August 1917 at a location the newspaper did not name, but it had occurred at HMEF, Pembrey, Camarthenshire. Four men and two women munitions workers had been killed instantly in an enormous explosion. The subsequent coroner's inquest failed to establish the cause of the explosion.

HMEF, Pembrey, was opened in early July of 1915 and this huge concern was initially managed by Nobel's Explosive Company Limited, until it was nationalised in June of 1917. This establishment built on the Pembrey Sand Burrows covered 760 acres and consisted of over four hundred separate buildings. It primarily produced TNT, tetryl and propellants.

There was also a National Filling Factory (NFF), the NFF Pembrey – Burry Port, built adjacent to the HMEF, Pembrey establishment. This NFF opened on 2 July 1915 was managed by the Explosives Loading Company until it too was nationalised in June 1917. It filled 4.5 inch, 6 inch and 8 inch shells.

The Explosives Loading Company's munitions factory at Uplees, near Faversham, Kent, at 2.20 p.m. on Sunday, 2 April 1916 literally blew up. For in the gunpowder mill some empty sacking had caught fire causing 15 tons of TNT and 150 tons of ammonium nitrate to explode. Initially 109 munitions workers including some boys had been killed by the sheer power of the catastrophic explosion that was heard many miles away. Seven further deaths occurred from secondary explosions which killed all the works' fire brigade members. On 6 April 1916, the 109 bodies that could be found though not individually identified were buried in a mass grave at Faversham Church. The remaining 7 bodies had been atomised. The site of this fomer munitions factory is now a nature reserve.

Even after the Armistice in November 1918, deaths due to explosions were continuing to occur to munitions workers in Wales. The *Herald of Wales* in their edition of Saturday, 14 December 1918, reported the deaths of three women munitions workers at a West Wales munitions factory, which most likely was HMEF Pembrey.

The *Herald of Wales* of Saturday, 18 January 1919, reported the deaths of two women munitions workers in a fatal explosion, again at HMEF, Pembrey. This HMEF, together with the adjacent NFF were certainly by the death count the most dangerous munitions establishments to work at in the whole of Wales during the First World War.

Today the site of this former HMEF Pembrey is a beautiful and vibrant country park set against the spectacular backdrop of the Gower Peninsula and overlooking the coastal scenery of Camarthen Bay.

The *Cambrian News and Merionethshire Standard* of 5 April 1918 carried this story:

PORTHMADOG
CONCERT – A concert in aid of North Wales Heroes Memorial and Porthmadog Nursing Association was held on Monday, promoted by a joint committee of railwaymen and munitions workers. Mr G. W. Yates, bookstall manager was chairman and acted as joint-

secretary with Miss Deborah Evans, a munitions worker. The singers were Miss Maggie Williams, Miss Blodwen Roberts, Miss Katie Lewis, Miss Blodwen Williams, Mr Tom Thomas and Mr Radford Jones, with Miss Theo Yates and Mr R. E. Jones as accompanists. A well sustained programme also included dances by Miss Beryl Logan, who was enthusiastically encored as were some of the other artistes. Choruses by a womens munitions workers choir, led by Mr Edward Evans were also well received by the large audience. The Rev T. Rees accompanied on the violin the singing of 'The Lost Chord' by Miss Blodwen Roberts.

The details of a wedding which had taken place in Cricieth a couple of weeks earlier, appeared in the *Cambrian News and Merionethshire Standard* of 26 July 1918, under news from Penrhyndeudraeth:

A quiet wedding took place on July 10, at Cricieth Parish Church, conducted by the Venerable Archdeacon Lloyd Jones, of Miss Gladys Bell, private secretary to the H.M. Factory, Penrhyndeudraeth, only daughter of the late Colonel James Bell of Bedford and Mr C. Gordon Williams, B.Sc., only son of Mr Coulsdon Williams of Croydon. The bride was given away by her mother in the absence of her brother, Major Bell, now in France. The bride looked lovely in white voile, bridal veil and orange blossoms. The bridesmaids were Misses R. Hughes and Lola Hughes Jones, Penrhyndeudraeth. Mr W. E. Evans, HM Factory was best man.

The presents were numerous and costly, including those given by the staff and workers of the factory. After luncheon at Thorn Hill, the happy pair where driven by Mr Greaves, Cricieth, to Chwilog Station to meet the train en route for Rhosneigr, Anglesey, where the honeymoon is being spent.

The women munitions workers at HMEF, Penrhyndeudraeth, known officially as 'the Factory', in order to maintain a level of secrecy, had a Young Women's Christian Association (YWCA) hostel opened to accommodate some of them in September 1918, as reported in the *North Wales Chronicle* of Friday, 13 September 1918:

MRS LLOYD GEORGE AT PENRHYNDEUDRAETH YWCA HOSTEL OPENED

On Tuesday, Mrs Lloyd George paid a visit to Penrhyndeudraeth, and spent a very busy time there. Immediately on her arrival by the afternoon train, she went to the local factory, where, at the main entrance, a group of girls acted as a guard of honour, and as Mrs Lloyd George entered they sang selections, under the conductorship of Mr R. D. Roberts. The youngest member of the staff, Miss Nellie Lloyd Davies, presented Mrs Lloyd George with a beautiful bouquet. Mrs Lloyd George in returning thanks, addressed the women workers in Welsh, and complimented them for coming forward to work in such an important department of national service. She was glad to hear they were willing and obedient workers, and had shown bravery under trying conditions. She was very proud of the Welsh women, especially as they now could stand side by side with English women. The Manager, Mr Potter, with Miss Jones, the Lady Superintendent, showed Mrs Lloyd George around the works, and she expressed delight at the skilful manner the women performed their duties.

A large crowd had assembled despite a heavy downpour. Mr Francis M. Potter, in Introducing Mrs

Lloyd George said the idea of a YWCA hostel originated when it became necessary to meet Government regulations by introducing female labour to the factory. The initial work was entirely in the hands of Miss Jones, Ynysfor, who was able to get in touch, through Mrs White Phillips, with the Headquarters Authorities, and the committee had throughout received strong support from the Welsh National YWCA. Council. Simultaneously, the YWCA movement was rapidly spreading in North Wales.

Mrs Lloyd George then formally opened the YWCA Hostel at Meirion House, a commodious building, well suited for the purpose, and the women's choir from 'the Factory' sang appropriate and patriotic songs under the leadership of Mr R. D. Roberts before dispersing.

The munitions factory of Messrs Powell Ltd of Wrexham, and its employees held a fete to raise monies for charitable war funds, as reported in the *Llangollen Advertiser* on 27 September 1918:

THE WREXHAM FETE
Substantial Gifts To War Funds
The fete promoted by the employees of Messrs Powell Ltd, Cambrian Iron Works, which attracted 18,000 people to Wrexham Racecourse on August Bank Holiday, has produced a profit of £1,513 13s. 11d. – a result upon which employers and employees at this progressive establishment are to be heartily congratulated. The proceeds divided to include – Wrexham War Memorial Infirmary £300; North Wales Heroes Memorial £300; the Mayoress of Wrexham's fund £300; the Boy Scouts £297; Queen Mary's Needlework Guild £60; the RWF Prisoners of War fund £160. The expenses were practically nominal, Messrs

Powell and their employees subscribed handsomely, and added to their gifts of money with those of labour, with the result that the fete was managed by a large band of well organised volunteers who have now the satisfaction of knowing that a number of valuable institutions have received substantial help as a result of their services.

With the Armistice came widespread rejoicing in Britain and the munitions workers of North Wales shared in that joy. The *Cambrian News and Merionethshire Standard* of 29 November 1918 reported this:

PORTHMADOG
THE SIGNING OF THE ARMISTICE – A correspondent writes stating how the news of peace was received at Boston Lodge Factory, Porthmadog: 'As soon as the news was received officially', he writes, 'the Union Jack was hauled up amidst great rejoicing. Everybody seemed to be electrified by the good news and the joy of peace shone on all faces there'. To commemorate the event a meeting was held between two shifts. It happened that Mr Parry, Coedmor Hall, Bethesda, was there. He is the auditor of the North Wales factories. Mr Williams, the manager, asked him to give the munitioners an address, and in introducing him, he gave a very timely address himself. Mr Parry gave an excellent address. The meeting was ended with the hymn, 'Aeth Heibio Dywyll Nos', tune of 'Dewi Sant', and 'God Save the King'.

The Armistice and the end of the First World War heralded the almost immediate cessation of work for females (women and girls) at the various munitions works in Britain. It was reported by the *Cambrian News and Merionethshire Standard* of 6 December 1918, under Penrhyndeudraeth news, that all the female munitions workers engaged at the local factory, the High Explosives Factory, Penrhyndeudraeth, had already received notices to terminate their engagements.

There is a simple explanation for the rapidity of the women munitions workers, not male ones you will find, being speedily made redundant, and it was not so much that the war was over and munitions were no longer needed to be made, but done to appease the Trade Unions. These immediate redundancies taking place for many thousands of female workers all over Britain in the many different trades and occupations. The male dominated Trade Unions had only agreed to 'allow' women workers to take over the jobs previously done by men as long as the women gave up (made to do so!) these wartime jobs immediately the men returned home from serving in the military. The Government and Employers did not want a fight with the Trade Unions and sadly women workers, who had done so much to help the war effort were now expected to quietly scuttle back to their homes and get on with being housewives now that they had 'served their purpose' for the country! For much of the First World War women in Britain had been the insiders, the achievers, the breadwinners, whilst so many men had been in the military, a vast number of them overseas.

The *North Wales Chronicle* of Friday, 13 December 1918, had this about the women workers at HMEF Penrhyndeudraeth, who were now required to swiftly leave their employment, as it changed from a wartime footing, and the final sentence engraved on the 'presentation gift' is a rather telling one:

PENRHYNDEUDRAETH
PRESENTATION – The women workers of HM Factory before ceasing duty held a farewell tea party in

their dining room, the Chief's of the Factory sections being present. Miss M. E. Jones, Ynysfor, supervisor, was presented by the women workers with a beautiful silver bowl on which was engraved: 'Presented to Miss M. E. Jones, Supervisor, by the Women Workers at HM Factory as a mark of esteem and appreciation of many kindnesses. It is only with the greatest regret that workers cease duty at the Factory'.

This is an extract from an article that appeared in the *Liverpool Echo* of Monday, 16 December 1918:-

RESETTLEMENT IN WREXHAM AREA
During last week, discharges of some hundreds of women have taken place from the munitions works in the area of the Wrexham Local Advisory Committee. The general attitude shows a pronounced tendency to postpone accepting any employment offered until after the Christmas holidays. The number of claims for out-of-work policies has increased daily, and the staff at the Employment Exchange, Women's Department, Lord Street, Wrexham, have been taxed to the utmost. Arrangements having been made whereby applicants signing the coupons call at prescribed hours, the work is evenly distributed over the day, obviating temporary dislocation owing to rushes.

Having speedily got rid of the female staff at the munitions works, a few men were kept on for the 'decommissioning' of the premises, before the machines, tools and equipment that were used there, were sold off, usually piecemeal.

Whilst carrying out this 'decommissioning' work after the Armistice, accidents to workers in the munitions factories continued to take place due to the volatility of the substances they were dealing with. One such accident was reported in the third week of March 1919, at the HMEF Penrhyndeudraeth: *Mr John Jones of Castle Street has met with a serious accident to his eye, whilst moving explosive flashes at the factory.*

The *North Wales Chronicle* edition of Friday, 3 January 1919, had this happier piece:

PENRHYNDEUDRAETH
Children Entertained – On Thursday at the National School, about 300 children were entertained to tea provided from the Munitions Workers Fund. The children were those of the local soldiers, munitions workers and the youthful members of the YMCA. They paraded the town and sang patriotic songs.

News of a particularly happy nature was also reported in the 7 February 1919 edition of the *Cambrian News and Merionethshire Standard*. A Victory Dance, a fancy dress dance had been held in Porthmadog. One of the prominent attenders was Mr K. C. Arbuthnot, the chief chemist at HMEF Penrhyndeudraeth. It was said that the floor of the dance hall was in perfect condition for dancing and that first class music was provided by a band with Mr Hazeldene of Rhyl as band leader. Earlier from 3.00 p.m. until 8.00 p.m., a children's fancy dress dance had taken place at the same venue. The master of ceremonies being Mr Yates and both events were said to have been well attended, and that great fun had been had by all.

During 1919, a number of public auctions took place for the various contents of the now defunct North Wales munitions factories. In the *Cambrian News and Merionethshire*

Standard of 21 February 1919, details were given for one such auction at the National Shell Factory (NSF), Caernarfon – the Vulcan Factory (Foundry):

G.R.

BY DIRECTION OF THE DISPOSAL BOARD

NATIONAL SHELL FACTORY, CAERNARFON

THE MACHINE TOOLS, &.C.,

In and upon the above Works.

Edward Rushton & Son and Kenyon are in receipt of
instructions to Sell by

Auction, piecemeal on the Premises, as above, On

THURSDAY, the 27th DAY

OF MARCH, 1919.

Further particulars will appear in future announcements
and catalogues may be had when ready from the
Auctioneers, 13, Norfolk Street, Manchester.

The *Cambrian News and Merionethshire Standard* of Friday, 4 April 1919 gave some details of the above auction, held at this former Caernarfon National Shell Factory:-

The contents of the Shell Factory fitted up at Messrs. H. Owen and Sons works at Caernarfon were dispersed by auction on Thursday by Messrs. Rushton & Son and Kenyon, of Manchester and Blackburn.

Erected in September 1915, the factory continued to work for about three years during which period the total output was about 120,000 shells.

Details were then given of some of the items sold and the prices they went for.

The *North Wales Chronicle* of Friday, 12 September 1919

informed readers of a general announcement in relation to munitions workers which would have probably greatly disappointed many of them:

The Ministry of Munitions has decided not to issue a medal to Munitions Workers.

An extensive article appeared in the *North Wales Chronicle* of Friday, 21 November 1919, which was now able for the first time with it being post-Armistice, to provide a real insight into the remarkable wartime activities of the extremely large HMEF Queensferry, Flintshire, and as to its future prospects as any kind of going industrial concern.

All attempts locally to keep this Queensferry factory open on any kind of peacetime footing were failing, and though the gates to it were open, it had but a skeleton staff, with nothing being produced there and it was already in decline. It was said that the whole district that had benefitted in jobs and prosperity, could now see those benefits slipping from their grasp and they were perturbed that this factory would become a national white elephant in their midst, and this potential industrial asset would just be broken up and sold off.

By November 1919, all of the female labour at the factory had gone with only a handful of male workers remaining. Yet at its peak only eighteen months earlier, this HMEF factory had been a huge employer – some 7,000 workers (one account has it as 7,325 at its peak) roughly made up of 4,000 males and 3,000 females. The figure of 7,000 included around 600 who were employed in the policing, welfare and medical sections. The welfare officers chiefly engaged in the care of the female workers. The women munitions workers accounted for approximately 70% of those who worked on the chemical processes here.

Unlike the enormous Gretna Factory, the large scale housing of its workers had not been considered. At Gretna two new towns had been created from scratch, which had permanent housing for tens of thousands of workers, together with the required infrastructure. Churches and chapels had been built and 'amenities' were provided such as cinemas and theatres, The Queensferry establishment had built for it a small garden village of only 160 houses for families, and hostels, six in total for unmarried or separated men and women. Three of these hostels were used by chemists who had been especially brought over from Australia. Two of the hostels were for women police officers and one hostel for the women supervisors of the welfare section. A small cottage hospital had been built at the site solely for the use of emergency cases from the factory and was not for the use of the local residents. This hospital had two wards, one male and one female, each containing six beds for the more serious cases that could not be safely removed to the nearest major hospital at Chester. Over 19,000 cases were treated at the Queensferry surgery during 1917 and 1918 alone, most being described as slight accidents. The official records (if they are to be fully relied upon) record only four deaths at the Queeensferry establishment during its wartime existence. Though four deaths is four too many, for such a vast and dangerous concern the fatalaties were extremely low. There also was a police station and a fire station at the site.

The Queensferry factory itself was spread over, after ongoing improvements, 343 acres of land, and comprised of over five hundred steel buildings, some of them gigantic ones. Housed within them were intricate and large plants that initially having produced guncotton, later primarily produced nitro cellulose, tetryl and TNT.

For all the various production processes, of great

importance was an enormous and constant water supply, that came from four distinct sources – Halkyn main, Hawarden main, the Aston reservoir and the river Dee. For the process work alone the Halkyn main supply was four million gallons of water per day and it was piped to the factory by means of an eighteen inch diameter pipe, eight miles in length. The large amount of effluent produced by the factory was carried to the Mersey estuary some eight miles away through a six-inch pipe, which on its way crossed the bed of the river Dee. This was later supplemented by a nine inch pipeline over the same course as the factory developed.

The electrical power generated at the time of the maximum production of the factory was a quite staggering 2,558,991 units for just one month, with cables carrying a voltage of 2,000 carried overhead by means of stanchions set in tons of concrete. The total horsepower of the motors used in the factory was 8,618.

To give some idea of the sheer volume of production achieved here at its peak of production, the Queensferry factory was costing to run the enormous figure then per month of £400,000, one fifth of which was for the wages of the employees. The value of the munitions products they produced if considered in commercial terms ran into the millions of pounds, back then one hundred years ago. Two jetties were quickly built and restrictions were put in place to prevent vessels from travelling at night on the river Dee, in the vicinity of HMEF Queensferry.

Providing transport for the workers here was a major task, partly because the factory was located in an agricultural district and not in an urban area, and partly because the Military Services Act meant many workers were officially deemed to live within the catchment area of the factory and claimed by the relevant authorities to work there. Special railway facilities here included the building of a railway station and stop, right outside the factory gates for passengers and goods. Also a fleet of sixteen charabancs (very early motor coaches that were usually most uncomfortable to travel in) were maintained, continuously running the shift workers for this twenty-four hours-a-day, seven days-a-week factory. These charabancs were used for workers on the Ellesmere Port, Heswall and Mold routes.

In the few years that this vast establishment at Queensferry had been operating, it had been a great source of employment, been vital economically to the area, and local residents had hoped it would continue in some shape or form. Such a notion had virtually been promised by politicians in government during the war. But this was not to be the case and one can fairly say Queensferry and the residents around it had all the hazards and inconvenience of the Gretna factory without virtually any of its longer term benefits. The Queensferry area gained a small garden village and that really was it. But with a huge industrial scar left on the landscape, much of which before the war was good, flat agricultural land.

The dangers and 'toxic legacy' for Women munitions workers

The book, *Shell Shocked Britain – The First World Wars' Legacy For Britain's Mental Health*, by Suzie Grogan has this piece on page 75:

> ... Of course many of the jobs assigned to the 1,600,000 women during the period 1914-1918 were difficult and dangerous, working in a munitions factory, as 950,000 women did by the time the Armistice was signed, was liable to create long-term health problems. The munitionettes working with TNT became known as

'canary girls', as the lengthy contact with sulphur found in TNT caused jaundice and consequent yellowing of the skin. Explosions and firearms accidents put them in constant danger and they knew their lives were at risk. In January 1917, for example, the Brunner Mond factory at Silvertown in the East End of London was the site of a huge explosion that killed 69 workers and injured 400 more. Eyewitness accounts bear witness to a horror, press reports of which were unable to escape the censors.

While propaganda posters of the day show attractive young women, smiling as they did their bit for the war, the reality was different. Women worked long hours in poorly ventilated factories, and those with children would have tucked them up at night in clothes covered with noxious chemicals. The argument that war work offered women financial independence is weighed against the fact that they invariably received lower wages than male workers doing comparable jobs. They had to supplement the family income whilst the men in their families were away at the Front on reduced pay and the armament industry made huge profits at their expense.

Another advantage of having women involved in the making of munitions was that they had slimmer hands and wrists 'generally' than their male counterparts, thereby finding it easier when filling by hand the interiors of shell casings.

It was indeed a dangerous occupation to make munitions, worsened by the requirement for them to be made speedily, with levels of output at such munitions factories always being keenly monitored thereby creating added pressure amongst the workforces. This was highlighted, when on 1 July 1918, at the National Shell Filling Factory, Chilwell, Nottinghamshire, an explosion occurred that could be heard as far as twenty miles away.

Eight tons of TNT had exploded killing 134 people, of whom only 32 could be positively identified. The unidentifiable bodies were buried in a mass grave at St Mary's Church, Attenborough, near Nottingham. A further 250 people had been injured in the explosion. But amazingly or shockingly, depending on your viewpoint, the very next day after the explosion, the NSF Factory at Chilwell was back in production again, and what is more, within one month it was able to record its highest ever figure for weekly output.

It is estimated that in total some 600 workers in the manufacture of munitions in Britain during the First World War were killed, and many thousands injured. This is almost certainly a very low estimate when one considers the many 'hidden deaths' – from all of the shocking side effects of handling the ingredients to fill the shells.

In the book, *The Great War – An Imperial History*, by John H. Morrow, Jr., on page 154, the matter of munitions workers and the perils they faced due to the mix of toxic substances they dealt with on a daily basis, is discussed:

Employment in munitions factories entailed hard and dangerous work. Female munitions workers contended with the toxic chemicals tetryl and TNT. Although less toxic than TNT, tetryl turned the skin yellow, an early form of toxic jaundice, a disease that killed hundreds of workers during and after the war and could lead to fatal disorders of the digestive, circulatory, and nervous systems. Prolonged exposure to TNT, black powder, cordite, acid fumes, varnish or aircraft 'dope' and asbestos could produce potentially deadly conditions, especially given the long hours and exhausting work. Common on-the-job hazards included nasal bleeding, burnt throats, skin rashes, blood-poisoning, severe abdominal pains and nausea, which doctors dismissed because they had no cure for toxic jaundice in any case.

Many of these working-class women had previously toiled as household domestics or in textile factories. They earned higher wages and the satisfaction of a job well done.

Two Porthmadog Sisters who were munitionettes working locally

Two of the women munitions workers dubbed by the British press as 'Munitionettes' who were employed at the National Shell Factory, Porthmadog, in the Boston Lodge Works were two local sisters, Laura Ellen Thomas born in 1895 and Mildred Thomas born in 1898. The sisters were born to Job Thomas, a Tremadog born general labourer and his Porthmadog born wife, Ellen Thomas (nee Williams). In 1901, this Thomas family lived at 33, Chapel Street, Porthmadog. Sadly, Job Thomas died in 1904, aged but thirty-five leaving widow, Ellen, to bring up three daughters alone, the third daughter being Eleanor, born in 1901. By 1911, Ellen Thomas and her daughters lived at 76, Madog Street, Porthmadog. So, when the First World War came, this Thomas family would have been glad of Laura Ellen, known as Laura and Mildred being able to have full time employment at the Boston Lodge Works, even if it was a munitions factory! The wages for the two young women would not have been great, and almost certainly only around a half of what the men who worked alongside them doing exactly the same job were getting paid. They were however better paid than if the two had been 'in service' – acting as servants to a local middle, upper middle or upper class family in the area. The hours were probably better also, but of course the risks they took working everyday with the explosives, risk of explosions and health wise were great.

Boston Lodge Works NSF, Porthmadog, munitions workers October 1915.
(L to R): First lady on front row is Mildred Thomas, eleventh lady on front
row is Laura Thomas.

Blodwyn Brookes Simon the inspirational former munitionette from Ruthin

Blodwyn Brookes Simon was born in Ruthin, Denbighshire in 1899. Her father was Denbigh, Denbighshire born William Brookes Simon, a carter, and her mother was Kyre, Herefordshire born Kate Simon (formerly Patten). In 1911 this Simon family consisted of the parents, one son and three daughters, and resided at 40, Clwyd Street, Ruthin. Blodwyn was keen to do her bit for the war effort in the First World War and decided to go to work in a munitions factory sometime around mid 1917.

In June of 1918, Blodwyn had been working for about twelve months as a munitionette in the English Electric Company's ordnance works in Coventry when an explosion of hundreds of detonators took place, and as a result nineteen-year-old Blodwyn was severely injured, being badly burnt about her head and arms. Initially one of her eyes had to be removed, but sadly the other eye was beyond saving and she was rendered totally blind. Blodwyn was a determined young woman and supported by her strong mother Kate, decided that she would make the best of the terrible thing that had befallen her. Initially she received training at the Henshaws Institution for the Blind in Manchester, where she learnt new skills and was soon producing fancy baskets and machining stockings in the family home at Ruthin.

A few years after the First World War there was some kind of fund raising effort for Blodwyn and perhaps others from the Ruthin area organised by the Mayor of Ruthin, which raised about £50, of which she received half.

Kate Simon wrote on behalf of her daughter in the early 1920's to St Dunstan's which was founded in 1915 and has now been renamed Blind Veterans UK. This wonderful charitable organisation for blind or partially sighted ex-forces personnel was founded as the First World War created so many such disabled soldiers, sailors and airmen. Kate Simon believing that her daughter as a former munitionette was to an extent ex-military wrote asking St Dunstan's if they could assist in obtaining a special typewriter for Blodwyn. They kindly sent Blodwyn such a typewriter and she became for many years involved with St Dunstan's, sixty-four years infact. She was only the second ever female to receive official status as a St Dunstan's 'beneficiary'. Blodwyn was for a number of years the secretary of the North Wales Blind Society. In the book *In the Mind's Eye: The Blinded Veterans of St Dunstan's,* by David Castleton, there is a quote from a Gwen Obern who was a fellow blind St Dunstaner, as they called themselves. She like many others who were blind found Blodwyn Brookes Simon to have been an inspiration to them. She said: '*I will always remember and appreciate everything she did to help me and others to come to terms with our blindness and other disabilities. She was blinded herself in the First World War, yet this in no way impeded her goodwill and generosity of spirit to those about her in similar condition, who I know have been very grateful for all she did*'.

Blodwyn spent the last year of her life at the St Dunstan's 'flagship' training and convalescent centre at Ovingdean, Brighton. The inspirational Blodwyn Brookes Simon, this former munitionette from Ruthin died at Brighton in 1988, aged eighty-eight. Her family placed a small memorial to her memory in the garden at St Dunstan's, Ovingdean.

Today there is a Blind Veterans UK centre in Llandudno, North Wales.

3

Lewis Edward Valentine and Moses Idwal Valentine – two very different brothers

From a 'very ordinary' Welsh speaking, working class Llanddulas (near Abergele) background emerged two quite extraordinary brothers, both with true leadership qualities. The elder brother, Lewis Edward Valentine became one of the founding members of Plaid Cymru, the Welsh Nationalist Party, and was to be its first ever candidate in a General Election. He was also to serve a prison term for his strong nationalistic beliefs. The younger brother was Moses Idwal Valentine, who would later make his own mark in a very different walk of life. As Moses Idwal Valentine who was gassed in the trenches of France on two occasions in the First World War, later rose in the ranks to become a highly respected 'no nonsense' police detective and ultimately became the Assistant Chief Constable of the Manchester Police Force.

Their family story begins with the brothers' grandparents, William Valentine, a shoemaker and his wife Hannah, living in Rhosllannerchrugog, near Wrexham, in the 1850's. The couple had a son, Samuel Valentine, born at Pen-y-cae, near Wrexham, in 1856. Samuel Valentine became a limestone quarryman and with his Llanddulas born wife Mary, lived and worked for a time in Newcastle-under-Lyme, Staffordshire. They then moved back to North Wales, to permanently live in Llanddulas, then in Denbighshire, where the 1891 Census shows they resided at 7, Ty'n y Wal, Llanddulas. They had according to their Welsh Census form of 1911, completed in Welsh by Samuel

Lewis Edward Valentine in his latter years

Valentine himself, a total of nine children, seven of whom were still living in 1911, but two children had sadly died by that year, one of them a son, Robert Charles Valentine before he had reached his first birthday. These surviving children included Lewis Edward Valentine, born at Llanddulas on 1 June 1893, and Moses Idwal Valentine who was born in June 1895, also at Llanddulas.

From an early age **Lewis Edward Valentine** showed a keen inclination towards the Church, and also a particularly strong feeling for the Welsh language. He began studying in order to enter into the Ministry of the Baptist Church at the University College of North Wales, Bangor. However, his studies were interrupted by the First World War breaking out, and though not wishing to take up arms, he was prepared to help in the fight, which at this time so many Welsh (British) people supported. Brigadier – General

Owen Thomas and Reverend John Williams, Brynsiencyn, Anglesey, the Senior Chaplain to the Welsh Army Corps created a new unit of the RAMC, the Royal Army Medical Corps – 'The Welsh Students Company, RAMC', a unit formed at Rhyl Town Hall, Rhyl, North Wales, on 28 January 1916. This new, specially created unit were to come to be nicknamed rather irreverently, but not with any malice, by the combatant soldiers who served alongside them as 'God's Own'. The Welsh Students Company consisted of some 250 men, many of whom were ministers of religion or theological students. But not all were Welsh, some joining the newly formed unit from theological institutions, universities and colleges in England. Some were teachers who joined them. They received some initial training in Llandrindod Wells, then in the old county of Radnorshire, now Powys. Their main training took place at the Hillsborough Barracks, Sheffield, Yorkshire, before they moved on to Aldershot, prior to being posted overseas. The Army service numbers given to these recruits ran consecutively from 81723 to 81983, with a few of the numbers not being issued. Lewis Valentine regularly sent letters home to his parents, some in English and some in Welsh, and one such letter in English he sent from 'RAMC Depot, 'E' Company, 'A' Squad, Sheffield Party, Aldershot', in September of 1916. It began: *'My dearest Parents'*, and included this: *'The training here is very strict and severe. I am glad you have heard from Idwal again. Now mother do try and be brave and for your own sake do not worry so much'*.

Lewis Edward Valentine just turned twenty-one was given the Corps Number 81908, and he was destined to be a stretcher bearer with a field ambulance unit on the Macedonian Front (also called the Salonika Front), a part of what was called the Balkans Theatre of War. He later in the war served on the Western Front.

A. E. Jones, Albert Evans-Jones who had the bardic name of 'Cynan' was born in Pwllheli, then in the old county of Carnarvonshire, on 14 April 1895. His father Richard Albert Jones was the proprietor of the Central Restaurant on Penlan Street, Pwllheli. He enlisted at the same Rhyl gathering as Lewis Edward Valentine. A. E. Jones (Cynan) was given the Corps Number 81725, and he also served on the Macedonian (Salonika) Front with a field ambulance unit, but on becoming a reverend he was on 4 September 1917, commissioned as a chaplain in the Royal Army Chaplains' Department (RAChD) and he served in France. He was a preacher, poet, dramatist and lecturer, but is I suggest best known for his tremendous connection with Welsh National Eisteddfodau over many, many years. He won the Crown Prize at three National Eisteddfodau, the first being at the 1921 Caernarfon National Eisteddfod, when he won with his poem 'Mab y Bwthyn' (in English: 'A Cottage Son'), the story of a young Welshman's experiences in the First World War. Then twice further at Mold (in Welsh: Yr Wyddgrug) in 1923, and at Bangor in 1931. He also won the Chair Prize on one occasion at Pontypool (in Welsh: Pontypwl) in 1924. He later became the Archdruid of Wales, was awarded the CBE in 1949 and he was knighted in 1969, to then be known as Sir (Albert) Cynan Evans-Jones, CBE. He died on 26 January 1970, aged seventy-four, and was buried in the churchyard of the beautifully located St Tysilio's Church, Church Island, Menai Bridge, Anglesey.

Some learned Welsh scholars believe that 'Cynan' is the premier Welsh war poet from the First World War, above 'Hedd Wyn'. For 'Hedd Wyn' of course was killed in his first action in battle, whilst 'Cynan', because he was at the Front over a period of time in the war and survived it, was able to write of his own experiences of the hell of war, and of the terrible impact that it has on the body and the spirit of an ordinary man.

Lewis Edward Valentine for his non-combatant military service subsequently received the British and Victory, War Medals. But his personal experiences of war at first hand greatly shaped his character and political views. Sometime in 1916, whilst he was serving in France he wrote in his journal: My hatred of the military deepens daily. Authority in the hands of the cruel gentry is a dangerous instrument. Though he survived the war physically unimpaired, psychologically his experience of war fighting for 'King and Country' left him fervently believing in Welsh Nationalism and the need for Wales to become a stand alone, nation state. Believing that Welshmen had fought and so many of them had died for the Monarchy and for England, without any discernable benefit to Wales or its people. He had great sympathy for the cause of Irish Independence, which became a particularly tense situation during the period of the First World War and for a number of years that followed. Lewis Valentine's military service, parts of it spent at the Front, had stirred within him a great Welsh Nationalistic fervour that sought an outlet.

In 1920, Lewis Edward Valentine publicly and controversially led a party of students at Bangor Railway Station, to pay 'homage' one could say, to the dead Irish Republican hunger striker, Terence Joseph MacSwiney, as his body travelled by rail from London, through Bangor, and on to Holyhead for the ferry to Ireland.

He also led a protest at the University College, Bangor, against the execution by the British authorities of eighteen-year-old Kevin Gerard Barry who had been convicted of complicity in the murder by ambush of three British soldiers. Kevin Gerard Barry was said by many at the time to have not actually shot any of the three British soldiers who were killed, but he was present and involved as a member of the IRA Volunteers who carried out the attack which had gone wrong. They were said to have been out to capture weapons and not to get involved in a 'shooting match' with British soldiers. Kevin Gerard Barry was hanged in Mountjoy Jail, Dublin on 1 November 1920.

On 5 August 1925, during the Pwllheli, Welsh National Eisteddfod, a meeting took place in an upstairs room of the Maesgwyn Temperance Hotel, Pwllheli. Lewis Valentine (elected President) and five other like minded men, namely, H. R. Jones (elected Secretary), Moses Gruffydd (elected Treasurer), Saunders Lewis, D. Edmund Williams and Fred Jones, met to establish a Welsh based political party. There had been talk of such a thing for many years without it actually happening. The principal aim at this time for this new Welsh Party, 'Plaid Genedlaethol Cymru' would be to bring about self-government for Wales. This new political party's business was to be conducted solely in the Welsh Language and its members should not continue to have links with any other political party – these being of course the Westminster, London based 'mainstream' political parties. At this meeting it was also decided to launch a Welsh language monthly newspaper *Y Ddraig Goch* (The Red Dragon). The new party had difficulty in the early years in attracting experienced Welsh and Welsh speaking politicians, but it had made a tenuous start.

Also in 1925, Lewis Valentine married Margaret E. Jones in the Conwy Registration District.

At the 1929 General Election, Lewis Valentine stood as Plaid Genedlaethol Cymru's first ever candidate, this being in the Caernarfonshire Constituency. He polled 609 votes, though only some 1.6% of the votes polled, it was nevertheless a beginning.

In the inter-war years, Plaid Genedlaethol Cymru proved

most successful as an educational and social pressure group within Wales, rather than as a bona-fide political party with any real clout. Lewis Valentine became the first President of the party, which of course is still going strong today in Westminster and in the Welsh Assembly in Cardiff, and is known today as 'Plaid Cymru – The Party of Wales.' There is no doubt that Lewis Valentine and Saunders Lewis were at the helm of this new political force and party, which sought eventual full Welsh independence from the Union that was England, Wales, Scotland and Northern Ireland.

In 1936, the Westminster based, United Kingdom Government were looking to set up a 'bombing school' somewhere suitable in the United Kingdom. Due to protests from locals and others, attempts to set up such a 'bombing school' in first the Dorset and then the Northumberland areas of England were abandoned. Instead, it was decided to set it up at Penyberth, near Penrhos, Llŷn, on the north-western peninsula. Protests against the 'bombing school' being sited here erupted, and when the Prime Minister, Stanley Baldwin refused to hear the case against it, despite a deputation that claimed to represent the views of some half-a-million Welsh people, matters escalated. The matter began to stir Welsh Nationalist fervour, and the protest known in Welsh as 'Tân yn Llŷn' ('Fire in Llŷn') took hold, which gave true recognition to Plaid Genedlaethol Cymru for really the first time since its inception. Lewis Valentine, Saunders Lewis and others involved in the protests were pacifists as well as Welsh Nationalists, who did not want the land of Wales to have upon it a place for promoting a barbaric method of warfare – aerial bombing. They believed the whole concept was against the grain of Welsh culture. Plaid Genedlaethol Cymru were at the forefront of the opposition, and issued pamphlets in the Welsh Language opposing the building of the bombing school. The old farmhouse of Penyberth was demolished to make way for the bombing school. But Penyberth was surrounded by Welsh myth, with it said to have been for generations the home of patrons of Welsh poetry, and had for centuries been used as a stopping point for pilgrims making their way to Bardsey Island.

Matters came to a head on 8 September 1936, when at 1.30 a.m. some timber at the 'bombing school' was set on fire as a protest by Lewis Valentine, Saunders Lewis, the Welsh dramatist, poet, historian and literary critic, and D. J. Williams, the Welsh scholar, poet and historian. The three men then made their way to nearby Pwllheli Police Station and confessed as to what they had done. There is a story, that the three 'miscreants' then spent the next few hours of the morning discussing poetry with the police sergeant who was on duty.

In their first trial at Caernarfon, the jury failed to agree upon a verdict on the three men. Saunders Lewis, a fine orator had appealed to this jury of Welshmen, that though the three had broken the law, what they had done had been morally right. The case was then sent with undoubtedly 'political motives' to the Old Bailey in London. In England and Wales, the Central Criminal Court Act of 1856 permitted the venue for 'certain high-profile cases' to be moved to the Old Bailey in London. It can be fairly said that the second trial of the 'Penyberth Three' being moved from out of North Wales, and to the Old Bailey, London, was probably the most controversial such 'change of venue' up to then to have taken place in British legal history.

At this second trial, all three men were found guilty and sentenced to nine months imprisonment each, which they served at Wormwood Scrubs Prison. Moving the trial out of Wales to London was seen by many for what it was, a purely political act, not a judicial one, and was also seen as a further slight against Wales and the Welsh Language.

David Lloyd George, now very much the elder statesmen, and approaching his seventy-fourth birthday had written to his daughter, Megan Lloyd George in late 1936, reflecting upon the second trial of the 'Penyberth Three' being moved out of Wales, and to the Old Bailey, London: '*They yield when faced by Hitler and Mussolini, but they attack the smallest country in the kingdom which they misgovern. This is a cowardly way of showing their strength through violence. This is the first government that has tried to put Wales on trial in the Old Bailey. I should like to be there, and I should like to be forty years younger*'.

Some Welsh Nationalists regarded the 'bombing school' action as the first violent act for five centuries by the Welsh against the English. Dafydd Glyn Jones, Welsh scholar has written that the setting fire to the Bombing School was: '*the first time in five centuries that Wales had struck back at England, with measure of violence ... To the Welsh people who had long ceased to believe that they had it in them, it was a profound shock*'. The action was called in Welsh, 'Llosgi'r Ysgol Fomio' – 'The Bombing School Burning'.

This Old Bailey Trial had been something of a sensation at the time and many sought to be present at it. Many Welsh people who attended this trial or read the details of it, felt that the Judge in the case had during it treated the Welsh Language with absolute scorn. The fact that the University College of Swansea had dismissed Saunders Lewis from his post there, even before he had been found guilty in the trial, did not go down well at all with many observers.

Plaid Genedlaethol Cymru, the political party, made great capital of the whole event and on the release of the 'Penyberth Three' from prison they were greeted as heroes by an estimated fifteen thousand Welshmen and Welshwomen at the Pavilion in Caernarfon. Plaid Genedlaethol Cymru issued a special pamphlet entitled,

'Coelcerth Rhyddid – Croeso i'r Tri' ('The Bonfire of Freedom – A Welcome to the Three').

The party was attempting to strengthen loyalty to the Welsh Nation by its people over their loyalty to the British State. However, with the onset of the Second World War in 1939, these strong sentiments felt by many in Wales, by and large, were set aside due to the menace of Hitler and the Nazi's. I believe that if the Second World War had not broken out and Britain, including Wales, had not gone to war, then the 'Penyberth Three's' action and its aftermath would have had a far greater and longer lasting resonance to many people in Wales. But Wales and its people did again what they did in the First World War, and that was to volunteer for military service in their droves and fully support 'Britain' in its fight against the vile Third Reich.

The members of Plaid Genedlaethol Cymru where given the freedom during the Second World War to choose for themselves their own personal level of support for the war effort. The Party was officially neutral, a stance I believe that ultimately set them back a long way. Many of the Party considered the Second World War as nothing more than an extension of the First World War. Their idea, or perhaps 'ideal' was that Wales as a nation had the right to decide independently as to its own stance in the Second World War, and that other Nations, they meant the English (British State), had no right to force Welshmen to serve in 'their Armed Forces'.

It was rather ironic that only a few months after the 'Penyberth Three's' release from prison after their action against aerial-warfare that the horrific bombing of the defenceless city of Guernica in the Basque country took place on 26 April 1937, during the bitter Spanish Civil War. Fascist bombers of the German air force's Condor Legion and the Italian Aviazione Legionaria, at the behest of the fascist Spanish Nationalist Government destroyed Guernica on its market day, killing many of its civilian inhabitants. The warnings given from the dock of the Old Bailey by Welsh nationalists had so soon been tragically proven correct in a European context.

Lewis Valentine was also a Pastor in the Baptist Church in Wales, and he edited the Baptist quarterly magazine, *Seren Gomer* from 1951 until 1975. He wrote of his own experiences in the First World War in *Dyddiadur Milwr: A Gweithiau Eraill* (A Soldier's Tale). In 1945, a book entitled, *Why we burnt the Bombing School*, was published, and was written by Saunders Lewis and Lewis Valentine. But perhaps his longest lasting contribution to Welsh culture will be his fine Welsh hymn, 'Gweddi dros Gymru' ('A Prayer for Wales'). This hymn is often sung to the tune of Sibelius's 'Finlandia' and is considered by some to be the second National Anthem of Wales after 'Mae Hen Wlad Fy Nhadau'. This hymn has been recorded and widely performed by such Welsh performers as Dafydd Iwan.

The Reverend Lewis Edward Valentine, M.A., continued for the remainder of his life to strongly support the Welsh Language, Welsh Nationalism and the need for Welsh Sovereignty from the United Kingdom. For many years he was a Minister at Capel y Tabernacl, the Welsh Baptist Tabernacle Chapel at the corner of Llewelyn Avenue and Upper Mostyn Street, Llandudno, Conwy. The Reverend Lewis Edward Valentine died on 3 March 1986, aged ninety-two.

Moses Idwal Valentine, known to family and friends as Idwal, for whom life most certainly at the conclusion of the First World War went in a completely different direction to that of his older brother Lewis. Moses Idwal Valentine was a quarryman, aged twenty years and four months when he volunteered to be a soldier in the First World War. He was very tall for that time, being just a quarter inch short of six feet tall, and he attested and enlisted at Denbigh, Denbighshire, on 26 October 1915. He was posted on this date to be with the Royal Regiment of Artillery (R.H. and R.F.A.), regimental number 113108. He was a gunner and later a signaller. He was on Home Service, which included his training, from 26 October 1915 until 24 June 1916, being then sent to the Front in France, where he served until 6 November 1917. During his active service in France, he was awarded the Military Medal for 'Bravery in the Field'. The official recognition of which appeared in the 21 December 1916 edition of *The London Gazette*.

One of the local newspapers in their 1 September 1917 edition printed this short piece: '*News has reached us that Signaller M. Idwal Valentine, the Llanddulas Military Medallist, son of Mr Samuel Valentine of Hill Side, has been seriously gassed and is now lying in Hospital in France. He was drafted out to France in June of 1916*'.

He had been first gassed at the Front on or around 27 July 1917, and he was again gassed sometime in September of 1917. By late 1917, Moses Idwal Valentine was out of the military hospital and he was now a gunner, qualified signaller and field telephone operator. Then from 7 November 1917, until 28 February 1919, he is recorded in military records as having served in Italy, now a corporal. On 29 February 1919, he returned to these shores. Rather disgracefully in early July of 1919, Moses Idwal Valentine, MM, had to write a letter from his family home at Hill Side, Llanddulas, requesting that the military authorities send him the Military Medal that he had been awarded some twenty-seven months earlier, and had yet to receive, let alone be 'properly' presented with. When he finally got notification that he was to receive his Military Medal, in his

Manchester City Police Detectives with their Chief Constable Sir John Maxwell (front row, centre). Moses Idwal Valentine looking imperiously at the camera is front row, second from left. Taken late 1930s.

second letter to the military authorities dated 19 July 1919, he chose to have his Military Medal sent to him via registered post, declining the rather belated offer of having the medal presented to him personally by a senior army officer.

Moses Idwal Valentine decided not to return to his pre-war occupation of quarryman. For he now post-war saw for himself a new direction, that of the police force and in England, not in his native Wales. On 9 April 1919, he became a police constable in the Manchester City Police Force. On 5 December 1923, he was promoted to the rank of sergeant, on 17 February 1930 to the rank of inspector, and on 24 January 1934 to the rank of superintendent. In the September Quarter of 1939 at Manchester, he married Ruth Kathleen Park, who though born in Ipswich, Suffolk, had spent most of her life up to this time residing in the

Manchester area. Later that same year Moses Idwal Valentine was promoted to the rank of chief superintendent, still being with the Manchester City Police Force.

In the Honours List of 1 January 1941, aged now forty-five, he was awarded The King's Police Medal (KPM) for distinguished service. The citation being: *Moses Idwal Valentine, Chief Superintendent, Manchester City Police Force, Regional Staff Officer, No. 10 Region.* He subsequently was appointed as the Assistant Chief Constable of the Force, under the renowned Chief Constable, Sir John Maxwell. Moses Idwal Valentine was one of the most famous Manchester policing figures of his day. His nickname was 'MI5' and he was known throughout the Force, and the City of Manchester as a formidable and indeed daunting figure, no doubt due in part to his experiences in the First World War. In 1958, Moses Idwal Valentine was awarded the OBE in the Queen's Birthday Honours.

Moses Idwal Valentine, OBE, MM, KPM, died in Cheshire, in June of 1972, aged seventy-seven.

4

Welsh Soldiers and their Soldiers' Eisteddfodau in the First World War

It would be fair to state that the Welsh as individuals, or indeed as a nation as a whole, would not have so deeply and wholeheartedly become embroiled in the First World War, albeit not initially, if it were not for David Lloyd George – his holding of high profile British government positions throughout the war, including from 6 December 1916 as Prime Minister – his rousing speeches that not only went down well with his audiences, but were also very widely reported in the newspapers – and his messianic aura to many people in Wales. Many Welsh people felt strongly that with Lloyd George, a fluent Welsh speaker being in political positions of power, before, during and after the First World War, that for the very first time 'they had one of their own' in the British Government that ran and ruled the British Empire.

Lloyd George, the 'Welsh Wizard' as he was known by many, was largely responsible for the establishment of the 38th (Welsh) Division, often referred to as 'The Welsh Army Corps', and colloquially known as 'Lloyd George's Army'. Many Welshmen did enlist to fight before conscription was brought in, yet there were many 'forces at work' against such a thing occurring: There was the strong Welsh Nonconformist tradition. For Welshmen had never really joined the British Army over the years in great numbers, not even that famous Welsh regiment, the Royal Welch Fusiliers. Over the years the Royal Welch Fusiliers were filled with Englishmen, and for a time were colloquially called with

Postcard c.1915 issued in aid of The National Fund for Welsh Troops. It depicts the great Welsh hero Owain Glyndŵr.

good reason, 'The Birmingham Fusiliers'. That liberalism was strong in Wales, and by the time of August 1914, socialism had become a force in Wales, most particularly in South Wales. Out of this socialism in South Wales came initially the No-Conscription Fellowship, and once conscription was brought in, came conscientious objection.

To rather prove the 'apparent' difficulties in obtaining volunteers for the British Army in the very early days of the First World War in parts of northern Wales, the *North Wales Chronicle* of Friday, 4 September 1914 had this:

STILL NO RECRUITS FROM LLANDDULAS
No amount of persuasion (writes a correspondent) will encourage the young men of Llanddulas to enlist under the colours, which is very singular in the face of the fact

that the majority of the men employed at the quarries are only working part time. The local recruiting officer has done his utmost, but so far he has not received a single recruit. An Army man, to whom I spoke on the matter, was very indignant. 'Yes', he said, 'they want Conscription slinging down their throats'.

With the hope of securing recruits, a meeting was held yesterday evening in the Church House, when addresses were delivered by Hon Mrs L. A. Brodrick, Major A. E. Priddle and Mr W. T. Ellis, Llanrwst, the last mentioned speaking in Welsh.

To further emphasize the lack of volunteers coming forward from specifically named parts of North Wales, Llanddulas especially singled out, an even more 'stinging' article was published in the *North Wales Chronicle* of Friday, 18 September 1914, with these headings for it, one of them of an incendiary nature:

CONWY MAGISTRATES
RECRUITING CAMPAIGN
LLANDDULAS MEN 'PREFER TO BE SHOT THAN ENLIST'
SIR FREDERICK SMITH'S COMPLAINT

This article began by stating that at the Guildhall, Conwy, a meeting was held on Monday morning, 14 September 1914: *To consider the best means for procuring suitable recruits.* This meeting was presided over by Mr Albert Wood. Eight Magistrates attended together with the Mayor of Conwy, Alderman Edward Jones and the Clerk, Mr James Porter. Mr Wood stated that the real struggle was when the British Army and its Allies reached German soil, but in the meantime they needed all the men they could to volunteer and enlist. The article continued:-

Referring to the question of organising meetings, Mr Wood said he believed the Welsh speakers did more good than the rest of them put together. Conwy, Deganwy, Penmaenmawr, and Llandudno, had already done very well indeed, but the response at Llanfairfechan, he was given to understand was miserable.

Mr J. W. Rayner said they could not get any recruits at Llanddulas. It was no use holding a meeting in the schools, but if the speakers would come round during the dinner hour he (Mr Rayner) would only be too pleased to render them every assistance. Some of the men said they would rather be shot on the spot than enlist.

Colonel Darbishire said the present operations in France were only incidents. The Germans were now in full retreat, but the trouble would come when they were within their own frontier. The situation was such that no one could look forward to any arrangements for peace. It was absolutely necessary to go on recruiting men. A man was no use under at least six months' training, and it would be at the end of that period that he would be required. A friend of his from Belgium told him that the German soldiers there were men with white beards. All the young men had been sent forward. That proved that Germany had put all their fighting men in the front rank. Speaking of the difficulty of procuring men, Colonel Darbishire said that for years ministers of the Gospel had been preaching peace, and the young men going to the different chapels and churches had got the idea ingrained into them – it was very difficult to disabuse their minds of it.

Colonel Darbishire had about as much clue as to what was actually happening on the Western Front at that time as a rock in one of the Llanddulas quarries! He and his ilk were sadly way out of touch. He would have recalled, with no doubt jingoistic pride, Britain's biggest conflict in living memory then – the Second Boer War, when the British Army faced less than a total of 80,000 Boer soldiers. At the outbreak of the First World War, Germany had some 3.7 million men under arms (mobilised to fight), with barely a 'white beard' in sight! Whilst in the early days of the war, Britain at best could only amass some 700,000 men – but was not only greatly outnumbered in men, but in all forms of weaponry, military training, and in strategy. Colonel Darbishire displayed the kind of 'Colonel Blimp' mentality that pervaded through the British Military Establishment, most especially in the first half of the war.

Llanddulas went on to provide many military personnel, quite a number of whom had volunteered and enlisted, long before conscription came into force. A number of these men were killed in action, whilst a number were awarded medals for gallantry. Welshmen from such places in North Wales as Llanddulas or Llanfairfechan wished to be properly informed as to why they as civilians, mostly working class, should enlist and fight on foreign soil, and were not prepared to be cajoled into doing so, by mainly old men (and women) from the middle and upper classes, many not even Welsh born, who would not have to go and fight themselves in this war they were so keen on, and who endlessly spoke of the need to protect the British Empire!

Colonel Darbishire was Charles Henry Darbishire, born in Lancashire in 1844, who resided for many years at Plas Mawr, Penmaenmawr. He was the manager and managing director of The North Wales Granite Company, a major concern which included the granite quarries at Penmaenmawr. Colonel Darbishire had been the commander in peacetime of 6th Battalion, the Royal Welch

Fusiliers for six years. He was seventy years of age at the outbreak of war, but was said to have tried to enlist as a private and go to the Dardanelles with 6th Battalion. Colonel Darbishire later in the war was responsible for the forming of a quarryman's unit for work behind the lines in French quarries.

A sea change in Welsh attitudes towards the First World War

Now with the war in its seventh week, on the afternoon of Saturday, 19 September 1914, at the Queen's Hall, London, David Lloyd George, then Chancellor of the Exchequer, delivered a powerful 'Call To Arms' for Welshmen. It was undoubtedly a brilliant, rousing, and I believe quite momentous speech, particularly directed at the many young Welshmen who were in the audience. Lloyd George stated he wished to see a good Welsh Army in the field, to imitate the deeds of the Welsh soldiers of old, and he was taking steps to effect this to a certain extent. That is to say he was heading a movement to raise a complete Welsh Army Corps. This speech reached a far wider audience, being reported upon in detail by many newspapers in Wales and beyond. The *Denbighshire Free Press* of Saturday, 26 September 1914, reported upon the speech in glowing terms with the headline of: *Trumpet Call to Young Welshmen.* A trumpet call it proved very quickly to be as the same article went on: *At the close of the meeting there was a big rush of young Welshmen to the recruiting station located close by, for enlistment.*

This speech was the first of many similarly stirring ones that Lloyd George delivered throughout the First World War. It was full of Welsh patriotism, with the wish that the new Welsh Army Corps should have Welsh speaking officers – indeed 'a wish' it proved only to be, not a reality.

For once the Welsh Army Corps came into existence it was very much integrated into the British Army as a whole – being given many English speaking only, or indeed English officers, full stop! But these speeches were not hollow ones made by a politician without belief, for Lloyd George passionately believed in the need for Britain to fight with all its might to defeat Germany, and that Wales must play its full part in the great struggle. He had an eye on Wales one day in the future being a totally stand alone, independent country, and having its own army he believed was an important requirement for this to happen.

Lloyd George also spoke of his wish for a different, distinctive uniform for this Welsh Army Corps – a hue of grey, not the khaki of the rest of the British Army. This notion of Welsh grey, 'Brethyn Llwyd' cloth began to happen, but due to primarily three factors it did not become established. Firstly, it was the higher cost of producing the uniform jackets by the thirteen mills that had been chosen, than the British Army khaki ones, though the uniform trousers were produced for around the same cost. Secondly, the difference in shades of grey between the different woollen mills that made the cloth, and thirdly, that these Welsh mills could not at that time produce enough of the uniforms to meet the numbers required. Still the term 'The Welsh Army Corps' had a cachet to it, with Welsh identity being to the fore.

But there was an additional factor in Welshmen attesting and enlisting in their droves, and the Welsh generally (though certainly not totally) approving of becoming deeply involved in the ongoing conflict. This factor was heavily played upon in many of Lloyd George's early wartime speeches – Belgium. For Lloyd George would speak of neutral Belgium, a small, proud country, not unlike Wales, being trodden on by the might of Germany. Even worse was that atrocities were committed in Belgium (which was true) by the marauding, brutal, juggernaut that was this German Army.

'After all', said Lloyd George, 'poor Belgium could have been Wales, Cymru'. Welshmen and Welshwomen were truly appalled at the plight of Belgium and Lloyd George and others, especially the British newspapers ensured that the world learnt of Belgium's terrible plight, in all of its gory details. Conveniently though, the atrocities of imperialism, such as the economic rape of the Belgian Congo were put to one side for the time being. For only a few years earlier, 'little Belgium' under the rule of the rapacious Leopold II had through aggression and genocidal policies taken control of and shockingly exploited land in the Congo region some seventy-five times larger than Belgium itself, in the process causing the deaths of millions of its black Congolese inhabitants.

On Saturday, 18 December 1915, General Owen Thomas (later General Sir Owen Thomas, MP) was interviewed at his Kinmel Park Camp Brigade Headquarters and he waxed lyrical about the many positive aspects of the new 'Welsh Army'. He began: *This is more distinctively a Welsh Army than has existed for over four hundred years. And by the term Welsh Army I mean all the units comprising that army today – the Welsh Guards, Royal Welch Fusiliers, South Wales Borderers and Welch Regiment – the last three have in addition to their service battalions, territorial battalions at the front doing excellent service. Then there are the Denbighshire, Pembrokeshire, Glamorganshire and Montgomeryshire Yeomanries. The Anglesey Engineers, Caernarvonshire RGA and the Welsh Horse. I do not think anything like it has been seen since the time of Sir Rhys ap Thomas of Abermarlais in Camarthenshire, who fought at the Battle of Bosworth. It was a*

Welsh Army which won that battle and made Henry of Richmond, grandson of the Welsh chieftain, Owen Tudor of Penmynydd, Anglesey, the King of England. Even that Army however can hardly be said to possess so strong a claim to be called a Welsh Army as has the one which has been raised for this war. Sir Rhys ap Thomas's army consisted almost entirely of men from Camarthenshire, Cardiganshire, Breconshire, Pembrokeshire, and a very small proportion of men from Glamorganshire. There could have been but few North Walians in its ranks except personal retainers of the Tudor family from Anglesey. But this is drawn from every county in Wales. Wales and Welshmen have cause to be proud of the fact'.

General Owen Thomas accepted that Wales had contributed in large measure to the British Army in years past, having for many years regiments of her own, such as the Welch Regiment with its noted motto, 'Gwell Angau na Chywilydd' ('Better Death than Dishonour'). The Royal Welch Fusiliers and South Wales Borderers also had proud and glorious records, but he contended that these were but regiments and never formed what could be called a Welsh Army, being at all times swallowed up in the English Army. But he said this new Welsh Army today was more distinctly Welsh than ever before and passed all the tests to prove this was so. The tests of from where the men were drawn, of their language, and of their religious observances. He regarded the present Welsh Army as more distinctly Welsh than the Welsh regiments of the past, for they were drawn from every county of Wales. Their officers were practically all of Welsh descent, or intimately connected with the Principality, either by residence, service or in other ways. In language two thirds of the officers were of Welsh nationality, with the majority of them knowing and habitually using the Welsh language, with Welsh being the common language of communication between the men and their officers. He also said that the religious predilections of the men in the Welsh Army had been most sympathetically considered by the military authorities. He continued: '*It grieves one to think that in the past the records of Wales, and particularly the more rigid and Puritanic section of Nonconformists had been wont to look upon membership of the army as entirely subversive to morality. This no doubt helped and emphasised the conscientious nonconformist objection to military service. I have no hesitation in saying that it constituted one of the greatest obstacles we had to contend with in earlier recruiting efforts. Men who had been brought up from their earliest childhood in the belief that war in itself was sinful, and to regard those who made the army their profession as having sunk deep in degradation both socially and morally, could hardly be expected to change all at once their point of view, even in the face of this great national crisis. The new Welsh Army allows for chaplains of every denomination to operate. Religious services are held as regularly in Welsh as is in the case of the little chapel in the heart of Wales. There is not a battalion, not a company in the Welsh Army of today, but could, and on occasion does, hold its own prayer meeting and Sunday school. I will undertake to say that the moral welfare and spiritual requirement of the men in the Welsh Army, are more carefully and systematically looked after than would be the case in hundreds of instances had they remained at home. We have in our ranks as non-commissioned or commissioned officers, Nonconformist deacons, lay preachers, theological students and ordained pastors in addition to those who hold the distinctive rank of chaplain. As I have already said, there has never been anything like it in the whole history of the British Army. This has tended to remove the last and the most serious objection of conscientious Welsh parents who feared to allow their sons to join the army*'.

In relation to recruiting, General Owen Thomas spoke of Wales to date having made a good effort in providing recruits: '*With some parts of the Principality having done better than others*', but still a large number of young Welshmen, particularly in the country districts had not yet enlisted. He blamed this largely upon their areas being somewhat out of the way in what he termed as, 'the more agricultural areas of Wales', and also that many did not yet thoroughly understand the Lord Derby Scheme for enlisting.

In the many books and diaries relating to the First World War that have been published over the years, written by both Englishmen and Welshmen, some have pondered over 'the Welsh Soldier' in the First World War. In *Goodbye To All That*, by Robert Graves, he wrote of the Royal Welch Fusiliers and of the volunteers from North Wales who served alongside him:-

In peacetime, the regular battalions of the regiment, though officered mainly by Anglo-Welshmen of county families, did not contain more than about one Welsh-speaking Welshman in fifty. Most recruits came from Birmingham. The only Harlech man besides myself who joined the regiment at the start, was a golf caddie. He had got into trouble a short time before for stealing clubs. The chapels held soldiering to be sinful, and in Merioneth the chapels had the last word.

Prayers were offered for me by the chapels, not because of the physical dangers I would run in France, but because of the moral dangers threatening me at home.

However, when Lloyd George became Minister of Munitions in 1915, and persuaded the chapels that the war was a crusade, we had a tremendous influx of men from North Wales. They were difficult soldiers, who particularly resented having to stand still while NCO's swore at them.

He wrote of the regiment he had just joined, the Royal Welch Fusiliers, of its history and the Army Council's view:

... As an additional favour it consented to recognise another defiant regimental peculiarity: the spelling of the word 'Welch' with a C. This permission was published on a Special Army Council Instruction of 1919. The ignorant *Daily Herald* commented 'strewth'! as though it were unimportant, but the spelling with a C was as important to us as the miniature cap-badge worn at the back of the cap was to the Gloucesters (a commemoration of the time they fought back to back in Egypt). I have seen a young officer sent off Battalion Parade because his buttons read 'Welsh' instead of 'Welch'. 'Welch' referred us somehow to the archaic North Wales of Henry Tudor and Owen Glendower, and Lord Herbert Cherbury, the founder of the regiment; it dissociated us from the modern North Wales of chapels, Liberalism, the dairy and drapery business, slate mines, and the tourist trade.

Charles Pritchard Clayton, MC, better known as C. P. Clayton was an officer on the Western Front with the Welch Regiment, who recorded his military service in a number of diaries during the First World War. These diaries were collated in the 1920's, and in 1978, C. P. Clayton's son, Michael Clayton, released them as a book entitled, *The Hungry One*. He made some interesting observations:-

The French and the Welsh
The French and the Welsh become very friendly. It is a hard job to prevent the exchange of helmets, bayonets, caps, puttees and whatnot, to such an extent as to have our men taken for French troops on the way back from

the line. In temperament the Welsh and the French seem to have much in common. The English worship the idea of the unbroken square, the unbroken line, at any rate some outward and visible sign of conformity. Not so the French and the Welsh. In the village of Loos the other day the French soldiers were strolling about in considerable numbers.

There was no trace of excitement, yet no sign of uniformity of movement. On the slopes of Hill 70 when the shelling was heavy and the attack was developing we could see French soldiers moving about with so little evident purpose or control that more than once some of our men, watching, called out 'the French are retreating'.

Yet they were not. They were probably adjusting themselves to the situation in a far more elastic, and possibly more effective way than was plain to the onlooker.

In the calm self-reliance and disregard of danger, and equal disregard of external discipline in a crisis; in their impatience with what they regard as the mere formalities of soldiering the Welshmen, especially the miners of whom there are so many in the Battalion, and the French in these parts at least, seem to see eye to eye. The English officer fails, I think, to do justice in his own mind to the Welsh miner-soldier, who has no use for the martinet officer, for clean buttons in the trenches, for arms drill and sentry-go, but who, when it comes to fighting, is absolutely imperturbable. In virtue of the very independence of spirit that makes him unhappy on the parade ground, he can be depended upon to take the initiative when there is no one at hand to command.

My own maternal side grandfather, Leonard Price, was a coal miner-hewer prior to his being a volunteer before conscription, when he attested and enlisted in March 1915, and I find the last few lines of the above extract rather apt for him. For Leonard Price, born on 8 February 1897, at Broughton, near Wrexham, Denbighshire, was proudly independent and 'his own man' from a young age. I know he was always more concerned with doing a job properly than looking smart or regimental whilst doing it. He served on the Western Front in France and Flanders as a Private, regimental number 8607, and

Private 201152 Leonard Price

later regimental number 201152, with 4th (Denbighshire) Battalion, the Royal Welch Fusiliers, a Pioneer Battalion. He fought with his battalion in the battles of Vimy Ridge in 1916, Messines and Cambrai in 1917 (helping to capture Bourlon Wood), and the Third Battle of Ypres in 1917 – Passchendaele, amongst others. His two brothers Joseph and Ernest, who had also been coal-miners, also served in the army in the First World War, Joseph seeing active service at the Front. In the early 1920's the three Price brothers, Joseph, Leonard and Ernest founded from scratch, and ran, their own motor coach company – Price's Motors, Wrexham – an early bus/motor coach company. Much of their work involved ferrying the miners to and from the collieries that abounded Wrexham in those days, with Leonard Price being a driver and mechanic in this enterprise. Price's Motors was efficient and resilient, but due to the economics of the period and abundant competition, sold out in April 1935 to the very much larger Crosville Motor Company.

Welsh soldiers integrated as well as any of the home nations into the British Army, whether they were part of the Welsh Army Corps or not. But sought to maintain their Welsh identities, and for many such soldiers they wished whenever possible to converse in their mother tongue – the Welsh Language. In certain regiments of the British Army the use of the Welsh language was frowned upon, but in some it was actually banned completely! Lloyd George got wind of this and stood firm to defend the Welsh language being used by Welsh soldiers, even threatening to resign over this matter at one time. Eventually, it was rightly accepted that the use of the Welsh language was to be permitted, though never on the parade ground!

The creation of 'Soldiers' Eisteddfodau', especially those that took place in England, were a tangible, communal way to maintain Welsh identity and proved very popular indeed with Welsh soldiers. A considerable number of these Welsh soldiers came 'from off the land', many having never been out of their own county, let alone to foreign climes such as France, the Middle East, or ... Southern England!

Many Welsh battalions went through their final training in the South of England before being shipped overseas to the theatres of war. Scottish soldiers, fellow Celts had the kilt and the bagpipes, whilst Welsh soldiers had their Eisteddfodau and for many of them, their native language Welsh – Cymraeg.

Many of the 'Welsh battalions' had large numbers of non-Welsh born soldiers, and many of the Welsh born ones, especially from the larger conurbations such as Cardiff, Swansea and Wrexham did not speak the Welsh language, but many of these men still enjoyed taking part in Soldiers'

Eisteddfodau, or were enthusiastic audience members at them.

A Soldiers' Eisteddfod took place at the Pier Pavilion, Llandudno, on the evening of Friday, 22 January 1915, which was reported upon in the *Flintshire Observer* of Thursday, 28 January 1915. *An Eisteddfod for the troops* as the paper reported, took place, managed by a committee, of whom Mr James Marks was chairman and Mr J. V. Humphreys, secretary. The Eisteddfod entries were restricted to soldiers who were undergoing their military training in the area, and it was said there was a very good entry for all of the competitions. Mr T. Osborne Roberts and Mr John Roberts were the adjudicators in the musical contests. Mr J. R. Jones, 'Teganwy' judged in the englyn contest, and the Reverend J. Irvon Davies, and the Reverend E. C. Davies judged in the recitation contest. Brigadier-General Owen Thomas, who at that time commanded the First Brigade of the Welsh Army Corps presided, and the conductor was the genial 'Llew Tegid', as he was described. Private W. Roberts, D Company, 13th Battalion, the Royal Welch Fusiliers, and Mr R. Eifion Jones, were the accompanists.

Brigadier-General Owen Thomas (later to become General Sir Owen Thomas, MP) was greeted with hearty cheers when he rose to speak. Looking around the audience he said they were Welshmen, and he preferred to address them in Welsh. That he was born a Welshman, had lived the life of a Welshman, and he was not ashamed of his nationality or language, and it was his intention to die as a Welshman. To this cheers then rang out. He continued that as Welshmen they should not forget they were Welshmen, and make sure of their own language, but that they ought to learn other languages too. But that all the young men listening to him should bear in mind that to be a Welshman was not a barrier to their climbing to the very top of any ladder in the British Empire. His speech continued in a patriotic vein and he finished by saying he wished the Eisteddfod well and hoped it would be a success. The newspaper gave a list of the soldiers who had been prize winners in the musical and literary competitions. These included the male voice party competition having been won by 16th Battalion, the Royal Welch Fusiliers, conducted by Sergeant-Major Singleton of 'A' Company, which had sung the popular, 'The Comrades' Song of Hope'. D. Davies and Alun 'Mabon' Edwards, both of 13th Battalion, the Royal Welch Fusiliers were adjudged equal first in the *englyn* competition.

On St David's Day, 1 March 1915, another Soldiers' Eisteddfod took place at Llandudno, and was reported upon in the *North Wales Chronicle* of Friday, 5 March 1915:-

MILITARY EISTEDDFOD
In the evening a Soldiers' eisteddfod was held in the Pavilion. A large and enthusiastic audience was attracted, the receipts amounting to over £62. Mrs Lloyd George presided, and the proceedings were conducted by Llew Tegid. The adjudicators were: Music, Major John Williams, Caernarfon; poetry, Mr J. R. Jones, 'Teganwy'; recitations, Llew Tegid. Mr Charles Hughes was the accompanist. As Mrs Lloyd George took her place on the platform there was a great outburst of cheering, which was heartily renewed as the Chancellor followed her. The Brigade Choir occupied the back of the platform, and sitting in front of them were: Mr & Mrs Lloyd George, Miss Olwen Lloyd George, Brigadier-General Owen Thomas, Miss Thomas, Miss Dilys Roberts, Sir

Osmond Williams and Lady Williams, Miss Gee and the Rev John Williams.

This article went on to report that the soldiers' choir under their conductor, Sergeant-Major Singleton delivered *a splendid rendering of the March of the Men of Harlech,* after which Mr David Lloyd George, then the Chancellor of the Exchequer, was presented with an album bound in Russian leather of khaki hide with gold decoration and bearing the seal of Llandudno Urban District Council, which had been especially cast for the occasion. Mrs Lloyd George was presented with a gold and enamel brooch, Miss Lloyd George with a box of chocolates, and Mrs Owen Thomas with a bouquet of flowers.

At this St David's Day Soldiers' Eisteddfod in Llandudno, Mr Lloyd George when addressing the audience of 4,000, men and women, soldiers and civilians, spoke of the need for increased recruitment in parts of North Wales and of his visits earlier in the day to military establishments in the locality. Here, he could not only render one of his stirring wartime speeches, knowing that it would be widely reported upon in the newspapers, but such gatherings also served the cause of recruitment into the military. Lloyd George also received confirmation here that in Wales there truly was an appetite for such literary and musical 'events' during wartime. Having earlier in this speech castigated a number of London based newspapers for having the temerity to question the volume of Welshmen then enlisting and attesting, Lloyd George then turned to speak to the audience in Welsh. He said: *'This is an Eisteddfod. My first experience of public speaking was here at Llandudno twenty-five years ago, and here for the second time I am addressing Eisteddfodwyr'.* He went on to say: *'I am glad that Wales has done so well towards raising an army. I believe the position of Wales at the end of the war will depend on what Wales does during the war. There is not a soldier on the battlefield more brave than a Welsh soldier, and I am glad to think that every regiment from Wales has been mentioned by our Commander-in-Chief. There is no fear of them running away, and they have plenty of grit to face the enemy. I am confident that these boys now in training will go and do likewise'* (cheers from the audience).

The various competitions then took place, after which the winners were presented with their prizes. The winners included Private G. Evans, 16th Battalion, Royal Welch Fusiliers for his englyn.

The *Cambrian News and Merionethshire Standard* of Friday, 6 August 1915, had this 'insight' into David Lloyd George, who had only a few weeks earlier on 25 May 1915 been appointed as the Minister of Munitions, for he had sent a personal letter to a wounded Welsh soldier bard:

WOUNDED WELSH BARD – Mr Lloyd George has sent an autograph letter to a wounded Welsh bard now in the military hospital at Croydon. The recipient is Mr Richard Joseph Parry (Ap Namor Wynn), Festiniog, and the letter was written from the 'Ministry of Munitions of War as follows':

Dear Mr Parry – Nurse Hodges has told me that you are being treated in the Convalescent Home at Croydon, after spending some time in the service of your King and Country on the battlefield. I have very great admiration for those who have sacrificed themselves in this manner, amongst whom you are included. The struggle up to now has been hard and severe, and it is due to the bravery and courage of yourself and thousands of others that we are not beaten. The task yet in front of us is harder still, and I am now trying to help in supplying our good fellows at the front with guns and munitions. I hope you will soon be well again, and please convey to your comrades my best wishes.

Yours faithfully, D. Lloyd George.

The *Cambrian News and Merionethshire Standard* of Friday, 10 September 1915, had this account of a Soldiers' Eisteddfod having taken place in 'Southern England':-

WELSH SOLDIERS IN TRAINING
AN EISTEDDFOD

A remarkably successful Eisteddfod was held on August 25th at the camp of the Welsh Army Corps in the South of England. Brigadier General H. J. Evans presided. The conductor was Corporal Gomer Evans of 13th RWF, and the secretaries were Lieut W. A. Evans, RE, (son of Dr R. D. Evans, JP, Blaenau Ffestiniog) and Gunner Bowen Davies, RFA. The Eisteddfod opened with 'Hen Wlad fy Nhadau' which was effectively sung by over 1,200 Welsh voices. The chairman in a rousing speech said it was an honour to be present among so many fellow-countrymen and fellow-soldiers, and praised the Welsh not only as singers, but as soldiers of the King. The General was given a great ovation as he sat down.

Mr Doodie, organist at Winchester Cathedral was the musical adjudicator. He remarked that he had never heard more beautiful singing. He was particularly taken up by the duet singing. The literary adjudicators were chaplains, the Revs P. Jones Roberts, formerly of Festiniog, and J. Hugh Jones. Special praise is due to Mr Jones Roberts for the great help he gave the men in promoting the eisteddfod.

A list of those who won the individual competitions was

then given and they included: Englyn: 'Galwad I'r Gad', Private David Davies, 'A' Company, 13th RWF. Penillion: 'Y Milwr Cymreig', Private O. T. Jones (Iorwerth), 'B' Company, 13th RWF and Private Rowlands (Myfyr Mon), 13th RWF first equal. Essay: 'Bywyd yn y Gwersyll', Privates O. T. Jones and G. Morgan, 'B' Company, 13th RWF, first equal.

The *North Wales Chronicle* of Friday, 1 October 1915, had news of a forthcoming Welsh Soldiers' 'Great Eisteddfod' to be held at Winchester Guildhall, Winchester, Hampshire, on Monday, 4 October 1915. Fifteen different competitions were to be held, open to soldiers in the 38th Division, Welsh Army Corps.

The *Flintshire Observer* of Thursday, 7 October 1915, had a first hand and rather insightful account of Welsh soldiers undergoing their military training in Southern England:-

THE SINGING SOLDIERS OF WALES
Eisteddfodau in Camps
Around Winchester are the Legions of Wales. Like the unseen armies of Elisha's time, they compass the city about. With Celtic zeal they are preparing themselves against the time when they will take their places in the great war.

Their days are full of work – hard, strenuous business, which is making them as capable as any regular that ever stepped.

But they seem to have but one hobby, music; and one enthusiasm, Wales. At every breathing space they sing. From Reveille to Last Post they sing.
PLENTY OF SOLOISTS
Almost every battalion has its male voice choir and every

company its quartettes and its madrigal singers, while soloists are as plentiful as blackberries.

So we have an Eisteddfod nearly every week at one or other of the camps. And because there are not enough, some of the choirs find their enthusiasm overflowing in the shape of charity concerts or open-air recitals.

To an outsider going among these sons of Wales, it would seem that they have no other thought, after war preparation, but music, compared with a bluff English regular they are somewhat shy, but talk to them about music, and see how their tongues will unloose.

AT THE CATHEDRAL

They are a Church and Chapel going lot too, most of them are Nonconformists, but they cannot resist the magnificent singing at the Cathedral. They admit it is fine.

Just one more picture. At the bottom of the town on a Sunday evening, beneath the shadow of the statue of the great Anglo-Saxon Alfred, a crowd of khaki-clad Welsh. On the kerb of the statue a Non-com. Using his swagger-cane as a baton, he leads off with a fine tenor in such a composition as 'All the Night', or 'Bryn Calfaria', or 'Hyfrydol'. Instantly the whole mass spring to the tune, taking parts by memory, singing the loved Welsh words.

'ABERYSTWYTH'

No sooner is one song finished than another is begun. If one particular tune is omitted, sooner or later it will be called for on all sides. 'Aberystwyth next Corporal'. 'Let's have Aberystwyth, Corporal', until with a smile the leader leads off with that weird memory.

The famous University Company of the 13th RWF has within the last few days lost some of its most popular members. Some of them have been commissioned, notably the popular conductor of the choir of the '13th', Private W. J. Owen, who has gone to a Lancashire Regiment.

Others, some of them with science degrees, have been drafted to the Engineers for skilled work in munitions at the base in France.

The 'Welsh Soldiers' Great Eisteddfod' as it was called, duly took place at Winchester Guildhall, Winchester, on Monday, 4 October 1915, and was open to Welsh soldiers in training at Winchester. It was held under the presidency of Brigadier-General Horatio J. Evans, with the Eisteddfod conductor being Lance-Corporal Gomer Evans. The Eisteddfod lasted for five hours and consisted of musical, literary and art (cartoon) competitions. The musical competitions included ones for choirs of Welsh soldiers. The prizes for which were £5 and a baton for the conductor. In the competition for choirs of sixteen, the Cardiff City Battalion, conducted by Corporal J. H. Davies were the winners with their singing of 'The Soldier's Chorus' from 'Faust'. In the competition for choirs of thirty members and over, 13th Battalion, the Royal Welch Fusiliers, the conductor for whom was Private Albert Roberts, were placed first for their interpretation of 'the test piece', De Rille's, 'Destruction of Gaza'. There were also a number of solo and quartette singing competitions.

In the literary competitions the winners included, for the 'Englyn to the President', Privates S. J. Phillips, 16th RWF and Alun 'Mabon' Edwards, 13th RWF, who were adjudged as first equal. The latter also won the prize for the Pryddest on 'The Soldier's Life' and was accorded Bardic Honours. He was crowned with a wreath of laurel by Mrs Pryce, wife of Lieut-Colonel H. E. Pryce, GSO, who together with Lieutenant G. Lloyd George, ADC, acted as the treasurers. The winner of the Welsh Recitation competition was Lance-Corporal Gideon Roberts.

Lance-Corporal G. H. Rees, 13th RWF and Chaplain P. Jones Roberts were the secretaries.

The majority of the Welsh soldiers who competed in this 'Welsh Soldiers' Great Eisteddfod' arrived on the Western Front or further afield by Christmas of that year. These included Private (later Lance-Corporal) Alun Edwards, who used the bardic name of 'Mabon' when competing. He had enlisted on 19 October 1914, and was a Private in 13th Battalion, the Royal Welch Fusiliers, regimental number 16386. Private Alun (Mabon) Edwards was the winner of the 'pryddest' (a long poem, not in full strict meter) competition and the joint-winner of the 'englyn' (a traditional short poem) competition, and he alone at this Soldiers' Eisteddfod was accorded 'bardic honours'. Private Alun (Mabon) Edwards first entered the theatre of war in France with his battalion on 1 December 1915. He served at the Front in France and managed to survive the war, though not unscathed. He was wounded on the Western Front resulting in him being returned home to recuperate. He was issued with Silver War Badge Number B/247917, and at the age of thirty-eight he was discharged from the British Army as a Lance-Corporal on 27 June 1919.

However, the winner of the Welsh Recitation competition, Lance-Corporal Gideon Roberts did not survive the war. Gideon Roberts was born at Broughton, near Wrexham in 1887, to Llandegla, Denbighshire, born coal miner, Robert Roberts and his Brymbo, near Wrexham, born wife, Mary. The family including Gideon all spoke Welsh as very much their first language. By 1911, Gideon Roberts was a bricklayer employed at the Lysaght's Iron and Steelworks in Scunthorpe, Lincolnshire. On the 1911 Census he was unmarried, and boarding at 37, High Street, Scunthorpe, with the Dean family. Later that year, aged twenty-four, he married Ellen (known as Nellie) Dean, from this household.

Though living in Scunthorpe, he chose to enlist in the

Royal Welch Fusiliers and was placed in 13th Battalion, and given the regimental number 19471. Like Private Alun 'Mabon' Edwards, after military training at Llandudno, and then in Southern England, he arrived with 13th Battalion in France on 1 December 1915. He received promotion to corporal and then to sergeant, being attached to 19 Pioneer Battalion in the Boezinge area, when he was 'Killed in Action' on 9 February 1917.

Sergeant Gideon Roberts was buried in the rather aptly named for him, Bard Cottage British Military Cemetery, Boezinge, near Ypres (now known as Ieper), Belgium, in Grave Reference 11.B.12. Though some official records show him at death aged thirty-three, he was in fact twenty-nine years of age. His widow Ellen was subsequently sent his Victory, British and 1915 Star, War Medals. He is remembered on the memorial tablet to the Fallen in the First World War of Lysaght's Iron & Steel Works, Scunthorpe.

Robert Graves in his book, *Goodbye To All That* includes his having attended a meeting in the Summer of 1916, at which both David Lloyd George and W. M. (Billy) Hughes, the Australian Prime Minister were present and delivered speeches. Robert Graves gave his forthright observations upon both men:-

From Page 178 into 179

> ... Later, in London, my father took me to a meeting of the Honourable Cymmrodorion Society – a Welsh Literary Club – where Lloyd George, then Secretary for War, and W. M. Hughes, the Australian Prime Minister, both spoke.
>
> Hughes was perky, dry and to the point; Lloyd

George was up in the air on one of his 'glory of the Welsh hills' speeches. The power of his rhetoric amazed me. The substance of the speech might be commonplace, idle and false, but I had to fight hard against abandoning myself with the rest of his audience. He sucked power from his listeners and spurted it back at them. Afterwards, my father introduced me to Lloyd George, and when I looked closely at his eyes they seemed like those of a sleep-walker.

At the end of February 1917, a Soldiers' Eisteddfod was held at the Knowsley Park Camp in the north west of England. This military camp was one of the camps created for the rehabilitation of soldiers deemed too fit for a convalescent camp, but not yet fit enough to be returned to active duties with their respective units. Knowsley could accommodate 30 officers and up to 5,000 other ranks. Many Welsh soldiers passed through here and at this Soldiers' Eisteddfod, a Welsh male voice choir of wounded soldiers contributed to the programme of musical and literary items. Awarded second place in the Recitation Competition was wounded soldier Corporal J. Davies, DCM of the Royal Welch Fusiliers.

He was Corporal Joseph Davies, 16th Battalion, the Royal Welch Fusiliers, regimental number 18275, a recovering hero formerly attached to 254th Tunnelling Company, the Royal Engineers. He was awarded the DCM (Distinguished Conduct Medal), a highly regarded gallantry medal for action in the Givenchy area of France during The Battle of the Somme (1 July 1916 to 13 November 1916). The action took place when he was attached to 254th Tunnelling Company, the Royal Engineers.

It was gazetted on 19 August 1916, and this is the citation:-

J. Davies, RWF, 18275

For conspicuous gallantry when acting as a bomber and leader of a party of miners, who followed a raid to destroy the enemy's shafts. He was heavily attacked and wounded badly in three places but stuck to his post and bombed till the enemy were either killed or driven away. The work of destruction was completed.

The *Llais Llafur* edition of Saturday, 26 May 1917, reported upon the first Welsh National Eisteddfod to take place in India, a bold claim for an 'Eisteddfod' that took place on a rather small and somewhat parochial scale. But the pride in what took place was wholly evident. Though it was in truth a Welsh Soldiers' Eisteddfod, rather than being a Welsh National Eisteddfod!

WELSH HOSPITAL IN INDIA

The first Welsh National Eisteddfod to be held in India took place on Easter Monday and Tuesday at the Welsh Hospital. Lieutenant – Colonel A. W. Sheen, the commanding officer presided each evening. The competitors were drawn entirely from the non – commissioned officers and men of the Welsh Hospital.

There were seven baritone solos, besides quartettes and instrumental competitions.

One of the most amusing events of the evening was the stump speech, the subject chosen being, 'Deolali and what you know about it', the adjudicator being Lieutenant Garfield Evans, Royal Army Medical Corps. At the end of proceedings Mrs Sheen distributed the prizes and 'Hen Wlad Fy Nhadau' was sung with enthusiasm.

On St David's Day a Welsh service was held in the Garrison Church at Deolali, India, which was largely attended. The Rev J. Jones, RN, preached, while Major John Owen, Royal Army Medical Corps (Liverpool) read the lessons. A concert was held in the evening for patients.

This Welsh hospital was 34th Welsh General Hospital (34 WGH), at Deolali, India. It originated in Wales, being mobilized in April 1916, and taken out to Deolali, India, by a number of British staff, including Welsh personnel. It grew at Deolali to become a 3,000 bed hospital. It was during the First World War staffed by many nurses of the Australian Army Nursing Service (AANS), who carried out their nursing duties with great distinction and under very difficult conditions.

Deolali was a hill station used for many years by the British Army as a barracks and transit camp for military personnel who served on the Indian sub-continent, and were awaiting transport home to Britain, or were convalescing prior to returning home. Deolali became notorious for its rather isolated location, boredom, heat and its propensity for causing many military personnel to have psychological problems. It is here that the sayings, 'Doolally Tap', and 'Gone Doolally' originated. Doolally meaning to have lost one's mind, with the word 'tap' being Urdu for a malarial type fever. A fever that many British military personnel came down with whilst at Deolali. This hospital in the First World War also treated enemy prisoners of war, including Turkish soldiers.

Colonel A. W. Sheen named in the above newspaper article who presided at, and supported the Soldiers' Eisteddfod was Cardiff born consulting surgeon, Colonel Arthur William Sheen, RAMC (Royal Army Medical Corps), who not only served as the Commanding Officer of 34 WGH, Deolali, but was also for a period of time the consulting surgeon to it.

Also at Deolali during the First World War was the smaller, 1,200 bed, 44th British General Hospital (44 BGH).

The *Llais Llafur – Labour Voice* edition of 7 July 1917, had news of a planned Soldiers' Eisteddfod:-

An Eisteddfod to be held at Kinmel Park Camp
Arrangements are well in hand for holding a Chair Eisteddfod on a large scale at Kinmel Park in September next and prizes of up to £100 are offered. The Prime Minister (the Right Honourable David Lloyd George) is expected to preside at one of the meetings.

Sadly, despite extensive research, nothing further can be found on this planned 'large scale Soldiers' Eisteddfod' at Kinmel Park Military Training Camp, Bodelwyddan, near Rhyl, or indeed if it did actually take place.

5

Welsh National Eisteddfodau 1914 to 1918 – the difficult wartime years

The Welsh National Eisteddfodau that did take place during the First World War gave their organisers, their competitors and their visitors, problems that pre-war and post-war did not exist. These 'problems' included financial ones, ones of duration, transport ones and concerted opposition from many quarters as to their actually taking place at all.

Following Germany's brutal invasion of 'gallant, neutral little Belgium', Britain declared war upon Germany on Tuesday, 4 August 1914. This declaration immediately had repercussions in Wales and the rest of Britain for all kinds of non-military organised events, national and local. So much was in a complete state of uncertainty that major future events began to be cancelled – one was the forthcoming 1914 Welsh National Eisteddfod, to have been held at Bangor, North Wales.

The cancelled 1914 National Eisteddfod, due to have been held at Bangor

The *Birmingham Daily Post* edition of Friday, 21 August 1914:-

WELSH NATIONAL EISTEDDFOD POSTPONED
At a meeting of the guarantors and executive of the National Eisteddfod of Wales, at Bangor, last night, it was unanimously decided to postpone the festival fixed for September 7, until September next year.

The 'Temple of Peace', the large temporary marquee 'building' due to house the main events of the forthcoming Welsh National Eisteddfod at Bangor was already set up, but now no longer required. A new and totally different use was found for it, as was reported by the *Exeter and Plymouth Gazette* of Friday, 11 September 1914:-

'TEMPLE OF PEACE'
AS RECRUITS DEPOT
Bangor, Thursday.
'The Temple of Peace' erected at Bangor to accommodate 7,000 people at the Welsh National Eisteddfod, which was to have been held this week, but has been postponed until next September on account of the war, was this afternoon examined by the military officers and the Finance Committee of the Eisteddfod. It has been agreed to let the building until next July to provide accommodation for the overflow of the Welsh recruits to Lord Kitchener's Army, for whom no room can be found in the now overcrowded depot at Wrexham.

The *Liverpool Echo* of Friday, 20 November 1914, had details of the latest plans for future Welsh National Eisteddfodau, with the First World War still in its infancy:-

THE NATIONAL EISTEDDFOD
It will be remembered that the Welsh National Eisteddfod which was to be held this year at Bangor, and next year at Aberystwyth, were postponed for twelve months, owing to the war, and that consequently the application for the holding of the Eisteddfod at Birkenhead in 1916, had also to be postponed. The provisional committee who have in hand the promotion of the Birkenhead movement have been in

communication with the Eisteddfod authorities, and as a result the request will be made at the Bangor celebration next year for permission to hold the festival in the Cheshire borough in 1917. It may be explained, that it is necessary to make the application two years in advance. Birkenhead's claim to the honour she seeks does not appear to have been contested, so far as 1916 was concerned, but the postponement for a year may bring forward other competitors.

The 1915 National Eisteddfod held at Bangor

With the cancellation at very short notice in 1914, of that year's National Eisteddfod, which was to have been held at Bangor, the 1915 National Eisteddfod, again to be held at Bangor, met with some vociferous opposition from prominent people in Wales as it approached.

The *North Wales Chronicle* of Friday, 25 June 1915, brought the rancour to the notice of the public. With passions running high, words were certainly not minced:-

THE BANGOR EISTEDDFOD
BISHOP OF ST ASAPH'S PROTEST
The following letter appeared in the Manchester Guardian of Thursday:-
Sir, – We are bidden to concentrate and mobilise the whole forces of the nation.

At such a moment, is Wales going to draw off from this life-and-death struggle the labour, the forces, the enthusiasm which are involved in the preparation for and in the holding of the Eisteddfod? The spectacle of Sir Henry Lewis and the Eisteddfod fiddling, while the Empire is on fire is not edifying – Yours etc. A. G. Asaph, The Palace, St Asaph, June 21st.

NATIONAL EISTEDDFOD NOT A HOLIDAY

A correspondent on Thursday, was able to ascertain the views of a number of prominent supporters of the National Eisteddfod regarding the protest of the Bishop of St Asaph against 'continuous fiddling while the Empire is in danger'.

The section of Welsh thought, admirably voiced by the Rev John Williams, Chaplain of the Welsh Army, claims that the postponement will bring home to Welsh people as nothing else possibly could that we are in the throes of an unparalleled struggle.

'Our language, our system of education, our national institutions, everything is in danger', one bard remarked, 'and sterner work than singing and musical competitions demand our attention'.

Sir Henry Lewis, who is the leading worker in connection with this year's festival, states that the Eisteddfod is no mere holiday gathering, but the meeting of the university of the common people of Wales, and therefore should be held in days of stress and tumult, even as the university capping ceremony was to be held.

The fact remains that the Bishop's protest may produce unexpected developments.

PREDICAMENT OF THE GUARANTORS

'Eisteddfodwr' writes: With reference to the Bishop of St Asaph's letter, the local guarantors find themselves committed to the expenditure of from £2,000 to £3,000. The further postponement of the Eisteddfod is quite out of the question. If it is abandoned will the Bishop and those who think with him raise a fund which will enable the guarantors to meet their obligations? If so, I feel sure they would welcome such a solution of their difficulties – difficulties which are unique in the history of the Eisteddfod.

A. G. Asaph as he styled himself in the letters he wrote, was Alfred George Edwards, then the Bishop of St Asaph (born 2/11/1848 – died 22/7/1937), who post-war in 1920, when the Church of England was disestablished, and the entity of the Church in Wales came into existence, was elected as the first Archbishop of Wales. He retired in 1934, and died in 1937, and was buried at St Asaph.

The Bishop of St Asaph had not approached the matter of the 1915 National Eisteddfod taking place with a neutral mind, but one sadly in great pain and turmoil, for only a few short weeks earlier his own son, Lieutenant Henry Laidley Garland Edwards had been 'killed in action' in France. He was killed on 16 May 1915, aged twenty-nine, when with 1st Battalion, the Royal Welch Fusiliers (formerly with 3rd Battalion), and was buried at Brown's Road Military Cemetery, Festubert, Pas de Calais, France.

During the First World War, Bishop A. G. Edwards held 'afternoon garden parties' at The Palace, St Asaph, the fine residence provided for the Bishop of St Asaph. On one occasion a large number of the officers from the nearby Kinmel Park Military Training Camp were invited to a particularly large such soiree, in order to meet with the Chaplain General, who was making a visit to the area that included his addressing the soldiers at Kinmel Park Camp. Perhaps, it would have been better in such dire times of war not to have held such garden parties, the officers' time better spent elsewhere?

As for the Reverend John Williams, better known as Colonel, Reverend John Williams, Brynsiencyn, senior chaplain to the Welsh Army Corps, well his comment one might say showed that he failed to grasp that the majority of the people in Wales did not need the postponement of their National Eisteddfod to bring home to them that they were in the throes of an unparalleled struggle, as many had already suffered the loss of loved ones, friends or work colleagues, plus the newspapers day after day, both national and local, brought to them bucketfuls of war related misery.

An extract from the *North Wales Chronicle* of Friday, 16 July 1915:-

THE NATIONAL EISTEDDFOD
WOUNDED CAPTAIN AND COMPOSER TO CONDUCT BANGOR CHOIR
Mr Cyril Jenkins the famous young Welsh composer, whose cantata 'Llewellyn' is to be performed at the final concert of the Bangor National Eisteddfod, on August 6th, has been selected by the Bangor Eisteddfod Choir to conduct the performance of this work. Mr Cyril Jenkins has only recently returned wounded from the front, where he held the rank of Captain in the Royal Field Artillery.

The *Denbighshire Free Press* of Saturday, 31 July 1915, had the programme of events for the following weeks National Eisteddfod at Bangor:-

THE ROYAL NATIONAL EISTEDDFOD BANGOR
2nd to 6th August
MONDAY; 2nd AUG. – Final Test Performances in the Dramatic Competition at the County Theatre. 2.00 p.m.: 'ASGRE LAN' by the Bethlehem Dramatic Company, Pentyrch, near Cardiff. 8.00 p.m.: 'BEDDAU'R PROFFWYDI' by the Red Dragon Drama Company, Carnarvon.
TUESDAY; 3rd AUG. – FEMALE CHOIRS COMPETITION; Welsh Folk-Song Competition for School Choirs, etc. CONCERT: MISCELLANEOUS.

Artistes: Miss Sybil Vane, Miss Dylis Jones, Mr David Ellis, Mr Evan Lewis, Mr Herbert Brown and Miss Olwen Rowlands, with full Orchestra (Band of the Royal Marines).

WEDNESDAY; 4th AUG. – CROWNING OF THE BARD. Children's Choirs Competition. Children's Action Song etc. CONCERT: 'ELIJAH'. Artistes: Miss Sybil Vane, Miss Dilys Jones, Mr David Ellis and Mr Herbert Brown. The Eisteddfod Choir conducted by Dr Roland Rogers, with full Orchestra.

THURSDAY; 5th AUG. – CHAIRING OF THE BARD. President: RT HON D. LLOYD GEORGE, MP CONCERT: 'THE DREAM OF GERONTIUS', etc. Artistes: Miss Phyllis Lett, Mr Gervase Elwes and Mr Ivor Foster. The Eisteddfod Choir, with full Orchestra.

FRIDAY: 6th AUG. – Welsh Folk-Song Competition for Mixed Voices etc. CONCERT: 'LLEWELLYN' (Cyril Jenkins) and MISCELLANEOUS. Artistes: Miss LAURA EVANS-WILLIAMS, Mr Seth Hughes, Mr Ivor Foster and Mr W. Herbert Davies. The Eisteddfod Choir, with full Orchestra.

Admission to each Eisteddfod Meeting or Concert, 1s to 5s. Military Men in uniform, half-price. Season Tickets, 20s to 30s.

For further information apply to the General Secretary, Eisteddfod Office, Bangor.

Despite the backdrop of rancour and opposition, the 1915 National Eisteddfod at Bangor did take place, for it had the backing of 'him' – David Lloyd George, the man who only weeks earlier had been appointed Minister of Munitions. Unlike the Bishop of St Asaph, Reverend John Williams, Brynsiencyn and their ilk, he saw for a number of sound reasons the need for the National Eisteddfod to take place.

So, on Thursday, 5 August 1915, at this National Eisteddfod gathering in Bangor, David Lloyd George, the pragmatic and charismatic orator arrived, and gave to those assembled in Bangor an incredibly rousing and patriotic speech, which also trumpeted the need for this 1915 National Eisteddfod to have been held. Many of the throng it was said, stood in awe of him, with this speech being widely reported upon in the newspapers of all the home nations and further afield, including the United States:-

The *Dundee Courier* of Friday, 6 August 1915, had a long article on the matter:-

CIVILISATION WILL BE PUT BACK A GENERATION SAYS MR LLOYD GEORGE AT WELSH GATHERING

Mr Lloyd George, accompanied by Mrs Lloyd George and his daughter, Miss Megan, was yesterday afternoon present at the ceremony of the Chairing of the Bard at the Welsh National Eisteddfod at Bangor.

The Minister of Munitions, who had a magnificent reception, passed from the station to the Eisteddfod building over a route lined by 4,000 people, who had been waiting for hours.

A resolution expressing the loyalty of the 10,000 Welsh assembled at the National Eisteddfod and their unalterable constancy to the Allied cause, having been adopted with enthusiasm. Mr Lloyd George, apparently commenting upon the controversy as to the advisability of holding the Eisteddfod during the war period, even after a year's adjournment, said he was glad the Eisteddfod had been held, because he did not relish the idea of the Welsh muse being placed in an internment camp, with barbed wire to keep her there till the end of the war. She was not an alien enemy, but a native of the hills; not a German spy, but a bonny lass from the Welsh glens; and he rejoiced that they had freed her once again.

THE UNCLEAN SPIRIT

He observed that this year they had omitted from the Bardic ceremony, the ancient Eisteddfod question, 'A oes heddwch?' (Is It Peace?) What was the good of asking that question? Everywhere the sounds of war trumpets rent the air from sea to sea. The land of Britain was trembling with the march of myriads preparing for war. On quiet nights he could, in his Surrey cottage, hear the sound of cannon fired in anger on the battlefields of France, and he knew with horror the work that was going on, and as he heard it, his lips uttered the old Gorsedd prayer, 'Oh Jesus, prevent wrong'.

'Is there peace?' cried Mr Lloyd George. 'No', he answered, 'and why not'? Because an unclean spirit had possessed the rulers of a great nation.

WALES' PART

Now and again he continued, a nation had to fight to win, sometimes had to fight to retain those elementary rights which lifted men from above the beasts of the field – justice, liberty, righteousness.

Mr Lloyd George went on to proudly state that many Welshmen had come forward: *'fully armed for battle and mightier than ever. Their three regiments had grown to 100,000 men, and more and more Welshmen were gathering to the camping grounds, as they heard that liberty was in danger. When Magna Carta was wrested from a tyrannical King there was a Welsh contingent amongst the forces that achieved that victory for English freedom, and there were Welsh names among the signatories of that potent document.'*

He concluded by speaking of liberty and that victory for

David Lloyd George

Britain and its Allies was certain, viewing the future with anxiety, but not with dread.

Not surprisingly the *North Wales Chronicle*, published in Bangor, had in their edition of Friday, 6 August 1915, several pages and numerous articles, long and short, devoted to that week's Bangor National Eisteddfod. A number of speeches were made during the week by prominent Welshmen. The one below from 'Llew Tegid', provided some light relief:-

Llew Tegid the conductor, remarked that the Bangor Eisteddfod Committee owed a debt to Mr Lloyd George that they would never realise fully, nor be able to repay. His faithfulness to Wales in the present circumstances would be of everlasting credit to him (*cheers*). 'I am not going to say anything', he added, 'of his value this moment to Britain, to Europe, to civilisation; he will tell you all that himself' (*loud laughter*).

'Llew Tegid' his bardic name, with the birth name of Lewis Davies Jones, was born on 3 November 1851, at Ffriddgymen, near Bala, then in the old Merionethshire. He was a most zealous supporter for many years of Welsh National Eisteddfodau. For twenty-seven years he was the headmaster of Garth School, Bangor, and relinquished the headship to organise the collecting of the funds needed for new buildings to be built at the University College of North Wales, Bangor. He wrote the Welsh words to many old folk songs that had been discovered. He first acted as conductor at a National Eisteddfod in 1902 at Bangor, and with one exception, 1905, he was a conductor at every National Eisteddfod until 1925. A conductor at Eisteddfodau is best described as being the Master of Ceremonies. 'Llew Tegid' was said to have had: *'the exceptional gift of being able to manage a large crowd. His voice was clear and penetrating. He had a fund of ready wit and considerable personal charm.'*

'Llew Tegid', Lewis Davies Jones, died on 4 August 1928, aged seventy-six, and was buried at Glanadda Cemetery, Bangor.

This article went on to state that the Gorsedd Prayer was offered by the Rev Ceitho Davies, who appeared in his military uniform as a chaplain in the Welsh Army. Since the commencement of the war in early August 1914, Nonconformists in Wales had been urging the Government and military authorities to appoint Welsh chaplains, because of the large numbers of members of evangelical bodies in Wales, now serving with the colours, as it was put. One of the very first such appointments was when in November 1914, Reverend Ceitho Davies, a native of Llanpumpsaint, Camarthenshire, was made a chaplain to the Welsh Army Corps.

The *Birmingham Gazette* of Saturday, 7 August 1915 reported upon the King, George V and the Welsh National Eisteddfod that was taking place at Bangor:-

KING'S REPLY TO WELSH
At the Welsh National Eisteddfod at Bangor yesterday the following telegram addressed to the Mayor of Bangor, was read –

'The King is greatly touched by the loyal, warm-hearted message addressed by you to His Majesty in the name of the ten thousand Welshmen assembled at the National Eisteddfod of Wales. The assurance it contains of the united and enthusiastic support of the Welsh Nation in these critical days strengthens His Majesty's unswerving conviction that victory will be ultimately secured to the Empire and our Allies'.

'STAMFORDHAM'

'STAMFORDHAM' who signed the communication was Arthur John Bigge, 1st Lord Stamfordham, who had been the private secretary to Queen Victoria in her latter years on the throne, and then to King George V. He was more than just a private secretary and was in reality King George V's chief advisor, especially through the First World War. Lord Stamfordham is credited with having the idea and then of persuading the King to agree to it – for the British Monarchy to change their very Germanic 'family name' of Saxe-Coburg-Gotha to the so English/British sounding, House of Windsor. This change occurred by Royal Proclamation in July of 1917, as after all the German aeroplanes dropping bombs on Britain and particularly London by this time, were German Gotha Bombers!

Leaving aside the 'ten thousand Welshmen' part in the Lord Stamfordham communication, with all and sundry in the country still oblivious to women and their growing contribution to the war effort, and that many women were in attendance at the Eisteddfod, it did show that many in Wales were patriotic towards 'Britain', the King and to the defeat of the enemy – Germany and its Central Powers cohorts.

In the Friday, 6 August 1915 edition of the *North Wales*

Chronicle an unnamed contributor penned an extensive and thoughtful article on the different aspects of the 1915 National Eisteddfod held that week at Bangor and of matters behind the scenes. It began by stating that it was a review of: The celebration of the High Festival of the Welsh Nation for 1915. It continued: The first thing that strikes any visitor to the Eisteddfod is that the war is responsible not only for the postponement for twelve months of the festival, but also for the very great changes necessitated in the manner of the holding. There can be little doubt had the local community twelve months ago been able to see what the circumstances would be at the present time, they would have taken the plunge then and held the Eisteddfod on the date originally announced. Then, whatever other difficulties would have had to be surmounted, the Committee would have not had to face the unprecedented disadvantage of being deprived of every special travelling facility always in former years available. It was to this cause more perhaps, than any other, that the decreased attendance this year, which will probably result in a financial deficit, must be attributed.

The contributor who seemed to have 'inside knowledge', informed readers that a special meeting of the National Eisteddfod Association, together with the Gorsedd Association had taken place, at which a number of important topics were discussed and voted upon. These included the likely financial loss that the 1915 Bangor National Eisteddfod would have to endure due to the difficult wartime circumstances of its holding. The National Eisteddfod Association normally made a grant to a National Eisteddfod of £100 or less in the form of special prizes for the competitions, in return for which it claimed half of any Eisteddfod surplus, when of course there was one, whether it be large or small. But with the exceptional circumstances of that years' National Eisteddfod, the secretary, Sir Vincent

Evans in his annual report felt it to have been the duty of the Association to extend substantial financial assistance to the Bangor Eisteddfod Committee should their financial deficit prove serious. A resolution was then unanimously adopted expressing admiration for the courage shown by the Bangor Eisteddfod Committee in holding the Eisteddfod under such unprecedented difficulties and pledging that the Association would render all possible assistance. It called upon all the friends of National Eisteddfodau everywhere to contribute according to their ability, in order to assist the Bangor Eisteddfod Committee, should the need arise. Mr Lloyd George who was in attendance was said to have given a fine speech supporting this resolution. During this speech he pointed out that there had been widespread criticism over the lack of excursion trains to and from Bangor for the National Eisteddfod. He explained that the Government had in wartime now taken over the running of the railways and putting on special excursion trains, even for the National Eisteddfod was not possible. He made an eloquent appeal to Aberystwyth to emulate the courage displayed by Bangor and to go ahead and hold their National Eisteddfod the next year, 1916. It was he said: 'Necessary if only to maintain the national spirit and confidence. The war might last another year, for the war must go on until the enemy was completely vanquished. But if the Eisteddfod were kept alive during the troublous period of war it would come out of the declaration of peace like gold purified by fire'. Mr Lloyd George was said to have never addressed a more earnest or more eloquent appeal to his fellow-countrymen and it was confidently anticipated that the courageous action of Bangor in holding the Eisteddfod in this year would be emulated by other towns for as long as the war lasted.

The contributor then went on to write of two innovations he, or perhaps it was a she, approved of, and deemed deserving of praise, which had taken place earlier that week at the Bangor National Eisteddfod. Firstly, the holding of a competition in performing a Welsh drama: The Bangor Committee had performed a national service by holding this competition and it had firmly established a dramatic competition as an essential part of the Eisteddfod programme, and no Eisteddfod in the future would be complete without it. That in an age of progress the country would not be satisfied with the drama as a mere side show to the Eisteddfod, for when all was said and done, that was the position accorded it at Bangor. The contributor bemoaned the drama had been pushed into the background of the Monday night before the visitors had come to the town. But believed that if it had been held later in the week, and at the Eisteddfod pavilion which could have been adapted to become a theatre stage, rather than their using a local building, the County Theatre, more money would have been taken than the £200 odd they took on the Monday. That the drama could have been substituted for an evening concert on the Tuesday or Wednesday, and would have crowded the pavilion to the utmost capacity of its accommodation.

The other innovation the contributor liked was the children's action song competition which apparently proved to be of a distinctly dramatic character, and the contributor believed was one of the most attractive and successful features of the week's programme. The contributor continued: The idea of Nonconformist ministers, with their Puritan leanings, not only attending but taking part in theatrical plays is a sign of the times. Among those who most applauded the dancing on the Eisteddfod platform on Wednesday were grave and reverend seigniors, who but a few years ago would have excommunicated their church members had they dared to witness so unholy an exhibition.

Writing of the Gorsedd, the contributor wrote, and it was

for that time a rather enlightened pro-female piece: There are two features in connection with the Gorsedd which deserve special notice. These are first, the unusually large number of Gorsedd graduates by examination initiated this year – a remarkable tribute in itself to the ever-increasing popularity of this the most ancient initiation in our land. Bangor has special cause to be satisfied. The city and district contributed a large proportion of the new graduates – and of these, an unusually large proportion were ladies. The male members of the Gorsedd must look to it or they will be outclassed and outnumbered by the ladies. The suffragettes should be gratified to find that the Welshwomen are the better 'men' in Wales. In passing, reference may be made to two Eisteddfod successes. A lady competitor shared the prize for Welsh lyrics with the bard who won the international crown at the great San Francisco Eisteddfod last month. Does not this foreshadow the possibility of our having shortly to welcome a chaired lady bard or a crowned queen of poets for Wales? Of a surety the men must look to their laurels. Indeed, had the Bangor Committee exercised the power, now possessed by Eisteddfod committees of counting the writing of a drama in Welsh, we should this year have had to crown a lady instead of a mere male man.

Another article from the same edition of the *North Wales Chronicle*:-

All the bardic addresses were not of necessity warlike, although they dealt with the war. One of the most striking and deserving to be placed on record was the admirable set of verses delivered from the Logan Stone by the Eisteddfod conductor 'Penar' in honour of the brave lads at the front. They deserve to be read and learned on every hearth in Wales. They read:-

Y BECHGYN YN Y FFOSYDD
(The Lads in the Trenches)

Mae'r bechgyn yn y ffosydd
Yn dal y cleddyf dur,
Yn enw Daw a chrefydd
A'n gobaith fyth yn bur;
Mae'r bidog yn disgleirio
Yn enw rhyddid dyn;
Y nef, y nef, fo'n cofio
Ein bechgyn ni bob un

Mae llawer cartre' Nghymru
A dydd ei aberth mawr
Yn cael ei ysgrifennu
Yn naear Ffrainc yn awr;
Y nef fo'n ymgeleddu
Yr aelwyd roes ei rhan,
I'an glywes utgorn rhyddid
Yn galw i helpu'r gwan

Mae'r bechgyn yn y ffosydd,
Ry'm ninnau wrth y fainc,
A'n gweddi ffyddiog beunydd
Yn cofio daear Ffrainc;
Daw rhyddid eto i ganu
Fel mwyalch yn y nen;
Daw'r bechgyn 'nol i Gymru
A'r goron ar ei ben

'Penar' who wrote the above verses was Griffith Penar Griffiths who was brought up at Ebenezer, Trecynon, Aberdare. He was ordained in 1884 and his first pastorate was at Merthyr Vale. He was as a congregationalist minister, and for the thirty-one years up to his death the pastor at Siloam, Pentre Estyll, Swansea (in Welsh: Abertawe). He became a well known Eisteddfodic conductor and adjudicator, in addition to being a well regarded writer of verse and prose in the Welsh language.

'Penar', Griffith Penar Griffiths, died aged fifty-eight on 22 December 1918, at this time residing at Penllwyn, Courtenay Street, Manselton, Swansea. He was buried at the Mynyddbach Burial Ground, Swansea. The *Amman Valley Chronicle* of Thursday, 2 January 1919, gave an account of his funeral, and one aspect of it was I proffer most unusual – a christening also took place.

> ... Prior to the cortege leaving the residence, the deceased's little grandson, Eryl Penar Griffiths was christened over the coffin by the Revs Samuel Williams (New Siloh) and W. Bowen (Manordeilo).

The Chair and also the Crown prize at the 1915 National Eisteddfod at Bangor, were both awarded to Dr Thomas Herbert Parry-Williams (generally known as T. H. Parry-Williams), who was born on 21 September 1887, at Rhyd Ddu, Caernarfonshire. He had also in 1912, at the National Eisteddfod held at Wrexham (in Welsh: Wrecsam) been awarded both the Chair and Crown prizes. He was a Welsh poet, author and academic, for many years professor of Welsh at the University College of Wales, Aberystwyth. In 1958 he was knighted and became Sir Thomas Herbert Parry-Williams.

But this well known Welsh public figure was also a great writer of essays in the Welsh language. He is credited with having introduced to the Welsh language, essays as a stand alone literary genre – a Welsh 'Montaigne' if you will – Michel Eyquem de Montaigne, the great French philosopher, writer and statesman of the French Renaissance, who had invented and popularised the essay, making it a literary genre to be respected. Montaigne's work influenced great philosophers and writers, such as Rene Descartes, Jean-Jacques Rousseau, Friedrich Nietzsche and our own William Shakespeare. During his lifetime, T. H. Parry-Williams had published between 1928 and 1966, seven volumes of his essays on such diverse topics as 'the mysteries of the universe', and the far more mundane, 'the strange complexities of a motorcycle engine'.

T. H. Parry-Williams' died on 3 March 1975, at the age of eighty-seven and was buried at the Beddgelert Cemetery, Beddgelert, Gwynedd. A collection of his essays was posthumously published in 1984, entitled 'Casgliad o Ysgrifau'. It is a book in the Welsh language of T. H. Parry-Williams' short essays, a number of which hark back to his childhood in Snowdonia – for he was of course born at Rhyd-ddu in the shadow of the highest mountain in Wales – our great mountain edifice that truly has the power to inspire – Snowdon (in Welsh: Yr Wyddfa).

The Bangor National Eisteddfod of 1915, which had fought through great difficulties to actually take place, made a deficit of £986 – a quite considerable loss.

At the final session of this Eisteddfod on the Friday, the conductor, 'Llew Tegid' revived into the Gorsedd proceedings the welcoming of Welshmen from overseas. Though with the ongoing world war he had only one Welshman, Mr David Jones, together with his daughter and niece to welcome and introduce to the audience. The three from Australia received a hearty welcome and Mr David Jones replying from the platform said he thanked the meeting on behalf of the Welshmen of Australia, where he had resided for the past thirty-five years. He said there were thousands of successful Welsh people in Australia and thousands more were wanted there 'to open the greatest country in the possession of Great Britain'.

The only address delivered was one by 'Dyfrig', Canon Davies, who said he had been greatly impressed by the short religious service at the Eisteddfod pavilion on the Wednesday of the Eisteddfod, followed by the united service at Bangor Cathedral, which was officially attended by members of the Gorsedd. As 'Dyfrig' put it: 'This happily combining Bardism with Christianity'. He went on to say another thing that had impressed him was the excellent speech by Mr Lloyd George and the hearty reception that had been afforded to him by both English and Welsh people. He was also convinced that the Eisteddfod was the strongest national bond of union at that critical time – cries of hear, hear, emanated from the audience to this. Some people he said complained that the Eisteddfod was too narrow and too rigidly Welsh, but that was not true for it paid occasional visits to England and was always glad to fraternise with the English. Others he said complained that the friends of the Eisteddfod indulged in too much self-praise, but having regard to the past achievements of the institution, who could not help praising it. That some of the masterpieces of Welsh literature and most successful researches were due to the Eisteddfod, and it was destined to enrich that literature in an increasing degree so long as its supporters remained loyal to it.

'Penar' then announced to loud applause that Madame Laura Evans-Williams would sing the Eisteddfod Song and as she appeared on the platform the applause renewed. She was said to have sung magnificently 'Gwlad y Delyn' ('Land of the Harp') and was 'uproariously encored'. This song is regularly performed today by the likes of the internationally renowned Welsh tenor, Gwyn Hughes Jones, and remains one of the Welsh nation's favourites.

The *North Wales Chronicle* further highlighted the great difficulties, especially financial, that the 1915 Bangor National Eisteddfod was held under. 'The Committee' being the Bangor National Eisteddfod Committee:-

> As evidence of their sympathy with the Committee in the face of the exceptional difficulties they have had to contend with, it may be mentioned that the musical adjudicators and artistes made a reduction of 25 per cent in their fees. Two of the paid door keepers have returned five shillings each from their pay towards the funds, and one of the poetical adjudicators has returned five guineas and another four. Rumour has it that others propose to follow their example.

The 1916 National Eisteddfod held at Aberystwyth

With the 1914 National Eisteddfod having been cancelled at short notice, and the 1915 National Eisteddfod having taken place under considerable opposition, even from a number of its normally most prominent advocates, the 1916 National Eisteddfod set for Aberystwyth also had a hard road to travel along.

It was on Friday, 10 December 1915, at the Town Hall, Aberystwyth, with the town's Mayor, Alderman John Evans in the chair, that an important meeting of the 1916 Aberystwyth National Eisteddfod Committee took place, during which a sub-committee's report was discussed at great length, as to the holding of the 1916 National Eisteddfod, but on a modified, lesser scale.

It had been ascertained that a marquee to seat 4,000 to 5,000 people could be hired for around £100, and that the total cost including seating accommodation would not exceed £200. This was indeed to be a 'toned down' National

Eisteddfod due to the ongoing war. A very full account of the proceedings was covered in the *Cambrian News and Merionethshire Standard* of Friday, 17 December 1915. An extract taken from it has Mr Jenkin James, the Honorary Secretary for the 1916 Aberystwyth National Eisteddfod, having written to Mr David Lloyd George concerning the proposed 1916 National Eisteddfod at Aberystwyth, and asking for his views upon it taking place:-

In view of the great interest evinced by Mr Lloyd George, MP, in connection with the matter, the sub-committee thought it desirable to communicate with him directly and to ask for his advice, and guidance with reference to the holding of the Eisteddfod during the war. The reply dated November 22nd was in the following terms:-
'Dear Mr James. – I have been considering the question you put to me regarding the advisability of holding the National Eisteddfod at Aberystwyth next Summer. The responsibility of deciding the matter must rest ultimately and principally on the Eisteddfod Committee, but my own opinion was expressed in the speech I delivered at Bangor in August last. I am firmly convinced that our great National music festival should not be put into a condition of suspended animation during the war. What possible reason is there for discouraging literature and music during the progress of the war? An Eisteddfod is not merely a frolic, it is a serious contribution to the best side of a nation's life. I quite realise you cannot give the same prizes and you cannot expect the same crowds as during the piping times of peace. Railway arrangements must be curtailed. But the most glorious days of the Eisteddfod were those in which the audiences were comparatively small and the menu restricted, but substantial. It would be a good thing for the Eisteddfod

itself to lead a simple life for a year or two. Let Aberystwyth give us a sample of what a real Welsh Eisteddfod used to be. One or two days at the outside would enable you to do that without incurring crushing liabilities for an elaborate show. I understand that the National Eisteddfod Association are offering the Committee substantial financial help in the event of a deficit, in addition to £100 in prizes, and if it is desired to eliminate some of the big choral contests and to reduce the time to (say) two days. I cannot help thinking that the Eisteddfod will turn out to be a great success. With regard to my being able to be present, I can only say at this stage that I consider it always to be a great pleasure, and even a duty to attend the National Festival of Wales, but you will readily understand that it is impossible for me to say what urgent calls there may be on my time at so distant a date'.

Yours faithfully, D. Lloyd George.

The Eisteddfod sub-committee felt certain that the strong expression of support for the event taking place in Mr Lloyd George's letter would carry great weight, especially with the inhabitants of Aberystwyth, and would materially assist the guarantors to arrive at a decision. The sub-committee had carefully looked at all the options, and they came to the conclusion that under the prevailing wartime conditions there was no alternative but to restrict the Eisteddfod as regards duration and programme. The net expenditure on the different sections of the Eisteddfod needing to be reduced – £50 in literature, £150 in music, and £50 in art. This reduction the sub-committee appreciated, would involve the abandonment of a large number of items particularly in the musical section, where the chief choral, second choral, male voice, orchestral, and brass band competitions, all of them most popular features, would have to be sacrificed.

This meeting of the Eisteddfod Committee went on to decide that a competition for mixed choirs be substituted for those events to be lost. But even at this time in late 1915, it was believed by many involved in the National Eisteddfod movement that not only the National Eisteddfod of 1916, if it went ahead would have to be reduced in duration, competitions and expense, but at least also the 1917 and 1918 ones. Those who were the guarantors financially for the 1916 and future National Eisteddfodau were now required to come up with monies based on the new expenditure and income estimates for mere two day, heavily curtailed ones. Estimates of the new expenditure and income were discussed.

It was quite obvious that in some quarters in Wales, and within the Welsh establishment, that there was quite vociferous opposition, as there was the previous year of 1915, to the 1916 National Eisteddfod taking place – full stop! Their main reasons for their opposition were two fold – firstly, that at a time of war such an event diverted people from the task of fighting the war on all fronts – secondly, that it was the cost involved in it being held.

With hindsight, looking at the expenditure of 'Britain' in this war, a quite staggering estimated £6 million cost per day, a few hundred pounds here and there, raised by the good people of Wales, backed by guarantors, for such an important annual cultural festival was but a tiny drop in a mighty, vast ocean.

On this December 1915 evening, two votes were held after the sub-committees findings had been fully debated on whether the 1916 National Eisteddfod at Aberystwyth should actually take place. The first produced a fourteen to thirteen result (it was not revealed which way) with some abstentions.

Strong appeals were then made by Professor E. Edwards, the Deputy Town Clerk, and by Mr D. C. Roberts. A second vote was then taken and it was decided sixteen to fourteen that the 1916 National Eisteddfod at Aberystwyth would go ahead, but in a modified form over just two days. This important Eisteddfod Committee meeting had lasted two hours, and a week later the guarantors of the 1916 event also met.

So it was by 'the skin of its teeth' that the 1916 Aberystwyth National Eisteddfod was to take place. If it had been cancelled as almost happened, what fate would have befallen the National Eisteddfodau for 1917, 1918 and beyond?

It was reported in the newspapers in early February 1916, that the guarantee fund for the forthcoming 1916 Aberystwyth Eisteddfod had far exceeded the sum that had been sought. Professor E. Edwards proudly reporting that they expected by the Eisteddfod itself to have an even larger guarantee fund. As a result, Professor E. Edwards of the Eisteddfod Committee proposed at a meeting of the Eisteddfod guarantors that the 1916 Aberystwyth National Eisteddfod be held during the week commencing 14 August, be of two days duration, and with three evening concerts. This was unanimously carried. It was also carried that any profits arising from this Eisteddfod would be donated to a national war fund.

In April 1916, at a meeting of the Executive Committee of the Welsh National Eisteddfod, a letter was read out from Mr W. M. Hughes, the Prime Minister of Australia, regretting that he was unable to accept the invitation to become the president of one of the Eisteddfod meetings, as he would have left Britain before 16 August 1916.

William Morris Hughes, known as 'Billy', though born in Pimlico, London, had been born to Welsh parents. His father, William Hughes, a Welsh speaker, was born in Holyhead, Anglesey, whilst his mother was a farmer's daughter born in Llansantffraid, then in Montgomeryshire. William Morris Hughes had emigrated to Australia in October 1884, aged twenty-two. On 27 October 1915, he became Australia's seventh Prime Minister, and held this high office until 9 February 1923.

At this meeting, it was also discussed that Welsh Members of Parliament should be approached for them: 'to use every endeavour to get cheap train tickets to Aberystwyth for the Eisteddfod.' Satisfaction was also expressed that Mr Lloyd George, the Chancellor of the Exchequer had informed them that the Eisteddfod would be exempt from the entertainment tax.

The question of prices for admission to the Gymanfa to be held on the day following the Eisteddfod was also discussed. It was decided that sixpence (6d) would be charged for each of the three meetings, and that the price of the reserved seats for the three meetings would be 2s 6d (also known as half-a-crown in 'old money').

It was announced that amongst the works which the Eisteddfod Choir would perform at the concerts would be Stanford's, 'Revenge' and David Evans', 'Deffro mae'n dydd'.

There was no doubt whatsoever from the tone of even the supporters of the 1916 National Eisteddfod that it was to go ahead in very difficult times, and in the teeth of considerable opposition. The future of National Eisteddfodau in wartime and beyond, were truly in jeopardy, like they had never been before!

Some months earlier it had been mooted in the press that at the next National Eisteddfod to be held later that year of 1916 in Aberystwyth, a special award would be made to 'the bravest Welsh soldier of the war'. How such an idea, however well meant it was could be fairly made to work is baffling. However, sense prevailed and the Friday, 17 March 1916 edition of the *Camarthen Journal and South Wales Weekly Advertiser* reported upon the latest thinking:-

THE NATIONAL EISTEDDFOD – GOLD MEDALS TO VC'S

At the Aberystwyth National Eisteddfod gold medals will be awarded to all Welsh soldiers and sailors who have won the VC in the course of this war. It was at first intended to offer a gold torque to the soldier or sailor who had performed the greatest act of bravery, as was done at the Llangollen Eisteddfod in 1858, a few years after the Crimean War, but as the war is still in progress it was considered impossible to decide at the present time, on the relative merits of the particular acts of bravery.

This idea, a rather nice 'Welsh one', was however opposed by many senior figures in the military, particularly by one or two General's, the most 'vocal' being General Sir Francis Lloyd, who was responsible for the defence of London (London District), and also in 1915 had become the Honorary Colonel of the Royal Welch Fusiliers. He stated that any such awards would undermine the country's highest award for gallantry – the Victoria Cross (VC), which where awarded in the name of, and by, His Majesty King George V. After this and other similarly deprecating opinions had been received, Professor E. Edwards moved that the idea be dropped, which was agreed to by the National Eisteddfod Association.

The Friday, 2 June 1916 edition of the *Cambrian News and Merionethshire Standard* had this:-

NATIONAL EISTEDDFOD
A PATRIOTIC OPPORTUNITY

Our advertising columns contain an announcement of the National Eisteddfod to be held at Aberystwyth on August 16th, 17th and 18th. The third day will be devoted to a unique feature in connection with the Eisteddfod, namely, a National Singing Festival which has been arranged on the suggestion of the Minister of Munitions. He is expected to preside. It is really through the initiative of Mr Lloyd George that the Eisteddfod is being held this year instead of being further postponed, owing to the war. The local promoters, backed up by the Eisteddfod Association, have to face unprecedented difficulties: but their course of action has been determined by their desire to make this years' gathering worthy of the opportunity and worthy of the patriotism of Wales. Not only is it intended to serve a patriotic objective by aiding war funds, but it is also intended that the Eisteddfod and Gymanfa will be a patriotic stimulus in the National Crisis.

This article went on:-

... Though it has been neccessary to curtail the competitions considerably, the programme of music arranged has been highly commended and interesting choral competitions are expected. The competitions will appeal particularly to local choirs. In addition to the competitions, rare musical treats will be provided at the three evening concerts, when the Eisteddfod Choir under the leadership of Mr J. T. Rees, Mus. Bac., will perform such works as: 'The Revenge', 'Deffro', 'Mae'n Dydd', 'Duw Sydd Noddfa', 'Life of Moses' and Welsh airs. Prominent artistes have been engaged.

The idea of holding the Gymanfa on the third day has

been approved of throughout the Principality, and will it is believed, attract a large and representative gathering. Professor David Evans has been offered and has accepted the conductorship for the day. Old Welsh hymn tunes, fifty-one in number, and two anthems, will be sung and copies of the programme will be ready shortly.

Congregational choirmasters are requested to apply to the General Secretary for a supply of copies of the programme which are sold at the following prices:- Old Notation, 6d each; Tonic Solfa, 4d each.

Entries for all the Eisteddfod Competitions close on July 10th. Season tickets, price £1, admitting to reserved seats at all the Eisteddfod meetings, evening concerts, and the Gymanfa are obtainable from the General Secretary and seats can be booked on or after August 1st at the Eisteddfod Office, Cambrian Chambers, Aberystwyth.

The ancient Gorsedd Ceremonies will be performed on Wednesday and Thursday mornings on the beautiful and historic Castle Grounds.

This advertisement for the forthcoming National Eisteddfod at Aberystwyth appeared in June 1916, in a number of Welsh newspapers:-

NATIONAL EISTEDDFOD OF WALES,
ABERYSTWYTH, 1916
AUGUST 16TH AND 17TH; Competitions.
AUGUST 18th: National Cymanfa.
THREE GRAND EVENING CONCERTS HAVE BEEN ARRANGED.
LAST DAY FOR RECEIVING ENTRIES: JULY 10TH.
Reserved Seats at all meetings of the Eisteddfod, evening concerts, and Gymanfa can be booked on or after August 1st. Surplus proceeds in aid of War Funds.

For Further Particulars and Season Tickets, Price £1, apply to
GENERAL SECRETARY
Eisteddfod Office
Aberystwyth.

The *Llais Llafur* reported in their Saturday, 17 June 1916 edition: It is interesting to note that five thousand copies of the special Welsh tunes to be sung at the Gymanfa Gerddorol in Aberystwyth during the Eisteddfod week are to be sent as a gift to Welsh Soldiers in the trenches.

The *Amman Valley Chronicle* of Thursday, 3 August 1916, had details of the forthcoming Aberystwyth National Eisteddfod:-

NATIONAL EISTEDDFOD
MR LLOYD GEORGE'S SUGGESTION
The executive of the Aberystwyth National Eisteddfod, at a meeting presided over by the Mayor, Mr John Evans, appointed Professor Edwards and Llew Meirion conductors of the Eisteddfod in conjunction with Llew Tegid. The following had been appointed presidents of the various meetings:- Tuesday night's concert, the Mayor of Aberystwyth; Wednesday morning's meeting – Lord Rhondda, afternoon – Sir Owen M. Edwards; evening concert, Mr Vaughan Davies, MP.

Thursday morning's meeting – Mr Herbert Lewis, MP, afternoon – Mr Lloyd George; evening concert, Lieut-Colonel David Davies, MP.

Dean Roberts, the Rev John Williams (Brynsiencyn), and Principal T. F. Roberts were appointed presidents of the morning, afternoon, and evening meetings respectively of the National Gymanfa, to be held on the Friday.

It was reported that 3,000 copies of the Gymanfa programme had been sent to Welsh troops on active service, and Mr Lloyd George had recommended that at least another 2,000 copies be distributed in this way. An intimation was made that Mr Lloyd George's suggestion would, in all probability, be carried into effect.

The committee decided to order 5,000 more Tonic-Sol-fa programmes, the 10,000 already ordered, having practically been sold out.

The Reverend John Williams (Brynsiencyn) had obviously 'undergone a conversion' of some kind, for only twelve months earlier he had been publicly vociferously opposed to that year of 1915's National Eisteddfod at Bangor taking place, let alone wishing to play an important role in the proceedings of a National Eisteddfod held in wartime. So, despite the ongoing war and difficulties facing the organisers, there was an increased appetite even from some of its previous detractors, for National Eisteddfodau to continue to be held despite the ongoing and worsening war.

Unlike the previous year's National Eisteddfod held at Bangor, this 1916 one to be held at Aberystwyth would have specially arranged 'excursion trains' to aid it. It was reported that arrangements had been made with the Cambrian Railways to run late trains to Devil's Bridge, Machynlleth, Barmouth and Dolgelley on the three nights. There were also to be special trains from and to Newtown and Llanidloes on Thursday. The Great Western Company was to run special trains from and to Camarthen, with connections to Aberaeron and Newcastle Emlyn on the Thursday and Friday.

The 1916 National Eisteddfod was held at Aberystwyth,

over three days duration as had been envisaged, with the third and final day given over to a National Cymanfa – a National Singing Festival. The *Liverpool Echo* of Thursday, 17 August 1916, reported upon it:-

A GREETING FROM WELSH TRENCHES

Mr David Davies, MP, Parliamentary Secretary to the War Minister, presided this morning at the Welsh National Eisteddfod at Aberystwyth, where about 10,000 people assembled to witness the great choral competitions.

The conductor, Professor Edward Edwards announced the receipt of a telegram from the Welsh boys now in the trenches conveying their best wishes for the success of the Eisteddfod and Gymanfa from Welshmen in the field: Next Eisteddfod we shall be with you, said the message, which was signed Thirty-eighth Welsh Division (*cheers*).

Professor Edwards added that evidently the boys in the trenches rejoiced that they had decided to go on with the Eisteddfod, and he was sure the audience would be very glad to see the boys at home next Eisteddfod (*hear, hear*). The Committee had decided to send a reply (*applause*). The telegram was read in English as written, but Professor Edwards gave a Welsh rendering of it, which elicited renewed applause.

Sir Owen M. Edwards in an afternoon presidential address at the Eisteddfod, spoke of 'the hundreds of sons of the Eisteddfod who were this day fighting for their country on the fields of Europe'. He referred to the victory that he had no doubt was coming for Britain and its Allies.

David Lloyd George had only recently been appointed as the new Secretary of State for War, and at this Aberystwyth

National Eisteddfod on Thursday, 17 August 1916, he made his 'keynote speech'. It was not for nothing in these years that the Thursday of a National Eisteddfod was colloquially known as 'Lloyd George Day'. In this speech he vigorously defended the holding of the National Eisteddfod in wartime and severely criticised a letter published in a major English newspaper objecting to this National Eisteddfod being held. Mr Lloyd George had received a great ovation as he entered the Eisteddfod Pavilion, which was renewed when he rose to speak. He spoke in Welsh and in English alternately. This was a fine rousing speech, witty in parts and on occasions distinctly acerbic. It was foremost an earnest and robust defence of National Eisteddfodau being held during wartime:-

I have come here at some inconvenience to attend and, if necessary defend this Eisteddfod. I have been a strong advocate of its being held. I was anxious that there should be no interruption on account of the war in the continuing of the Welsh National Eisteddfod (*applause*). It is too valuable an institution – it has rendered too great a service to our country to risk its life by placing it in a state of suspended animation for an indefinite period. There are a few people who know nothing about the Eisteddfod, who treat it as if it were merely an annual jollification which eccentric people indulge in. A letter appeared in the *Times* this week written by a person who seems to hold that opinion. He signs himself 'A Welshman'. He evidently thinks that the publication of his name would add nothing to the weight of his appeal, so he has wisely no doubt – withheld it. That gentleman makes it clear that he has no objection to common people attending, but he expresses the hope that important people like the Welsh Members of Parliament will not encourage such an improper assembly. His notion of the Eisteddfod is a peculiar one, and as there may be a few outside Wales who hold the same views I think I must refer to this estimate of its purport and significance. He places it in the same category as a football match or horse race, and a good deal beneath a cinema or music hall performance (*laughter*). These are kept going afternoon and evening without the slightest protest. To this egregious Welshman the competing bards are so many racehorses started round the course by Mr L. D. Jones, the chairing day being, I suppose, the bardic Oaks (*laughter*). Sir Vincent Evans would be the Grand Bookmaker - (*loud laughter*), who arranges the stakes and, of course, we all have something on one or other of the starters (*more laughter*). The meetings of the Cymmrodorion, the Gorsedd of the Bards, the Arts Section, the Folk Song Society, the Union of Welsh Societies, and the Bibliographical Society are the sideshows which amuse the Eisteddfod larrikins whilst the race is not on (*laughter*). That is where the thimble rigging and the coconut shies, and games of that sort are carried on. No wonder this intelligent gentleman is ashamed to avow his name. I challenge him to give it (*cheers*). Prizes for odes, sonnets, and translations from Latin and Greek literature. Essays on subjects philosophical, historical and sociological. An adequate treatment of some of these subjects necessarily involves a good deal of original research. Art is encouraged. Even agriculture is not forgotten (*hear, hear*). Forsooth, all this effort should be dropped on account of the war? To encourage idle persons to compose poetry during the war is unpatriotic? Promoting culture amongst the people – a futile endeavour at all times – during the war is something every Welsh Member of Parliament ought to snub? To give a prize for the study of the social and industrial conditions of a Welsh village is dangerous at any time; during the war it is doubly so! To excite the interest of the people in literature during the war is a criminal waste of public money? Above all, to sing during a war, and especially to sing national songs during a war, is positively indecent, and the powers of the Defence of the Realm Act ought at once be invoked to suppress it (*laughter*). Hush, no music please! There is a war on. Why should we not sing during this war? Why, especially should we not sing at this stage of the war? The blinds of Britain are not down yet, nor are they likely to be (*loud cheers*). The honour of Britain is not dead (*loud and prolonged cheers*). Her might is not broken; her destiny is not fulfilled, her ideals are not shattered by her enemies (*cheers*). She is more than alive. She is more potent. She is greater than she ever was. Her dominions are wider. Her influence is deeper. Her purpose is more exalted than ever (*cheers*). Why should her children not sing? (*hear, hear*). I know war means suffering. War means sorrow. Darkness has fallen on many a devoted household; but it has been ordained that the best singer among the birds of Britain should give its song in the night, and according to legend that sweet song is a song of triumph over pain. There are no nightingales this side of the Severn. Providence rarely wastes its gifts. We do not need this exquisite songster in Wales. We can provide better (*cheers*). There is a bird in our villages that can beat the best of them. He is called Y Cymro. He sings in joy, he sings also in sorrow. He sings in prosperity, he sings also in adversity. He sings at play, he sings at work. He sings in the sunshine, he sings in the storm. He sings in peace. Why should he not sing in war? He sings in the daytime, he sings also in the night. Hundreds of wars have swept over these hills, but the Harp of Wales has never yet been silenced by one of them, and I should be proud if I contributed something to keep it in tune during the war by the holding of the Eisteddfod today (*loud and prolonged cheers*). Our soldiers sing the songs of Wales in the trenches, and they hold their little eisteddfodau behind. I heard a good deal of them when I was there last week. There is not one of them who would not be sorry if we gave up our Eisteddfod. They want to feel that when they are upholding the honour of Wales, we are doing our best to keep alive all the institutions; educational, literary, musical, and religious, which have made Wales what it is (*cheers*). They want the fires on every national altar kept burning, so that these shall be alight when they return with the laurels of victory on their brow from the stricken fields of this mighty war in Europe, Asia, and Africa. That is why I am in favour of holding the festival of Welsh literature and of song, even in the middle of Armageddon (*cheers*). But I have another and even more urgent reason why this Eisteddfod should be kept alive during the war. When this terrible conflict is over, a wave of materialism will sweep over the land. The urgent needs of the hour will create it. Nothing will count but machinery and output. There is nothing more fatal to a people than that. I have done my best to improve machinery and to increase output; but it is not all. That is why I believe in keeping alive during the war, and to the end of the war, an institution like the Eisteddfod. National ideals without imagination are but as the thistles of the wilderness; fit neither for food nor fuel. A nation that depends upon them must perish (*cheers*). We shall need at the end of the war better workshops; but we shall also need more than ever every institution that will exalt the vision of the people above and beyond the workshop and the counting house. We shall need every national tradition that will remind them that men cannot live by bread alone. I make no apology for advocating the holding of this Eisteddfod in the middle of this great conflict, even though it were merely a 'carnival of songs', as it has been stigmatised. The storm is raging as fiercely as ever; but now there is a shimmer of sunshine on the waves (*cheers*). There is a rainbow on the tumult of the surging waters. Let us sing (*cheers*). The struggle is more terrible than it has ever been; but the legions of the oppressor are being driven back, and the banner of right is pressing forward (*cheers*). Why should we not sing? It is true there are thousands of gallant men falling in the fight; but let us sing of their heroism. There are myriads more standing in the battle lines facing the foe, and myriads more behind ready to support them when their turn comes. Let us sing to the land that gave birth to so many heroes (*cheers*). I am glad that I came down from the cares and labours of the War Office of the British Empire to listen and join with you in singing the old songs of Wales (*cheers*), which our brave countrymen on the battlefield are singing as a defiance to the enemies of human right and liberty (*prolonged cheers*).

David Lloyd George then alluded to the telegram which had been received by the secretary of the Eisteddfod from Welsh soldiers fighting on the Western Front. This telegram he said gave greetings and best wishes for the success of the Aberystwyth Eisteddfod and Gymanfa from Welshmen in the field and included the words: 'Next Eisteddfod we shall be with you' (*great cheers from the audience*). David Lloyd George then responded with: 'Please God they will. That telegram is from the 38th Welsh Division. They don't ask us to stop singing during the war'.

An official reply was despatched to the Commandant of the 38th Welsh Division from the Eisteddfod at Aberystwyth to the telegram received from Welsh soldiers of the 38th Division. It was worded: The Eisteddfod assembled was much touched by the hearty greetings from the Welsh soldiers in the field, and wishes them a safe and speedy return, and promises a great welcome when the time comes. Welsh soldiers will be glad to know Aberystwyth Eisteddfod is a great Success.

Fine sentiments but sadly for many Welsh soldiers of the 38th Welsh (Infantry) Division fighting on the Western Front there would be no 'safe and speedy return' – indeed for many there would never be a return, for by the time the content of this telegram reply had reached the Western Front many of them had already a few weeks earlier been mowed down in the hail of machine gun bullets at 'Mametz Wood', that glorious nadir which inflicted so many casualties upon the 38th Welsh Division, that it was over a year until they were ready again to fight a major action, and that was on 31 July 1917, at The Battle of Pilckem Ridge – a part of the hell on earth that we call Passchendaele – The Third Battle of Ypres.

The *North Wales Chronicle* of Friday, 18 August 1916 had this:-

THE NATIONAL EISTEDDFOD
A MODIFIED PROGRAMME
HYMN-SINGING AS A FEATURE
The Royal Welsh National Eisteddfod was opened at Aberystwyth on Wednesday, and will continue until today (Friday) evening. Shorn on this occasion of much of its old glory, the festival still bids fair to justify the courageous policy adopted by the Cardiganshire resort

in the face of the opposition of a loud-voiced minority of townspeople who urged its abandonment this year on account of the war.

Influenced largely by Mr Lloyd George, the promoters decided to 'carry on' with a less ambitious programme, to which three days are being devoted in place of the usual five or six days. In the circumstances a number of competitions have been dropped and the prize money offered is substantially smaller. Pageants have disappeared, and little other than essentials occupy the attention of Eisteddfodwyr.

A noteworthy feature introduced this year is the conspicuous place given to hymn singing. A book of about fifty tunes has been published for the festival and the singing of these favourite old compositions tomorrow is calculated to put new life into the Eisteddfod, in more than one respect.

There are about 10,000 visitors at Aberystwyth, and though the weather has broken up somewhat there are great hopes for the complete success of the festival.

Another article from the same edition:-

MR LLOYD GEORGE AND THE WOUNDED SOLDIERS

When Mr Lloyd George was about to enter the Eisteddfod marquee on Thursday, he noticed two of the wounded soldiers from the Aberystwyth Auxiliary Hospital.

He immediately went to them and after enquiring about their welfare, asked in what battle had they received their wounds. One of the men showed his arm and said the wound had been caused by a German explosive bullet. 'Are you sure'? asked the War Minister.

'Well, the doctor say so', replied the soldier. Mr Lloyd George's face hardened. 'We will give them explosive bullets before we have done with them'.

The Chair at this 1916 National Eisteddfod, held at Aberystwyth, was awarded to J. Ellis Williams on the topic of 'Ystrad Fflur' (Strata Florida), the former Cistercian abbey at Pontrhydfendigaid, near Tregaron. Reverend J. Ellis Williams, a native of Nefyn on the Llŷn Peninsula was educated at Clynnog and at Bala-Bangor. For a number of years he was the Minister of Pendre Congregational Chapel, Bangor. He had on three previous occasions been placed second for the chair prize at National Eisteddfodau. However the Crown Prize was withheld and not awarded this year – in Welsh 'Neb yn Deilwng' ('No One is Worthy').

The specially organised Cymanfa Ganu Genedlaethol (In English: National Singing Convocation) was held on the Friday at Aberystwyth under the auspices of the National Eisteddfod, and brought together a body of some 3,000 members of choirs and congregations from ostensibly three counties of Wales. A committee had earlier selected for this festival a number of the best known Welsh hymns, 'wedded' as it was put, to old tunes, all rendered as far as was possible in their original forms. Care was taken to include the denominations of both the Anglican and Nonconformist churches in Wales. Lloyd George then Secretary for War was openly credited with having come up with the idea of a singing festival as part of the Aberystwyth National Eisteddfod, and to show his approval of it taking place he took an active part in the day's proceedings. However, on the downside it was said that the Aberystwyth Eisteddfod Pavilion was found to have been quite inadequate to accommodate the 6,000 or perhaps a little more, who attended.

The morning session was held under the presidency of the Dean of Bangor, who was supported by Mr Lloyd George, Mrs Lloyd George and their daughter Megan. Amongst those also on the platform were Sir Herbert Lewis, MP, Sir Frank Edwards and the Reverend John Williams (Brynsiencyn). This singing festival was opened with prayer by the Archdeacon of Cardigan, the Venerable David Williams of Aberystwyth. The Dean of Bangor in a short address stated that the singing festival was a new departure in the history of the National Eisteddfod and was just what was required during such grave times. The singing then commenced, under the conductorship of Mr David Evans, Cardiff.

In the afternoon session, the Reverend John Williams (Brynsiencyn), the Calvinistic Methodist minister and honorary chaplain to the Welsh Division presided. He was in relation to the 'need for the fight against the German foe', a very close ally of Lloyd George. The Reverend John Williams did on many occasions during the First World War, wearing his colonel's uniform, preach in the chapels and market places of rural North Wales, that Welshmen, especially those from the country areas should come forward and fight the enemy, and uphold the rights of small nations such as Belgium. For he regarded this war as a 'Holy War', one that Welshmen, Christian Welshmen, needed to fight in, to bring about defeat for Germany and its Central Powers allies. His eagerness for Welshmen to enlist and fight, plus his 'recruiting drives' in full military uniform from the chapel pulpits did not go down well with many in Wales. He was disrespectfully referred to by his detractors as being 'Lloyd George's Chaplain'. Post-First World War many Welsh veterans vociferously derided Reverend John Williams (Brynsiencyn) for having used his great eloquence to encourage so many young Welshmen to enlist and fight, many of whom were subsequently killed or wounded. They were saying in effect that 'he had their blood on his hands'!

The opening service at the afternoon session was conducted by the Reverend D. Tecwyn Evans, Birkenhead. The Reverend John Williams (Brynsiencyn) in his address described this singing festival as being the first of its kind in which all the religious denominations of Wales were represented and he hoped that it marked the beginning of a new epoch, as their aims were the same, so why should they not sometimes unite to achieve it? Cheers resounded from the audience to this statement. He went on: 'There must be something out of place in a religious body which rendered it impossible for it to join with others in a campaign against the common enemy of mankind. The festival was really the forerunner of many blessings that would result from the war. The action would, perhaps, be poorer in material wealth, but infinitely richer in character. I have no idea what the people of England or Scotland or Ireland might be doing these days, but in Wales at any rate, they had the spectacle of the people assembling in their thousands to praise God in the midst of the war, with the Minister of War on the platform'. Cheers again resounded to this.

Principal W. H. Hadow of Armstrong College, Newcastle, and Dr H. P. Allen, spoke at the evening session.

The *Cambrian News and Merionethshire Standard* of Friday, 25 August 1916 had this light hearted story relating to Lloyd George and the recently held Aberystwyth National Eisteddfod:-

A PENNILESS WAR MINISTER

While Mr Lloyd George was waiting to enter the Eisteddfod marquee and for a competing choir to finish, he was tackled by little Miss Dolly Owen, daughter of Mr Owen, builder, Penglais Road, to buy a flag in aid of the wounded soldiers fund. He took a flag, but found that he had not a penny in his pocket to pay for it.

He, however, soon raised a loan for that amount from Colonel David Davies, and smilingly completed the transaction much to Dolly's delight at having sold a flag to Mr Lloyd George.

The first meeting of the Executive Committee of the 1916 Aberystwyth National Eisteddfod to take place post-Eisteddfod, did so on Monday, 2 October 1916. Here the accounts were discussed and votes of thanks were awarded to Mr W. H. Williams, superintendent of the Cambrian Railways and Mr John Rees, the divisional superintendent of the Great Western Railway, for the special railway facilities both companies had provided on the Eisteddfod days – no mean feat in wartime. Commemorative cards were to be issued to all of the stewards at the Eisteddfod, expressing the gratitude of the Eisteddfod Committee for their voluntary service.

Mr T. Lewis was pleased to report that copies of the Cymanfa programme continued to be sold and that 100 had lately been sent to Welsh soldiers serving in Egypt.

A letter had been received by the Eisteddfod secretary from a Gunner Jarman: I was reading in my bivouac 'somewhere in Macedonia' of the great speech made by Mr Lloyd George at your Eisteddfod in Aberystwyth. The heading was 'Song in War Time'. The grand little man was denouncing the gloomy ones. I thought it great the way he put it before them, hoping I will be there next time it is held. I was very glad to hear it was a success. I am a Welsh Tommy who is delighted to hear some singing and never more pleased than when I am on the stage with a good male voice party. Cymru am byth.

Another letter had been sent by a Private A. T. Lee,

writing from Salonika to RSM Fear, who resided in the Aberystwyth area: We still have it warm here and still got the flies, so that we are kept pretty lively with one thing and another. I have been reading all about the Eisteddfod in the Cambrian News. It must have been a wonderful thing to hear 10,000 voices. I would liked to have been there. I am glad it was a success. Aber rarely fails when it takes things up. I was also pleased to hear there were so many visitors.

The *Cambrian News and Merionethshire Standard* of Friday, 1 June 1917 published the final accounts of the previous years National Eisteddfod, held at Aberystwyth:-

THE NATIONAL EISTEDDFOD
A meeting of the Executive Committee of the Aberystwyth National Eisteddfod was held on Friday night to receive the balance sheet. Alderman T. J. Samuel presided. The total receipts of the Eisteddfod and Gymanfa amounted to £3,373 13s 0d, and the payments to £2,116 4s 7d. The Gymanfa receipts amounted to £777 19s 1d, and the payments to £347 3s 8d. The balance in hand from the Eisteddfod and Gymanfa is £1,216 18s 2d, the Eisteddfod balance being £786 2s 9d. After paying £393 to the National Eisteddfod Association, the Committee will have £823 18s 2d to divide between the various war funds. A committee has been appointed to report as to the division of the surplus.

The 1917 National Eisteddfod held at Birkenhead

The *North Wales Chronicle* of Friday, 7 September 1917 had details of the opening of the 1917, Welsh National Eisteddfod, held at Birkenhead. Birkenhead in Welsh being 'Penbedw':-

NATIONAL EISTEDDFOD

The National Eisteddfod of Wales opened at Birkenhead on Wednesday, with the procession of bards to the Lower Park for the Gorsedd Ceremony. The Archdruid, Dyfed, presided, and among the interested spectators were Lord Leverhulme and the Mayor and Mayoress of Birkenhead (Mr and Mrs James Merritt), who were introduced to the Chief Eisteddfodwyr. Being wartime the Gorsedd was opened for the third time without the Ceremony of Unsheathing the Gorsedd Sword, and the old challenge: 'A oes heddwch' (Is there peace?) was not raised.

The Archdruid, in his address, said half the world was on fire, but the Eisteddfod, after a fainting fit at Bangor, had recovered itself at Aberystwyth, and appeared strong and reinvigorated at Birkenhead. 'Here is a message from the trenches', he added – 'from the boys of Wales undergoing the ordeal of fire somewhere in France': Success to the National Eisteddfod at Birkenhead. Many of us here are thinking of it and singing the old songs of Wales in the trenches. When God willing we return, our songs will have a new and more tender note, and our patriotism will burn with a brighter flame (*cheers from the audience*).

The Crown Prize at this 1917 National Eisteddfod, held at Birkenhead was awarded to Wil Ifan for his 'Pwyll Pendefig Dyfed'. 'Wil Ifan' his bardic name, was William Evans, born on 22 April 1883 at Cwmbach, Llanwinio, then in Camarthenshire. He was like his father before him a congregationalist minister, being over the years such in both North and South Wales. But he had many talents – a poet and author in both Welsh and English, a playwright, newspaper columnist, broadcaster, lecturer, musician and an able artist.

In total he was awarded the Crown Prize at National Eisteddfodau on three separate occasions – Abergavenny in 1913, Birkenhead (Penbedw) in 1917 and Pwllheli in 1925. He was the Archdruid (in Welsh: Archdderwydd) of Wales in the Gorsedd of Bards from 1947 to 1950. 'Wil Ifan', William Evans died at Bridgend on 16 July 1968, and was buried at Rhydymain, near Dolgellau, then in the old county of Merionethshire.

A National Eisteddfod story of pathos, which later led to some controversy

At the greatly curtailed National Eisteddfod, held at Bangor in 1915, the male voice choir competition had been scrapped as it was put, owing to the lack of cheap rail excursions to and from Bangor for prospective choir members to be able to attend from around Wales. This competition's scrapping was said to have been one of the most regretted of the Eisteddfod's musical victims of wartime. However a late decision was made by the Eisteddfod Committee to extemporise a male voice choir competition on the Friday, offering the smaller than usual first prize of £15 for choirs of about thirty voices. Each choir to sing a piece entirely of their own choosing, rather than them being issued with the usual 'test piece'. The result was six 'local choirs' of an excellent quality it was said, turned up on the day to compete – two soldiers' choirs in their khaki uniforms from battalions of the Royal Welch Fusiliers and four civilian choirs.

The first to perform was the 'B' Company choir of 17th Battalion, the Royal Welch Fusiliers who had chosen to sing 'The Comrades' Song of Hope' and did so in splendid style. They were vigorously cheered by the audience as they marched smartly onto the stage and after they had finished singing the conductor of the Eisteddfod, 'Penar' cried out, 'God bless them', as they left the platform area. He then called for them to be given another cheer to which the audience gladly responded. Though all the choirs received cheers, the loudest were given to the two soldiers' choirs. The one from 16th Battalion, the Royal Welch Fusiliers was up next and they were loudly cheered as they marched onto the stage to also sing 'The Comrades Song of Hope'as their chosen piece. Another of the choirs chose this song whilst one sang Cyril Jenkins', 'The Assyrians came down', another 'The Martyrs of the Arena' and one 'Y Delyn Aur' ('The Golden Harp'). Dr Vaughan Thomas, a fine composer himself adjudicated, acting as such with Major George Miller. Dr Vaughan Thomas announced the result as being: The winners with 88 marks – 16th Battalion choir, RWF, conducted by Private Tom Ll. Tucker from Skewen (in Welsh: Sgiwen), near Neath. In second place – Llanrwst and Trefriw with 85 marks. Third equal with 79 marks was the 'B' Company choir, 17th Battalion, RWF, conducted by Private Samuel Evans of Rhosllanerchrugog, near Wrexham, and the Ebenezer choir. Fifth equal with 73 marks the Bangor and the Arfon choirs. Dr Vaughan Thomas congratulated and thanked the choirs for having come forward at such short notice and upon the excellence of the performances they had given.

It was then at the suggestion of 'Penar' that both of the choirs in khaki were invited back on to the stage to sing together their chosen piece of 'The Comrades' Song of Hope', under the direction of Major Miller. It was said: Both the khaki choirs marched with brisk military tread to the platform, amidst ringing cheers, and rendered the work with thrilling effect. Their joint rendition was said to have electrified the audience. The National Anthem was then sung and the meeting was brought to a triumphant conclusion.

Now forward two years to an event that took place during the 1917 National Eisteddfod, held at Birkenhead. A number of Welsh and English newspapers had this account, though slightly varied in their exact content:-

THE SACRIFICE OF WALES

The pathos of an incident at the Eisteddfod meeting at Birkenhead will live forever in the memory of everyone who was present. Two years ago at Bangor, two male voice choirs in khaki, both from the Welsh Army Corps in training at Llandudno, competed for a male voice choir prize and one of them was drawn from 17th Battalion, the Royal Welch Fusiliers, under the leadership of Private Samuel Evans of Rhosllanerchrugog and took part receiving great praise. The battalion soon afterwards went to France and on Thursday morning, 'Llew Tegid' announced in the Eisteddfod pavilion to the large audience that the conductor of this choir was now the sole survivor and that he was present amongst them at the Eisteddfod. Furthermore, that the relatives of the fallen men of 17th Battalion, R.W.F. had sent to the Eisteddfod Committee a decoration for him, this survivor. The decoration being a black and white rosette – the black to represent their mourning for the dear ones fallen and the white for the untarnished honour of 'the Lads'. General Sir Owen Thomas who was himself in deep mourning after the loss of two of his sons in the war was called to the platform to invest Corporal Evans with the rosette. Corporal Evans was invited to come forward and a 'bent and broken man arose' with difficulty, walking forwards slowly, leaning heavily on a stick. The feeling of the vast audience was intense and tears were in many eyes.

A controversy then arose from out of the above Birkenhead National Eisteddfod related incident, due to a simple misunderstanding and most certainly not anything that was done in an underhand way. The *Cambrian Daily Leader*, Tuesday, 25 September 1917 edition, sought to clarify matters through their publishing an exchange of letters:-

AN EISTEDDFOD STORY
Some Fresh Details of Pathetic 'National' Scene.
The Rev J. Evans Jones, Congregational minister, Skewen, writes us to the following effect:-
To the Editor
Sir, – May I presume on your usual courtesy in order that a matter be set right, to which public attention was called at the recent Birkenhead National Eisteddfod, and, as I am anxious to show, in a decidedly misleading manner. In the course of the proceedings there was a pathetic scene, when the Eisteddfod conductor called to the platform a certain wounded soldier who, it was announced, had led his male voice choir to victory at the Bangor National. The incident was given great publicity by the newspapers, from one of which let me quote the following:
'Two years ago at the Bangor Eisteddfod, two military choirs from the Welsh Army, under the fostering wing of General Sir Owen Thomas, competed. One of the choirs was from the 16th Battalion, the other from the 17th'. I have now before me a letter signed by Mr T. R. Roberts, general secretary of the Bangor National which he sent to Pte T. Ll. Tucker, 16th Battalion, Royal Welsh Fusiliers, of Skewen and handed to me by Mr John Tucker, the father, which conclusively proves that the above account is totally misleading. The letter is as follows:
Eisteddfod Offices, Bangor,
31st August 1915

Dear Sir, – In reply to your letter, the following is a copy of the adjudication in the singing of the male voice party from the 16th Battalion of the Royal Welsh Fusiliers, which won the prize of £15 under your conductorship at Bangor on the 6th inst: Good tone and colour. More sostenuto could have been secured, and this even when the chording was quite good. Good enunciation of words. Start was good. Nice pace. Good tempo chosen for both movements. A very fine crescendo was secured on page 5 and they were accurate in the chromatic bass passage, which is so frequently sung inaccurately. The rendition showed organic development. Good steady rhythm. Good conducting. Marks, 88. – D. Vaughan Thomas.

Yours faithfully,

T. R. Roberts

In justice to this talented young musician, Pte T. Tucker, 16th Batt., RWF, who is now on active service, it is only fair that the true facts of the case should be published.

The *Herald of Wales* of Saturday, 6 October 1917, sought to clear up this matter, once and for all:-

THE SURVIVOR

More About an Eisteddfod Incident

In view of the widespread interest taken in the incident at the recent National Eisteddfod, when, as reported in the 'Herald of Wales', Corporal Samuel Evans, Rhos, the conductor of a Military Choir, which had been awarded a prize at the Bangor National Eisteddfod two years ago, as the sole surviving member of that choir was invested by General Sir Owen Thomas at Birkenhead with an In Memoriam emblem. Our North Wales correspondent has interviewed Llew Tegid, the Eisteddfod conductor, who acted as master of ceremonies at Birkenhead.

Exception has been taken by the Rev J. Evans Jones, Skewen, and Mr L. J. Roberts, his Majesty's Inspector, Swansea, to the announcement officially and publicly made at Birkenhead that the winning choir at Bangor was that of the 17th Battalion of the Royal Welsh Fusiliers. The prize, they declared, was awarded not to the 17th Battalion Choir, under Mr Samuel Evans, Rhos, but to the 16th Battalion Choir, under the baton of Pte Tom Ll. Tucker, of Skewen.

Llew Tegid while admitting that a mistake was undoubtedly made at Birkenhead in announcing the 17th Battalion choir as 'the victorious choir', disclaimed all personal responsibility for the misstatement. 'It was not correct to announce as was actually done', he said, 'that it was the 17th Battalion Choir which had carried off the prize at Bangor. The information on which he acted was contained in a letter addressed to the Eisteddfod Secretary and was stated to have been sent by the family of two members of the choir of the 17th Battalion. I have ascertained since', he added, 'that it was the choir from the 16th Battalion that won the prize.

Still the 17th Battalion Choir was also a prize winner, a prize having been made up for it by the audience. The competition was an open one for male voice choirs and was not confined to military choirs. I have also ascertained that there are members of both choirs still alive, some still on active service, others discharged'.

Some newspaper accounts of the results of the hastily arranged male voice choir competition at the 1915 Bangor National Eisteddfod were incorrectly printed, with the added confusion that both choirs 'in khaki' were awarded 'prizes' on the day. The 16th Battalion choir as the winners received the £15 prize money and 17th Battalion were awarded a 'special prize' donated by Dr Owen Prichard of London for being a choir in khaki. These factors resulted in the announcement at the 1917 Birkenhead National Eisteddfod of the wrong choir as having been the overall 'winner' of the male voice choir competition back in 1915. This obviously was important to those involved, but in the great scheme of things bearing in mind the 'Hedd Wyn' chair ceremony grief of that same Eisteddfod week, it was but a minor matter.

It was not in fact true that Lance-Corporal Samuel Evans was the last surviving member of that 17th Battalion, RWF choir from 1915, as some were still in military service and others discharged. But a number of the choir had fallen in battle and quite a number of them including Lance-Corporal Samuel Evans himself had been wounded in action. Surely this detracts little from the sheer pathos of that black and white rosette presentation?

The 1918 National Eisteddfod held at Neath

It has been the custom for the venue for a National Eisteddfod to be chosen in advance of between eighteen months and two years. The *North Wales Chronicle* had this in their edition of Friday, 18 August 1916:-

EISTEDDFOD OF 1918
The Archdruid and Mr Llewellyn Williams, MP, presided at the joint meetings of the Gorsedd and Eisteddfod Association, held at the County School, on Wednesday. The question of holding the Eisteddfod in 1918 was considered. It was stated that no application had been received, though there were applications in former years from Barry, Aberdare, and Neath. It was decided to postpone the question for three months to give an opportunity for one of these towns to apply.

Mr Llewellyn Williams, in supporting the proposition, spoke in favour of adopting the Aberystwyth Eisteddfod as a model, so as to enable even small towns to entertain the festival.

On Tuesday, 19 December 1916, Sir Vincent Evans sent out circulars to the members of the two committees dealing with the Welsh National Eisteddfod, asking them to vote upon the claims of Neath, Barry and Porthcawl, for the venue to host the 1918 National Eisteddfod.

In the event, it was the town of Neath which was chosen as the venue for the 1918 National Eisteddfod.

Sir Vincent Evans was a particularly important and noteworthy figure for Welsh National Eisteddfodau, especially during the difficult times of the First World War. He was Sir Evan Vincent Evans to give his full name, born on 25 November 1852 at Nancaw, Llangelynnin, then in Merionethshire. In 1872 he left Wales for London, for a career initially as an accountant, to later become a journalist and author. On 30 June 1881, at St Augustine's Church, Highbury, London, he married London born, Annie Elizabeth Beale, and they went on to have two children together, Gladys and Lewis. He went into the business sector and became the managing director of the Chancery Lane Safe Deposit and Office Company Limited, and in 1909 was knighted.

But it is for his outstanding work over many years for Welsh cultural organisations and for wartime charities, that he is best remembered. For many years he was the secretary of the National Eisteddfod Association and also of The Honourable Society of Cymmrodorion (in Welsh: Anrhydeddus Gymdeithas y Cymmrodorion), the London based, learned Welsh society, which is still in existence

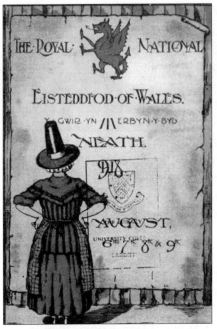

The official programme of the 1918 Neath National Eisteddfod

today. This society was prominent in the establishment of our modern annual Welsh National Eisteddfodau, which began in 1861 at Aberdare, South Wales.

During the First World War, Sir Vincent Evans was very active for good and important causes, as the honorary treasurer of The National Fund for Welsh Troops, 1915-1918; a trustee of The Welsh Troops' Children's Fund; and the treasurer of The London Welsh Belgian Refugees Fund, 1914-1915.

He was also for a period the chairman of the Royal Commission on Ancient Monuments in Wales and Monmouthshire, a member of the Royal Commission on the Public Records, and many more such appointments especially in the field of education councils.

Sir Vincent Evans, as he was generally known, was a very well known public figure, especially in Wales. He was a lifelong friend of David Lloyd George and no doubt this relationship did no harm to the important societies and charitable funds Sir Vincent Evans was so closely connected with. Sir Vincent Evans was said to have been: A man of massive and dignified bearing, with a leonine head and a genial smile. In 1922 he was made a Companion of Honour, and he died on 13 November 1934, aged eighty-one. He was described in the national press following his death as: One of the most worthy and useful representatives of Welshmen of his generation. He most certainly during his lifetime had done a great deal for the Welsh National Eisteddfod movement, for Welsh troops and their families, and to further the Welsh language and Welsh literature.

A meeting of the Neath National Eisteddfod Committee was held on Wednesday, 1 May 1918, under the presidency of Alderman H. P. Charles, JP. It was declared by a unanimous vote that despite the ongoing war that the Neath Eisteddfod would carry out the full four day programme, as had been originally arranged. This was announced with the backdrop of the war now going very much in favour of Britain and its Allies – allies that now included the powerful United States, who were sending thousands of troops every week to the Western Front, together with large amounts of military equipment and supplies. The German Spring Offensive of 1918 had failed to provide the German's and their Central Powers allies with victory. Now with the United States becoming ever more deeply embroiled in the war against them, and problems mounting back home in Germany, the war was close to being lost, with the momentum being very much against them, and with Britain and its Allies.

The National Eisteddfod duly took place in 1918 at Neath, South Wales, the first occasion for it to be held in this South Wales town. As had been expected, large crowds of people attended the opening on the Tuesday morning. The presidents for the day were Mr T. J. Williams, MP and Sir Henry Jones. 'Llew Tegid' and Professor Edward Edwards ('Pencer') were the conductors. The *Herald of Wales* in its special supplement issue of Saturday, 10 August 1918 stated: The irresistible attraction which commenced the day was of course the Gorsedd in Victoria Gardens at 8.00 a.m. Perhaps the Gorsedd collects, centralises and typifies the great Welsh characteristics of the Eisteddfod, which, form after all, the basis of the conception and growth of the Eisteddfod.

The main competitive event of the first day being the chief choral competition for which there were twenty entries, with the first prize being a handsome £70. The five adjudicators for this competition included two noted composers – Welsh born Dr David Vaughan Thomas and London born Mr Granville Bantock. These two men also adjudicated upon the orchestral competition for which two orchestras had entered.

There was a note of disappointment, for the Prime Minister, David Lloyd George was 'owing to important matters of state' unable to preside at the Eisteddfod on the Thursday, as was his usual way. However, he spent the entire following day, the Friday in Neath. He attended the Gymanfa and earlier in the day he had officially received the 'Freedom of Neath'.

Proudly it had been announced that this Neath National Eisteddfod would be a financial success for all the reserved seats for the Thursday had been sold before the Eisteddfod was even opened. Wales and the Welsh flow to this Palestra of Song, as the *Herald of Wales* put it, and continued: Financially alone, that is a significant and heartening omen to the promoters and to all Wales that owes so much to, and feels so much for the National Eisteddfod, wherever it is held.

The Presidential Address was given by Mr T. J. Williams, MP, who in his speech said: 'The Neath Eisteddfod would be memorable because of many circumstances, not least of which was that it had the honour of offering welcome to one whom he considered the greatest man in the world – Mr

Lloyd George'. Cheers rang out from the audience for those words of high praise for Lloyd George, the Prime Minister.

This *Denbighshire Free Press* article in their edition of Saturday, 10 August 1918, provided details and some financial figures for the Neath National Eisteddfod which had been held that week:-

THE NATIONAL EISTEDDFOD
The National Eisteddfod has been held this week at Neath, and has been a great success, although a deluge of rain on Monday night seemed likely to ruin the prospects, but the weather cleared and the attendance was very large at every gathering. On the opening day it was computed that 9,000 persons were in the pavilion and over £1,000 had been taken in the pay boxes, so that the financial success was assured thus, early in the week. One great event of the week was the Chair day on Thursday when the Prime Minister was to have presided, but was unable to be there until the evening. But he remained throughout Friday after the Psalmody Festival. The Gorsedd proceedings were a great attraction under the direction of the Archdruid Dyfed.

The article went on to state that the *'Crown Poem Bard'* winner was Mr D. Emrys Lewis, a Port Talbot journalist who was *'crowned by Dyfed with all the quaint ceremonial attaching'*. It also informed readers that with the subscriptions, season tickets and reserved seats sold prior to the Eisteddfod, they had covered all the expenditure of the Neath Eisteddfod which amounted to £4,000. The article also gave the result of the Friday's Male Voice Choir competition: 1st Williamstown (conductor Mr Ted Lewis). 2nd Welsh Guards (conductor Corporal J. Davies).

The Chaired Bard was the Reverend J. T. Job, formerly of Bethesda, who had now '*for the third time won the position of Chaired Bard*'. He was John Thomas Job, born 21 May 1867 at Llandybie, Camarthenshire, a Calvinistic Methodist Minister, who was also a noted hymn writer and poet. He was awarded the Chair at three National Eisteddfodau – Newport (in Welsh: Casnewydd) in 1897, Llanelli in 1903, and Neath (in Welsh: Castell-nedd) in 1918. He also won the Crown Prize at the Liverpool (in Welsh: Lerpwl) National Eisteddfod of 1900. Reverend John Thomas Job died on 4 November 1938.

In the *History of the Welsh Guards* by C. H. Dudley Ward, DSO, MC, an account is given of a choir of the Welsh Guards taking part in the male voice choir competition at the 1918 Neath National Eisteddfod, which was keenly contested by both military and non-military male voice choirs. This choir of the Welsh Guards, formed only in April 1918 at the Guards' Depot, Caterham, Surrey, was personally organised and supervised by Capt G. C. H. Crawshay, with Corporal J. Davies No. 3,707 as conductor, and Guardsman J. Witcomb No. 2928 as accompanist. It did contain a number of 'old soldiers', but its formation was credited to the Government's final recruiting rally of early 1918, which resulted in thousands of miners throughout Britain, including Wales, being released for Army service. Now with sufficient numbers and a confidence that many of the new men would prove to be able singers, and with nearly four months for them to practise before they would leave the Guards Depot, an opportunity presented itself for the formation of a choir, the standard and strength of which past circumstances had not permitted. The choir members during the period of their training at Caterham practised singing for two hours per day, including at the weekends.

Their first big public performance was when they sang at a regimental concert held at the Apollo Theatre, London, on 11 June 1918, and here a total of £500 was raised for the Regimental Prisoners' of War and Comforts Fund.

It was on 5 August 1918, that this eighty strong Welsh Guards choir left Caterham for Neath, to compete in the male voice competition at the National Eisteddfod. On their arrival in Neath they were met by some 3,000 people and amidst considerable excitement were fittingly played to their quarters by the band of the HM Welsh Guards under Lieutenant Andrew Harris, ARAM.

On Tuesday, 6 August and Thursday, 8 August 1918, they proudly took part in the Ceremony of the Gorsedd, joining in the procession and forming a circle around the Maen Llog (Logan Stone) to keep the ground while the addresses were being delivered. This action on the part of the authorities in having asked them as representatives of the Army to guard the sacred Gorsedd Circle was said to have been without precedent in the annals of Eisteddfodau and that they could have paid no greater compliment to the regiment.

The Gorsedd had from time immemorial been regarded as a purely civil and religious ceremony, from which the military had been rigorously excluded, but it was believed that in the Welsh Guards the Druids saw not the old-time band of hired assassins, but Welshmen of their own blood whose ideals, love of home, and pride of race, were also theirs. Welshmen fired with all their ancient ardour, once more fighting for Hen Wlad.

On Thursday, 8 August, the choir competed in the male voice competition. As they marched onto the platform they received a wonderful welcome from the vast audience of some 15,000 people, who rose to their feet, cheering them again and again. The result of the competition was not announced until nearly 6 o'clock, by which time the audience were said to have been in a state of the utmost excitement. Dr David Vaughan Thomas gave the adjudication in the test piece, 'Here's to Admiral Death', of which he was the composer. Fourteen choirs had competed and the Williamstown Choir was placed first with ninety-two marks and the Welsh Guards Choir second, with eighty-two marks. This result was received with acclamation, for it was recognised by the audience that the Williamstown Choir had given the finest sustained rendering of the piece, but that the Welsh Guards Choir with the exception of the opening phrases had been of equal merit. It was believed that initial nervousness was largely responsible for their disappointing opening phrases together with the fact that the first tenors had suffered from the loss of their leader, Guardsman S. Jenkins No. 5,376 who was said to have been suffering from a severe cold and was unable to sing. As their first practice of the test piece only took place at the end of June, in just two months they proved at Neath their ability to hold their own and more with the best male voice choirs in Wales, who had had six months in which to practice. Much credit for their fine performance was given to their conductor, Corporal J. Davies of whom it was said: His natural genius and Celtic temperament enabled him to bring out in each individual member that sense of artistic interpretation with which Welshmen are born. But great credit was also given to all the members of the choir, for they had never failed to attend daily practices after parade hours, when most men had only been too glad to rest.

This Welsh Guards Choir though did not leave Neath empty handed, for owing to the large number of competitors, a special prize was offered for the choir which had proved to be the quickest and smartest in mounting and leaving the platform. Mr Thomas Powell, Inspector of

Schools, Neath, announced after the adjudication that the Welsh Guards Choir had been awarded this prize.

Dr David Vaughan Thomas was born at Ystalyfera, then an industrial village in the Upper Swansea Valley, on 15 March 1873. He was a fine composer and musician, composing a large volume of anthems, songs and part-songs for both Welsh and English lyrics. A proud Welshman, he was a pioneer in the movement to lead one might say Welsh music away from their then limited choralism to a more sensitive practice and appreciation of other musical forms. To this end, when he gave his many recitals and lectures, and particularly when he planned the music programmes for several Welsh National Eisteddfodau, he always gave the most rigorous of leads towards the attainment of higher standards in music.

As a National Eisteddfod adjudicator he was very forthright in his pronouncements, whether delivering favourable or unfavourable ones. It was said of him that: His musical work was pervaded by an imaginative enthusiasm for the characteristic qualities of the Welsh National Culture and its distinctive expression of music. Perhaps his best known work is the cantata, 'Llyn y Fan' (1907), based on an old Welsh folktale associated with the South Wales lake, Llyn y Fan Fach. Other well known works of his include, 'The Bard' and 'A Song for St Cecilia's Day'.

His reputation is said to rest mainly upon his development of a distinctive approach to the word setting in his songs. He concentrated on the Welsh genres of choral and vocal music.

In 1906, Dr David Vaughan Thomas had married Morfydd Lewis, she being a daughter of Daniel Lewis, a weaver and a poet, who in July 1843 had led the "Rebecca Riot" at Pontarddulais which destroyed the hated Bolgoed Tollgate. Daniel Lewis was one of the leaders of this movement and it was said of him: Daniel Lewis was a man of unusual culture who fostered the radical ideas of the time.

One of the three sons born to Dr David Vaughan Thomas and his wife, Morfydd was the well-known and much liked Welsh newspaper journalist, author, broadcaster and raconteur, Wynford Vaughan Thomas, CBE.

Dr David Vaughan Thomas, composer, scholar and poet, died in Johannesburg, South Africa, on 15 September 1934, aged sixty-one. A large number of his instrumental compositions remain as yet unpublished. There is a fine slate plaque to his memory to be found at 141, Walter Road, Swansea, where he resided from 1918 until his death.

Official confirmation of the financial success of the Neath National Eisteddfod of 1918 appeared in the *Denbighshire Free Press* of Saturday, 17 August 1918:-

NATIONAL EISTEDDFOD

Neath Eisteddfod has proved the greatest financial success for many years; the receipts were £7,421, as against an expenditure of £5,021, leaving a surplus of £2,400. The previous largest surplus was at Carnarvon in 1877, of £1,400.

Considering the matter from a musical point of view, the Neath National Eisteddfod may also be credited with having achieved a decided success in the matter of the singing in the chief choral competition and in the male voice choir competition. Not that the choirs in the chief choral competition at Neath excelled or even equalled their rivals at the great Llanelly Eisteddfod of 1895, or those at Carnarvon in 1886, Wrexham in 1888, or London in 1909, in their appeals to the public ear. But that their interpretation of severer test pieces, plus a high degree of merit in pure singing, entitle them, speaking generally, to the higher ecominiums.

Judging from the remarks of the adjudicators the literary sections at the Neath Festival may be classed as somewhat commonplace compared with those at some previous Eisteddfodau, but both the chair ode and the crown poem seem to have been of considerable merit.

6

'Hedd Wyn' and 'The Black Chair Eisteddfod' of 1917

The 1917 National Eisteddfod, held at Birkenhead is best remembered for the awarding of the Chair prize that year. It is now of course legend, a Welsh legend, that the winning entry for the Bardic Chair at this National Eisteddfod of 1917 was announced by one of the adjudicators, T. Gwynn Jones, as being 'Yr Arwr' (In English: The Hero). The winning entry on this topic was written by 'Fleur-de-lis', the nom-de-plume of the winning author whose bardic name was 'Hedd Wyn' and whose actual name was Ellis Humphrey Evans. 'Fleur–de–lis' was then called upon to come forward to accept his award. The fanfare of trumpets sounded, but no one came forward. The Archdruid Dyfed then solemnly informed the expectant throng of the winning Bard's recent death on the battlefield. Shock and an eerie hush gripped those in the pavilion, followed for many by tears. Archdruid Dyfed later commented: *'The festival in tears and the poet in his grave'*. The finely carved bardic chair was empty, bereft of the winner. 'The Chair' had been hand crafted by the Flemish refugee Eugeen Vanfleteren, who had fled to Britain at the outbreak of the war and had settled in Birkenhead. 'The Chair' was now 'Hedd Wyn's' to keep by right, but his bright light had gone from this earth. 'The Chair' was ceremonially draped with a black sheet, and from that day onwards this Birkenhead, Welsh National Eisteddfod of 1917, has been known as 'The Eisteddfod of the Black Chair', or in the first language of 'Hedd Wyn' himself – 'Eisteddfod y Gadair Ddu'.

Yr Ysgwrn – the family home of 'Hedd Wyn'

'Hedd Wyn' – Ellis Humphrey Evans

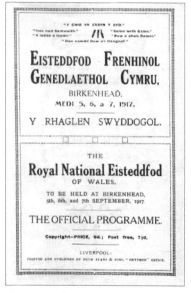

Official programme for the 1917 Birkenhead National Eisteddfod

The 'Black Chair' awarded to
'Hedd Wyn'

The CWGC headstone upon
'Hedd Wyn's' grave

The statue of 'Hedd Wyn' in
Trawsfynydd

Darlun olew J. Kelt Edwards, 'Hiraeth Cymru am Hedd Wyn'.

Painting depicting the great sorrow felt
at the death of 'Hedd Wyn', c. 1917

Madame Laura Evans-Williams, a fine contralto, who was born and bred in Henllan, near Denbigh, Denbighshire, had been invited to sing the Chairing Song, but after it had been announced that the winner of the Chair prize had been slain in battle a few weeks earlier, she sang instead the more appropriate 'I Blas Gogerddan' ('To the country house of Gogerddan'), which contains words of the battlefield, of fighting and of the loss of blood. Sung to an audience in which by this time in the proceedings, barely a face of any male or female did not have tears uncontrollably streaming down it.

This momentous chair ceremony was drawn to a close with the audience uniting in singing the funereal Welsh hymn, 'Bydd myrdd o ryfeddodau' ('There will be myriad wonders'), regarded by many as the national funeral service/burial service hymn of Wales.

'The Chair' was subsequently presented to the Evans family still draped in the black sheet that had been placed upon it at the Chairing Ceremony. 'The Chair', his 'poetic works' and his memory, having to suffice instead of a grave near to them, for those closest to him who mourned his loss – his family, his sweetheart Jennie Owens of Pant Llwyd, Blaenau Ffestiniog, and his friends. But a nation, the nation of Wales felt his loss fervently too, and today some one hundred years later, he is most certainly not forgotten and never shall be – mourned still as a potent symbol of what Wales lost in human life, talent, and in innocence, in the carnage that was the First World War.

Imagine if you will, the scene of the noble Archdruid Dyfed announcing the death, killed in action of the winner of the Chair prize, to a large, expectant audience, in the midst of a bloody world war in which members of their own families were at the Front on some godforsaken foreign field, or had already like 'Hedd Wyn' made the ultimate sacrifice. Even today the thought of the scene engenders a mixture of sadness and pride, together with a strong feeling that something most profound occurred that day on the stage of the 1917 Birkenhead National Eisteddfod.

'Dyfed' was the bardic name of Evan Rees, born 1 January 1850, at Puncheston, near Fishguard, Pembrokeshire. His parents were James Rees, a collier and his wife Eunice. James Rees died in 1858, when Evan Rees was but eight years of age. Both he and elder brother Jonathan (who later became a fine poet, essayist and eisteddfodwr) became colliers at a young age. The Rees family moved to reside for many years in Aberdare. Evan Rees showed an aptitude for the writing of poetry in the Welsh language and after early successes at provincial Eisteddfodau was awarded the Chair prize at four National Eisteddfodau – in 1881 at Merthyr Tydfil; 1884 at Liverpool (In Welsh: Lerpwl); 1889 at Brecon (in Welsh: Aberhonddu), and 1901 at Merthyr Tydfil.

Evan Rees became a Calvinistic Methodist minister, and was the Archdruid of the National Eisteddfod of Wales from 1905 until his death in 1923. He also acted over a span of some forty years as an adjudicator at National Eisteddfodau. His literary prowess resulted in his having a number of books published. He became a renowned lecturer, and he travelled the world widely, including visiting other parts of Europe, North America, South Africa and parts of Asia.

In 1911, as Archdruid, he was the first to wear the 'stola', the form of headwear, which had emblazoned upon it the eye of the sun and its rays, a rampant red dragon and a dove.

'Dyfed', Evan Rees, died on 19 March 1923, aged seventy-three, and forever his name would be synonymous with that of 'Hedd Wyn', and 'The Black Chair Eisteddfod of 1917'.

Ellis Humphrey Evans, 'Hedd Wyn', was born on 13 January 1887 at Pen Lan, a row of stone fronted terraced houses in the centre of the village of Trawsfynydd (now in the county of Gwynedd). He was the eldest of twelve children born to Evan and Mary Evans, nine of whom were still living in April 1911. Evan Evans had inherited Ysgwrn from his father, Lewis Evans and his mother, Mary Evans.

Ellis Humphrey Evans very reluctantly enlisted for military service in the First World War being forced to do so by the terms of the Military Service Act of 1916, and doing so rather than his younger brother Robert Llewelyn Evans having to. Robert was then left (for a time) undisturbed to continue working on the family's farm 'Yr Ysgwrn', located some 1.5 miles from Trawsfynydd. In February 1917, Ellis received his initial military training at Litherland Camp, Liverpool. The Royal Welch Fusiliers' 3rd (Reserve) Battalion were based here as part of the Mersey Defence Force. But this military camp's main function was to train new recruits like Ellis Humphrey Evans, to prepare them to join the frontline battalions of the regiment. Here, also soldiers returning from having been wounded or on sick leave were 'toughened up' prior to being returned to frontline duties.

However, only one month later in March 1917, there was a general call for farm workers to return to the land, especially to carry out ploughing work. Ellis was temporarily released from military training and duties at Litherland Camp to return to his haven that was Yr Ysgwrn – a case for him of 'going from the ridiculous to the sublime'. Ellis whilst home worked on his awdl, 'Yr Arwr' (the Hero) which he intended to submit for that years Chair competition at the National Eisteddfod at Birkenhead. He wrote it according to his proud nephew, Gerald Williams, 'on the table by the fire'. Ellis overstayed his release by a week and he was posted as being a deserter. As a result some military police attended at Ysgwrn and took Ellis from the fields into custody. After spending a time in a cell at Blaenau Ffestiniog police station he was escorted back to Litherland Camp. As he had been so swiftly removed from Yr Ysgwrn he had left the pages of his awdl, 'Yr Arwr' on the table in the farmhouse. Happily he could remember this work of his, and he wrote out a second copy when back at Litherland Camp. That is why two handwritten copies of his 'Yr Arwr' with annotations exist today – one is held at the National Library of Wales in Aberystwyth and the other at Bangor University.

Ellis Humphrey Evans, regimental number 61117, was sent out to serve with 15th Battalion, a frontline infantry battalion of the Royal Welch Fusiliers who were in the area of Flechin, France. Ellis completed 'Yr Arwr' and on 15 July 1917, posted it back to Wales from Flechin, before they moved on into Belgium and the area known as the Ypres Salient. The British Army were planning a major offensive in this area to begin in the early hours of 31 July 1917. Pilckem Ridge held by the Germans was an arc of small but strategic hills that formed a saucer shape around the British positions. The Germans here had been shelled for days by British artillery prior to the planned major offensive, which (not for the first time!) gave away any element of surprise and the Germans knew that an attack against them was in the offing in that area. But the British artillery bombardment had not been as effective as those in command had thought (again, not for the first time!), for the Germans were holed up in craters made by the British artillery shells, and here they concealed their machine guns and their snipers. The Germans had also been able to construct some concrete pillboxes, but the worst obstacle of all in reality for the British attack to come was the terrain itself, and the shocking conditions underfoot due to the heaviest rain in the area it was said for forty years. In this area famously the conditions were so extreme that if a soldier, carrying on his person up to one hundred pounds of equipment slipped off the pathways or duckboards, he fell into muddy water craters and drowned, without a hope of being able to extricate himself from the mire – this sadly was the fate of many British soldiers here at what later became a byword for the horrors of the trenches of the First World War – Passchendaele.

The 15th Battalion, Royal Welch Fusiliers including Private Ellis Humphrey Evans at 3.50 a.m. on Wednesday, 31 July 1917, were one of five battalions who were to attack the German hill positions around Pilckem Wood and beyond. Ellis and his comrades despite heavy enemy fire and the awful cloying mud and swamp-like terrain succeeded in taking Pilckem Ridge, and now advanced towards what was called 'Iron Cross Ridge', a German stronghold. It was approaching here under heavy enemy fire, according to eyewitnesses, that Ellis was hit in the stomach by an enemy nose cap shell, which caused him to fall to his knees, and when down, for him to grab two fistfuls of earth. He was very badly hit – he was in fact dying. None of the soldiers with him could stop to assist him, but fairly quickly he was carried to a nearby first-aid post by stretcher-bearers. There he was conscious and asked the doctor attending him: 'Do you think I will live'? A short time later at approxiametely 11.00 a.m. he died.

I have researched this matter and I strongly believe that Private Ellis Humphrey Evans, 'Hedd Wyn', was initially buried near to the battlefield, but was some days later moved and re-buried at the Artillery Wood British Cemetery.

There were even worse ways to die that day than to be hit by a bullet or shell, or to be drowned in the quagmire, as an account of that morning at The Battle of Pilckem Ridge which appears on page 25 of *A History of the 38th (Welsh)*

Division, edited by Lieut-Colonel J. E. Munby, CMG, DSO reveals:-

> The neighbourhood of Iron Cross was strongly held and the 14th Welsh Regiment suffered somewhat heavily in rushing it. They had, however, the satisfaction of killing with the bayonet some twenty of the enemy and taking forty prisoners and three machine guns in this neighbourhood.

Chilling words – 'They had, however, the satisfaction of killing with the bayonet some twenty of the enemy'. Exemplifying that it was truly 'life or death', 'kill or be killed'. The Germans bayoneted to death were the enemy – but they were also of course someone's husband, brother, friend ... Their killing would also become someone's future horrific nightmare – days, weeks, or perhaps years later – for having been 'the one' who stuck in the bayonet, then twisted it, as they had been hard trained to do. Then to hear the agonising cries of your 'victim', and see his intestines ooze out as you withdraw your bayonet, and life then swiftly drains from him – but it truly was a case of 'you or him' to perish – 'better him than you'!

The account continues lower down the page:-

> ... The 15th Royal Welch Fusiliers commenced their advance from the Blue line at the correct time but on nearing Battery Copse were met there with such fire that in a short time, only a few officers were left and our barrage began to run away from the men. The men, however, struggled forward and established themselves on the Iron Cross Ridge.

Private Ellis Humphrey Evans, 'Hedd Wyn', had advanced from 'the Blue line' that the Generals had so kindly plotted back, a long way back in their Headquarters – but he never reached Iron Cross Ridge, then again – neither did so many others ...

The copy of 'Hedd Wyn's, Yr Arwr' held at the National Library of Wales in Aberystwyth is a precious treasure, and part of a twenty-five page original manuscript in his own handwriting with corrections made in pencil. On the back of this priceless work can be seen written his original nom-de-plume of 'Y Palm Bell' that he had chosen for his entry in the 1917 Welsh National Eisteddfod at Birkenhead. But just prior to submitting it, he had changed his nom-de-plume to 'Fleur-de-lis'. It is believed that he chose Fleur-de-lis for he had posted it off whilst serving with his battalion of the Royal Welch Fusiliers in the northern French village of Flechin. The copy of 'Yr Arwr' in the Bangor University Archives has annotations of criticism added to it by adjudicator, T. Gwynn Jones, who himself had been awarded the Chair prize at the 1902 Bangor National Eisteddfod with his ode 'Ymadawiad Arthur' (In English: The Departure of Arthur) – a seminal work of Welsh literature. T. Gwynn Jones was also awarded the Chair prize at the 1909 National Eisteddfod held in London (in Welsh: Llundain).

'Hedd Wyn's', 'Yr Arwr' was written in four parts and contains two main characters – 'Merch y Drycinoedd' (in English: girl/daughter of the Tempests) and 'Yr Arwr' (in English: The Hero). A number of scholarly interpretations of the true meaning of this fine and highly regarded work have been made and perhaps the truest of them is that 'Hedd Wyn' like his favourite poet, Percy Bysshe Shelley, was a romantic who longed for a perfect harmony and a perfect world. Whilst of course during the First World War when 'Yr Arwr' was written the world was full of great uncertainty and instability. 'Yr Arwr' has 'Merch y Drycinoedd' as a symbol of love, being the beauty of nature and creativity. Whilst 'Yr Arwr' is a symbol of goodness, fairness, freedom and justice, and that it is through his sacrifice and union with 'Merch y Drycinoedd' that a better age or time will come.

Sadly, for 'Hedd Wyn', that better age or time did not come on that fateful morning of Wednesday, 31 July 1917, at what was later to be called The Battle of Pilckem Ridge (31 July – 2 August 1917), the opening attack on the first day of the main part of The Third Battle of Ypres (now Ieper), better known to us as Passchendaele.

A petition was organised and submitted to the CWGC (the Commonwealth War Graves Commission) for extra words, Welsh ones, to be added to his standard CWGC white Portland stone headstone at his grave, Grave Reference 11. F. 11. at the Artillery Wood British Cemetery, near Boezinge, Belgium. This was granted and these extra words may be found below the cross at the base of the headstone and read: 'Y Prifardd Hedd Wyn' (in English: The Chief Bard Hedd Wyn).

Ellis Humphrey Evans, 'Hedd Wyn' (in English: 'Blessed Peace'), was adjudicated to have been second for the Chair prize at the previous year's National Eisteddfod, held at Aberystwyth, with his awdl (a long Welsh poem which has a single end rhyme) on the topic of 'Ystrad Flur'. This awdl written in honour of the fine, former Cistercian Abbey ruins of Strata Florida Abbey (in Welsh: Abaty Ystrad Fflur), located near Tregaron, Ceredigion, Wales.

Following the 1917 Welsh National Eisteddfod at Birkenhead, a committee was formed under the leadership of Mr J. R. Jones, the Headmaster of the village school in

Trawsfynydd. Its aim was to collect together all manuscripts in the hand of 'Hedd Wyn' that could be found. This shrewd idea proved a success, and in the following year of 1918, the first anthology of 'Hedd Wyn's' work, fittingly entitled, *Cerddi'r Bugail* (in English: The Shepherd's Poems) was published. In 1934 the original manuscripts collection was donated to the National Library of Wales in Aberystwyth.

In the *Welsh Outlook* monthly for October 1917, was this thoughtful piece:-

> The incident will be known in history as 'The Black Chair of Birkenhead'. Hedd Wyn, the young poet of Merioneth, failed to appear to claim the chief Bardic prize which his ode to 'The Hero' had so brilliantly won. For six weeks before the Eisteddfod he had been sacrificed to the madness of the miscreants who pretend to govern Europe. He was one of the most lovable of men, a quiet, mystic dreamer, who loved to tend his sheep on the mountains of Merioneth, to read his books and dream his dreams. He had won five chairs already at provincial eisteddfodau and many other bardic honours. He was the second best last year in the Chair competition at Aberystwyth – the best according to one of the adjudicators. Now the guns in Flanders have hushed his song for ever. He is mourned by all who knew him, for he was the idol of the Trawsfynydd district. He died at 29, and Wales has lost in him one of her best poets. The week after the Eisteddfod the War Office published in the press:
>
> Killed: Evans 61117, E (Trawsfynydd)
>
> To the relentless juggernaut Hedd Wyn was only a number. To the Welsh Nation he will ever live as the 'Hero' of the Black Chair of Birkenhead.

The Hedd Wyn Memorial was unveiled at Trawsfynydd, in a ceremony held on 11 August 1923. This bronze statue, proudly unveiled by his mother, of 'Hedd Wyn', Ellis Humphrey Evans, still stands proudly today in the centre of the village of Trawsfynydd. Upon it is written an englyn (a traditional Welsh verse or stanza, short and concise), which 'Hedd Wyn' had written in memory of a fallen comrade, killed in battle. This englyn:-

Ei aberth nid â heibio – ei wyneb
    Annwyl nid â'n ango
    Er i'r Almaen ystaenio
    Ei dwrn dur yn ei waed o.

Translated into English:-

His sacrifice was not in vain, his face
    In our minds will remain
    Although he left a bloodstain
    On Germany's iron fist of pain

Many believe that this now famous englyn was written in memory of Griff Jones, but this rather interesting piece appeared in the *Cambrian News and Merionethshire Standard*, 7 September 1917 edition:-

NORTH WALES POET
Pte Ellis H. Evans (Hedd Wyn), the brilliant North Wales poet, killed in action, is said to have entered for the chair at Birkenhead this week. He was second for the chair at Aberystwyth last year according to two of the adjudicators, while the third adjudicator, Rev J. J. Williams placed him first. Hedd Wyn composed the following englyn to the late Lieut D. O. Evans, Festiniog,

and this may now, with pathetic interest, be said of himself.

Lieutenant D. O. Evans, was Lieutenant David Owen Evans, 17th Battalion, the Royal Welch Fusiliers, who was killed aged twenty-four on 12 February 1916, and is buried at St Vaast Military Cemetery, Richebourg L'Avoue, Pas de Calais, France, Grave Reference 11.P.5. Lieutenant D. O. Evans, known by friends as 'Deio' was a keen supporter and organiser of Soldiers' Eisteddfodau. He was a son of Dr Robert David Evans, JP, of Blaenau Ffestiniog and a brother of Major Dr Sir Thomas Carey Evans, MC, KB, who married Olwen Lloyd George, a daughter of David Lloyd George. Another brother, William Arthur Evans another serving officer was also deeply involved in the organising of Soldiers' Eisteddfodau during the First World War.

Today, the fine Bardic Chair awarded posthumously to 'Hedd Wyn' at Birkenhead in 1917, remains on display at Ysgwrn, the traditional Welsh farmhouse near Trawsfynydd. 'Hedd Wyn's' nephew, Gerald Williams has done much to preserve his uncle's 'memory and legacy', and in December of 2012 he was awarded an MBE for his exceptional contribution 'to the poet Hedd Wyn's heritage'.

The *Cambrian News and Merionethshire Standard* of Friday, 25 July 1919, had this poignant post-war piece:-

AT HEDD WYN'S GRAVE.
PEACE DAY ON PILCKEM RIDGE.
Capt Cox who prior to the war was on the staff of the 6th RWF, at the Caernarfon Barracks, gives an account of an impressive ceremony which took place on Peace Day on Pilckem Ridge. The young poet Hedd Wyn fell a few

weeks before the Birkenhead Eisteddfod at which he was declared to be the winner of the bardic chair.

On 28th June, Colonel Vaughan, DSO, better known by his pen name of 'Owen Rhoscomyl' invited a number of men of the Royal Welch Fusiliers serving under him to the graves of the poet and other British soldiers who defeated one of the ex-Kaiser's crack regiments on Pilckem Ridge two years previously. At an hour of the day when Colonel Vaughan thought the Germans 'were brought to their knees and were signing a just peace', he accompanied by a number of other officers formed up at the four corners of a grave containing the remains of several Welshmen, and there saluted the dead while the padre read part of the 90th Psalm.

A flag with a Red Dragon upon it was also placed at the head of the grave, and Mrs Vaughan, wife of Colonel Vaughan placed some flowers on the sacred spot.

Robert Llewelyn Evans, a younger brother of 'Hedd Wyn'

Like many thousands of other families in Wales and in Britain generally, the Evans family of Yr Ysgwrn farm, near Trawsfynydd, suffered in the war, with the tragic loss of their Ellis, 'Hedd Wyn', but were not left alone to mourn on their mountain farm. For the British Army claimed another of their sons to their ranks under the Military Service Act – Robert Llewelyn Evans, born 24 November 1898, at Trawsfynydd. He was required to attest and enlist, and did so in the Royal Welch Fusiliers at the Wrexham Depot of the Regiment, on 14 June 1918, where he was initially placed in 3rd Battalion. The war was now going Britain and its Allies way but it was not yet won and the younger brother of the late 'Hedd Wyn' had to leave the tranquillity of the family farm in the Welsh hills near Trawsfynydd for the army and its routines to receive his military training. On his army record Robert Llewelyn Evans described his occupation as farm horseman, and he was declared to be five feet, two inches tall. His military record file is a thick one for a soldier who did not serve long in the war, or actually did much during it! But there is a good reason for this, for though once the Armistice had passed and the war was over, the British Army including 2nd Battalion, the Royal Welch Fusiliers were still required, in the case of 2nd Battalion in Ireland, for 'the problems' that were taking place there. Private Robert Llewelyn Evans, regimental number 91959 was posted to Limerick, Ireland with 2nd Battalion. The commanding officer of 2nd Battalion, the Royal Welch Fusiliers in Ireland was Major F. J. Walwyn, DSO. Private Robert Llewelyn Evans was then allowed, strangely like his late brother Ellis had been two years earlier, what was called an 'agricultural furlough' – for a limited period to be allowed home to assist on the farm. He was 'officially' granted this from 10 September 1919 to 7 October 1919. However, due to a number of complications and misunderstandings, he did not return, instead staying on at the farm. Finally, between the War Office, St James' Park, London and No.2 Infantry Record Office, The Riding Stables, Shrewsbury, it was realised that he had not returned to his unit as was required, so he was immediately posted as a deserter, a most serious military offence even in peacetime (relative peacetime bearing in mind the difficulties in Ireland), which usually resulted in military prison time having to be served. The War Office were not happy either that 2nd Battalion, the Royal Welch Fusiliers, though having Robert's home address, had not bothered to post him as absent or send him orders to promptly return to them. The army drew up a long list of all the military clothing and equipment – War Office property that Robert as an alleged deserter had illegally in his possession – as if they were of any use to him on the farm at Ysgwrn! The Army sent a first wire (telegram) addressed to 'The Chief Constable', Trawsfynydd, for the police to formally arrest and detain Private Robert Llewelyn Evans for desertion from the British Army. This first wire appears to have been ignored, for a less than pleased army official then sent a second wire and this produced a result. At 10.00 a.m. on 6 July 1920, police constable A. H. Williams from Trawsfynydd police station, formally arrested Robert at Ysgwrn and took him into custody. Robert was held until a military escort arrived to take him back to Limerick to face a court martial for desertion. Military records quaintly record that 'Private Robert Llewelyn Evans joined 2nd Battalion, the Royal Welch Fusiliers on 6 July 1920 in Limerick, Ireland, from Desertion'. Meanwhile, a number of persons set about trying to help Robert and his family in a difficult and worrying situation. The Ruthin, Denbighshire, born Member of Parliament (MP) for Merionethshire from 1900 until 1945, Mr Henry Haydn Jones, who during the war years had often interceded on behalf of soldiers in difficulties with the military authorities, made representations on Robert's behalf. A former army chaplain, R. Peris Williams (Reverend Robert Peris Williams), a congregationalist minister kindly wrote a letter to the military authorities on behalf of Robert and the Evans family:-

9/7/20
2nd RWF
91959 Evans, Pte R. L.
In view of the fact that this man's people have been hit hard by the war, allow me to appeal to you to deal leniently with him. Would it not be possible to deal with him under A.F.a46 and get him demobilised. His brother, Pte Ellis Evans of 15 Btn. RWF was killed at

Pilckem. His father is a country farmer in a small way and is much in need of this man's help on the farm, especially just now in the harvest.

R. Peris Williams

Hon Late-Chaplain

38th Welsh Division – BEF

R. Peris Williams had in wartime been a much respected and liked Welsh Army chaplain who had been an adjudicator at the 'Welsh Soldiers' Great Eisteddfod', held at Winchester Guildhall, Winchester, on Monday, 4 October 1915.

Representations had been made on Robert Llewelyn Evans' behalf, and it was obvious that bureaucratic glitches had played a part in the matter. These included certain army records having Private Robert Llewelyn Evans' regimental number incorrectly recorded as being 91998 (actually a Percival Robert Evans), and also as 91973. The court martial held in Limerick, Ireland, rendered a most lenient verdict – Private Robert Llewelyn Evans was to forfeit 273 days army pay, which was not unreasonable as he was for this period of time working on the family farm! Perhaps Lloyd George or someone of that stature in the establishment had also positively become involved in this matter which produced a kind court martial result for Private Robert Llewelyn Evans – due to the 'Hedd Wyn' factor?

So, Robert Llewelyn Evans was able to return to Yr Ysgwrn and live out the rest of his natural life. He died in 1977, aged seventy-eight, having had a most reasonable life span on this fair earth, something of course his elder brother, Ellis Humphrey Evans, 'Hedd Wyn', was deprived of in the mud and blood of Pilckem Ridge – Passchendaele.

7

'Pack Up Your Troubles' – courtesy of two St Asaph born brothers

Two of the most popular songs to have come out of the First World War which survive even today are 'It's A Long Way To Tipperary', by Irish born Jack Judge and 'Pack Up Your Troubles In Your Old Kit-Bag' by the St Asaph, North Wales, born and bred, Powell Brothers – Felix Lloyd Powell and George Henry Powell. Felix the elder brother was born on 23 May 1878 and George on 27 April 1880.

The 1881 Census shows that the Powell family of John Morris Powell, a thirty-eight year old West Bromwich born house painter and his Bootle, Liverpool born wife, Sarah Powell (nee Snelson), lived on the High Street, St Asaph, North Wales. By 1891, this Powell family lived at 11, Gemig Street, St Asaph.

The father, John Morris Powell, who was said to have been musically gifted, was also a lay clerk at the nearby St Asaph Cathedral. Both Felix and George sang in the Cathedral's choir, with Felix playing the organ from the age of twelve. At an early age they had both shown an aptitude for music, singing and the playing of musical instruments. Their father John Morris Powell had died in 1882, aged but forty. Sarah Powell remarried at St Asaph in 1896, Frederick Fear, but only five years later in 1901, he died aged forty-seven, leaving Sarah a widow again, and she reverted to using the surname of Powell, not Fear from then on.

Felix Powell's first proper employment was in the 'town office' in Leamington, Warwickshire, of the coaching department of the London and North Western Railway (the

LNWR), from 29 April 1895, until he resigned on 3 October 1896. At Scarborough Register Office, Yorkshire, on 11 June 1911, Felix Powell married Mabel Florence Rush, who had been born in London and was a fellow musical artiste.

They had prior to their marriage, a son together, born at Bingley, Yorkshire, on 5 December 1910, whom they named Harley Felix Powell, named Harley after their concert troop 'The Harlequinaders'.

George Powell had married at Exeter Register Office on 15 July 1905, Leila Byron, the daughter of Thomas Byron, a tailor and outfitter.

Prior to 1914, Felix Powell who was said to have been something of an introvert, and brother George Powell who was said to have been more the extrovert, did have a few minor successes which included the song 'Queen of Summer' in 1913. The music was by Felix, with lyrics by the Powell Brothers' elder sister, Constance Mary Powell who was born at St Asaph in 1877.

In 1915, conscription had not yet arrived, and Felix and George Powell were still touring the theatres and music halls of Britain as part of their entertainment troupe 'The Harlequinaders'. Their six person troupe consisted of Felix on piano and vocals, George on vocals, plus their respective wives and two other young men. Whilst appearing at various theatres in Britain, the Powell Brothers would try out new songs they had written during breaks in daily performances. During one of these breaks when appearing at the London Hippodrome Theatre, they tried out a song for which Felix had written the music and George the lyrics. It was called 'Pack Up Your Troubles', but George in particular regarded the song as 'piffle' and it was initially consigned to a drawer they had for 'duds'. However, they learnt of a competition being organised with a winners prize of 100 guineas by a Tin Pan Alley (name given to an influential collection of New

The Harlequinaders

York music publishers and songwriters who dominated the popular music scene in the United States and beyond in the late 19th and early 20th centuries) music publishing company – the successful Francis Day & Hunter Ltd, for a marching type song, suitable for soldiers. One of the judges of the competition was the famous Scottish music hall comedian and singer Sir Harry Lauder. It is said that 'only for a joke' the Powell Brothers sent in their 'dud, Pack Up Your Troubles' expecting to hear no more. Then, later in 1915, when appearing at the Grand Theatre, Birmingham, a wire (telegram) arrived for them. Upon it was written: 'PACK UP YOUR TROUBLES FIRST PRIZE'. The Powell Brothers realised they had a success on their hands with the song, and soon incorporated it into their act, the first occasion being at Southampton, when it was sung by George's wife, Leila. The song went down a storm and soon became a hit in the United States as well as in Britain. The song featured in the 1916 hit Broadway Show, 'Her Soldier Boy'. It really did catch on and service personnel could be heard singing and whistling it. The Powell Brothers declined offers to sell the song, and this proved to be a very shrewd move as over the years it made then in royalties many thousands of pounds. The story is that Jack Judge who wrote 'It's A Long Way To Tipperary' sold the rights to it for a mere £5, not realising its potential – That's Showbiz Folks!

The 'Pack Up Your Troubles' song has a catchy melody, a perfect 'marching song' with cheeky, cheery lyrics:-

Pack up your troubles
in your old kit bag
and smile, smile, smile
while you've a Lucifer
to light your fag
smile, boys, that's the style

What's the use of worrying
it never was worthwhile
so, pack up your troubles
in your old kit bag
and smile, smile, smile

The full song was the repeat of the above lyrics a further twice. The 'lucifer' referred to was the old name for a match and 'fag' was of course the old name, indeed which is still often used today, for a cigarette. Interestingly George Powell wrote songs and appeared under the pseudonym of George Asaf, a firm nod to his birth and upbringing in St Asaph.

By early 1916, conscription had been introduced in Britain. This was to have a major effect upon the Powell Brothers, as of course it did upon millions of others in the country. George Powell now aged thirty-five was a pacifist and when conscription was brought in he became a conscientious objector, which the authorities ensured was not an easy path to take. He steadfastly refused to enlist in any shape or form, and later in life became a Christian Scientist. So it truly was a strange situation for him through two World Wars, that as a staunch pacifist he and his family benefitted greatly from royalties that came in from the 'Pack Up Your Troubles' song – especially in wartime!

Felix took a different course altogether to his younger brother, and for the following few years the Powell Brothers went their separate ways. Felix attested and enlisted at Leeds, Yorkshire, on 5 February 1916, aged thirty-seven years and nine months. He gave his occupation as music composer, and his army records show that he was five feet, five inches tall, and his home address at this time was 11, St Margaret's Avenue, West Green, South London. He became a Private with the RASC (Royal Army Service Corps), Motor Transport Section, Service Number 315948, and was a lorry driver. But he also would entertain the troops on occasions in both Britain and on the Western Front.

The *Liverpool Echo* of Friday, 28 July 1916, had this:-

Felix Powell composed the 'Pack Up Your Troubles' song and he has done something equally good if not better. He has collected some Harlequinaders and banded them together in a beautiful musical turn, which roams hither and thither, and all the time pleases the ear. His company leads the Argyle Theatre's show next week, and on the same bill I note a Ragtime Drummer and a number of good turns, and a topper in Fred Culpitt, the Magical Comedian.

In 1917, with Felix still in the Army, 'The Harlequinaders' had to be disbanded and Felix formed another concert party, this one to tour the front lines on the Western Front, which he named 'The White Knights'.

Felix Powell came to find it difficult to hear the soldiers off to the front happily singing 'Pack Up Your Troubles' as they went along, knowing that many would soon perish, mown down by machine gun fire or obliterated by heavy shelling – these things weighed heavily upon his mind. Also, he felt 'guilt' that the song which was raking in money for him and George, was also being used to aid recruitment. It all preyed on his mind, and he had a virtual nervous breakdown whilst serving in France. Felix Powell was demobilised on 28 June 1919, and subsequently received the Victory and British, War Medals.

Aubrey Powell, a grandson of Felix Powell, still has Felix's tambourine which was inscribed with the names of the various First World War battlefields of Flanders. Strangely when the British occupied the Rhine area post-Armistice, Felix not only heard British soldiers singing 'Pack Up Your Troubles', but also German soldiers who sang the words translated into German – the melody truly is a catchy one.

A broken man mentally by the end of the First World War, Felix was unable to write anything for a number of years. Until in the mid-1930's he was back writing again, particularly musicals and operettas.

Charles William Neville, a Darlington, County Durham, born entrepreneur and promotional genius, born into a showman family, had travelled the world, living in Canada and Australia amongst other countries. In 1916, he bought land which was on the coast near Newhaven, Sussex. He became a property developer and decided to build a brand new town and resort which he decided initially to name 'New Anzac-on-Sea'. But after the failed Gallipoli Campaign of the First World War he was persuaded to rename it

'Peacehaven'. It was a kind of garden city by the sea, and Neville encouraged Felix Powell and his wife, along with a number of other 'celebrities' of the day to buy plots of land from him, build their own houses, and settle permanently in Peacehaven. George Powell subsequently moved with his wife to live near to Felix and his wife, in Peacehaven. The Powell Brothers produced two songs to promote this brand new resort, one entitled 'Come to Peacehaven' and the other called 'Lureland Waltz', named after Peacehaven's specially built dance hall and theatre, 'Lureland Hall', on Phyllis Avenue, Peacehaven. Here, Felix and George put on musical productions, and tried out new entertainment projects before taking them to the larger Brighton theatres, and ultimately to the West End, London. Felix also owned an estate agents business, an enterprise which was later to prove an important factor in his downfall.

Gracie Fields, a great star of the time, though a 'Rochdale Girl' was also persuaded by Neville to reside in Peacehaven, which she did for a time. Gracie Fields during the Second World War gave many concerts, performing a medley of songs that nearly always included 'Pack Up Your Troubles', which was a firm favourite of audiences both military and civilian.

Felix and George ran the local paper, well more of a news sheet, the *Peacehaven Post*, and were well known 'celebrities' in the area.

Felix wrote a musical he entitled 'Rubicund Castle', which received favourable reviews when it opened in a Brighton theatre. The well known actress and musical director, Anne Croft, mother of the 'Dad's Army', 'It Ain't Half Hot Mum' and 'Hi-De-Hi' creator David Croft, was looking for a hit for the West End, London, and she encouraged Felix to take the musical which she changed the name of to 'Primrose Times', to London. To finance this production Felix was introduced to William Quilliam, who unbeknown at the time to Felix was in fact something of a shyster and gangster. Just prior to the show opening, Quilliam demanded his money back, which at this time Felix was unable to do.

Felix Powell having only recently recovered from pneumonia and with financial difficulties causing him to 'take monies' from the estate agents business, mainly due to having William Quilliam on his back, he was facing mounting problems. Then add to these that with the Second World War in full horrific flow, 'the song' was again popular and like the previous world war was being used as a rallying call to arms for British military personnel. In the midst of all this on 10 February 1942, Felix dressed in his uniform as a staff sergeant in the Home Guard, went to the Lureland Hall, near his home in Peacehaven, locked the doors, left 'notes' to his family and friends, and shot himself through the heart with his service .303 rifle. He died later that same day in the Royal Sussex County Hospital, Brighton. A most sad end to his life at the age of sixty-three for Felix Powell, a man who found it very difficult over the years to be able to 'pack up his own troubles'.

Brother, George Powell, after a long illness, died at the age of seventy-one on 3 December 1951, at 10, Palmeira Square, Hove, Sussex, the home he shared with wife, Leila.

'The song' has been translated and sung in many different languages and over the years has appeared in numerous films and television programmes – at least sixty fully credited ones. The 1932 Laurel and Hardy film entitled 'Pack Up Your Troubles', has Stan and Ollie as soldiers in the First World War. More recently, Eliza Doolittle, the British singer-songwriter heavily 'sampled' the song in her 2010 'Pack Up', featuring Lloyd Wade, which reached number five in the UK Singles Charts.

'Pack Up Your Troubles' was also the inspiration, though not in a good way for Wilfred Owen's hard hitting, anti-war poem, 'Smile, Smile, Smile'. He chose for the title of this poem the chorus line of "Pack Up Your Troubles", believing (rightly) that it had become ubiquitous.

Aubrey 'Po' Powell, son of Harley Felix Powell, and grandson of Felix Powell has truly carried on the 'Powell' family tradition of being in the entertainment business. Aubrey 'Po' Powell co-founded the iconic album cover design company Hipgnosis with Storm Thorgerson in 1967. Hipgnosis through the late 1960's, the 1970's and early 1980's created some of the greatest, innovative, and often surreal record cover art that I suggest has ever been produced. Hipgnosis were nominated on five occasions for Grammy awards. Their 'clientele' included Pink Floyd, Led Zeppelin, Genesis, Emerson, Lake and Palmer, Paul McCartney, Black Sabbath, Peter Gabriel – to name but a few. Perhaps their most well known album cover was the gatefold design album cover for Pink Floyd's, 'The Dark Side of the Moon' in 1973, produced with their associate George Hardie, with its prism design. An estimated fifty million copies of this album were sold.

Aubrey 'Po' Powell has been the set designer for many rock shows and concerts and is a successful film-maker and producer – this grandson of Felix Powell, who was of course born and bred in St Asaph, North Wales.

8

The Terrible Shell Explosion at Moss, near Wrexham

Of all the stories of tragedy, sadness and deep loss I have come across, I believe that none surpass this story of the Bagnall family and their relations, from the Moss area of Wrexham, North Wales.

William Bagnall (senior) was born in 1864 at Hanley, then in Staffordshire, and he moved to the Wrexham area for the coal mining work. In the December Quarter of 1889, William Bagnall (senior) a coal miner-hewer, married seventeen-year old Hannah Davies of Broughton, Wrexham. The couple in 1891 lived in the Broughton area of Wrexham, with their first born child, Eliza. William and Hannah had further children, all boys, but sadly in 1899, William Bagnall (senior) died aged only thirty-six, leaving Hannah a widow by then with one daughter and four sons. The 1901 Census shows that Hannah did housework for others to make-ends-meet, took in colliers as lodgers, and had her mother Eliza, also a widow, living with her at 1, Eagles Place, Francis Road, Broughton, Wrexham.

By the 1911 Census, Hannah, and now eight sons and one young daughter were living at 16, Hill Street, Pentre Broughton, Wrexham, with a John Thomas Mathias, a thirty-six year old coal miner-hewer. Her two eldest sons, John Bagnall, known as Jack and William Bagnall (junior) were now both coal miner-hewers, whilst the third eldest son, Hugh was soon to follow them for a short time down the local pit. The eleven members of the Bagnall (and Mathias) family also had with them a lodger, Hugh Thomas

A typical WW1 shell fuse

Davies, who not surprisingly was also a coal miner. Life was hard for this rather 'unconventional Edwardian Family', but with the First World War came horrors beyond comprehension for them, not on the battlefield, but in their own midst in the Moss, Wrexham.

William Bagnall (junior), the second eldest son enlisted in the Royal Welch Fusiliers on 9 January 1912, at Summerhill, near Wrexham. He was but seventeen years and eight months of age. In the months leading up to the start of the First World War, he was on 25 April 1914, transferred to 5th Battalion, the Manchester Regiment, regimental number 1871. On 9 September 1914, he was sent with the British Expeditionary Force to firstly Egypt, being there until 2 May 1915. Then on 3 May 1915 until 30 June 1915, he was part of the ill-fated Dardanelles/Gallipoli Campaign. He returned to these shores on 1 July 1915, and stayed in this country continuing in the military, until on 7

April 1916, he was medically discharged as being unfit for military service. He was to later receive the British, Victory and 1915 Star, War Medals.

The third eldest son, **Hugh Bagnall**, born 5 July 1895, was but five feet, two inches tall when he enlisted in the British Army prior to the First World War on 11 March 1914 and being so young he was initially a drummer. But later in 6th Battalion, the Welch Regiment, regimental number 267065, he served in the trenches of France and Flanders. On 11 September 1916, on The Somme he was wounded for the first time. It is recorded as a gunshot wound, probably sustained when either capturing an enemy trench, or when retreating from a British trench under German close quarter attack. He had been at the front on The Somme from 10 July 1916, until wounded, and was then repatriated home on 14 September 1916. Though rather patchy records exist it is believed that Hugh Bagnall returned to the Front in France and Flanders, and that he sustained a further gunshot wound, this time to his right knee that required him to be at the Military Hospital, Pembroke Dock from 20 March 1917 until 27 July 1917. He was discharged from military service on 17 August 1917, due to his wounds. Now home for good, Hugh Bagnall married in late 1917. He died in the June Quarter of 1972, in the Wrexham area, aged seventy-six.

But it was the eldest son of Hannah Bagnall, **John Bagnall**, known as Jack, for whom fate had terrible things in store, but not on the battlefield in a foreign country, but in his own home! John Bagnall (Jack) was born in 1892, and in the September Quarter of 1912 he married a local girl Mary E. Williams. He served like his two younger brothers, William and Hugh, on the Western Front, first arriving there on 6 November 1914.

On Monday, 6 March 1916, John (Jack) Bagnall,

regimental number 6738, returned home on leave to the Moss, Wrexham, from active service with 4th (Denbighshire) Battalion, the Royal Welch Fusiliers, a pioneer territorial battalion. He had brought back with him in his soldier's kit, a souvenir from the Front, a rather innocuous looking, quite shiny shell fuse. On the following Thursday, 9 March 1916, there was a gathering at his Moss home of family members, especially to see him before he returned to active service a few days later. The next part of the story has elements that are disputed, but the shocking outcome is most certainly not. John (Jack) Bagnall proudly exhibited his shell fuse souvenir and later claimed it had just accidentally fallen off the table onto the hard floor below. But, one of the visitors Mary Ann Roberts, who personally suffered terrible injuries, and the shocking loss of her two young children, later stated that John (Jack) Bagnall had told everyone that the shell fuse was harmless and proceeded to drop it on the floor. Then to show all present just how harmless it was, proceeded to pick it up and drop it to the floor again, as if to prove his point. However, the second time it was dropped it exploded with devastating effect in the small enclosed room. Two of the children died almost instantly from blast injuries, whilst two others dreadfully mutilated died from their injuries within a few hours. The four young children who died were John (Jack) Bagnall's own two-year-old daughter Sarah Hannah Bagnall, Violet Williams, aged seven, whom I believe was a niece, and Mary Frances Roberts aged four, and her sister Ethel Roberts aged fifteen months. The latter two sisters being the daughters of Mary Ann Roberts who had been holding Ethel in her arms when the force of the explosion blew Ethel from her grasp and through a door, killing Ethel instantly. Mary Ann Roberts herself lost both legs in the blast, whilst Mary Bagnall, wife of John (Jack) Bagnall lost one foot and half of her other foot. As for John (Jack) Bagnall himself, well he sustained the loss of one leg and it was feared that he would also lose his other leg. A local newspaper stated at this time that: '*Mrs Roberts who lies in Wrexham Infirmary, is begging to see her two children of whose fate she has not yet been told*'.

The Inquest upon this truly shocking incident that had resulted in the needless death of four young children, and three adults maimed for life, was opened and then adjourned on Monday, 13 March 1916, by Mr Llewellyn Kenrick, the Coroner for East Denbighshire.

On the following Friday, 17 March 1916, the Inquest proper was held by the coroner Mr Kenrick. The full harrowing details of this most shocking incident came out fully into the public domain. The coroner began by stating that the injuries inflicted upon those still alive and undergoing treatment at the Wrexham Infirmary were so terrible that: '*they also might terminate fatally*'. During the Inquest, George Samuel Roberts, father of two of the dead children, and husband of the terribly injured Mary Ann Roberts, gave evidence as a witness. He stated that on hearing an explosion coming from the direction of Private John (Jack) Bagnall's house, he had rushed over to the house, and the rest of his evidence was short but chilling: '*I was met by my Wife. She was crawling out of the house. She said to me, let me alone, look after the children. My legs have gone*'.

In his summing up, the coroner said that whilst it may seem presumptuous for a civilian to criticise military procedure, one could only judge of their procedures in this case being extraordinary. That men returning from active service should be allowed to bring back with them such dangerous articles as the one which 'Bagnall' had in his possession. The baggage that soldiers brought back with them could be but very small, and he pleaded that surely it would not take long to overhaul it and see that no dangerous articles were concealed within? The Coroner had been told that 'the Enemy, the Germans' would dish out severe punishment to one of their soldiers returning or trying to return home with such an item. As the four deaths were due to an explosive device, the coroner said that it was necessary that he gave the Government Inspector of Explosives due notice of this shocking incident. The Inquest Jury returned the verdict upon the four deceased young children as: *The deceased were accidentally and by misadventure killed.*

This tragedy attracted much press attention at the time. The local newspapers reported the incident itself with such headlines as: *Fatal Bomb Explosion* and *Four Children Dead in Moss Tragedy.* Whilst after the Inquest proper had concluded they had headlines such as: *The Dangers of War Mementos* and *Dangers of War Relics.* Newspapers as far a field in Britain as the North Devon Journal, and abroad as the Australian and New Zealand ones reported upon this terrible event, and accounts of the Inquest which followed.

We can only guess at the physical and mental trauma that ensued for the survivors of this truly shocking and totally needless incident. The term, 'I don't know how they managed to go on', certainly springs readily to mind. The perpetrator John (Jack) Bagnall was not surprisingly medically discharged from military service very soon after this incident on 20 March 1916. He subsequently received the Victory, British, and 1914 Star, War Medals. What thoughts he had over the following years we can only imagine. He died in the March Quarter of 1943, in the Wrexham area, aged fifty-one. His mother Hannah Bagnall, the matriarch of the family had died in the June Quarter of 1939, aged sixty-seven.

9

The adept, brazen, 'Bogus Army Staff Captain' – Henry Alexander Chamberlain

This is the story of an adept brazen fraudster, conman, bigamist and bogus Army Staff Captain – namely, one Henry Alexander Chamberlain, born in about 1861, who hailed from the county of Suffolk. Chamberlain over the years used a plethora of aliases, including those of Henry Noel Cuthbert, Staff Captain Stewart and a couple of Scottish Earls!

In February 1914, Henry Alexander Chamberlain was appointed as Head Gamekeeper to the Llanbrynmair (then in Montgomeryshire, now Powys) Estate of the very wealthy landowner, Sir Watkin Williams Wynn. To obtain this position he tendered at his interview a glowing reference from a Major Faulkner who had apparently served in the British Army with Chamberlain. This reference was an especially glowing one because Chamberlain had written it himself, and Major Faulkner did not in fact exist. As Head Gamekeeper, Chamberlain received monies from shooting parties on the estate that were supposed to be passed on to Major Scott who held the tenant rights to the shooting on the estate. He was also given monies in order to pay the wages of several under-keepers on the estate. But instead, Chamberlain kept the monies for himself, and after pocketing three lots of money via bank cheques, he disappeared from the area. But Chamberlain did not go too far, for he soon resurfaced in Wrexham, North Wales, where he was now Army Staff Captain Stewart, and he wore the uniform, and had all the trappings of a British Army Officer of that rank. He stayed at a Wrexham Hotel for the well-heeled, the Wynnstay Hotel on York Street, Wrexham. Here he 'held court' as he made the acquaintance of a number of local well-to-do gentlemen, and some locally based army officers. Chamberlain posing as Staff Captain Stewart told one local businessman that he should not trouble himself about the War Office, which he said was composed of a lot of old fools and promptly gave this businessman a large order for materials for an army camp!

So successful was Chamberlain in his bogus Staff Captain persona that he became bolder and bolder. From somewhere, probably hired with the monies he had recently purloined, he produced a motor car which he said was his staff car, and he 'ordered' a genuine, locally based army private to drive him all the way to the army military camp near Rhyl, North Wales, which was Kinmel Park Military Training Camp. At this camp upon his arrival he carried out certain inspections, and according to a later military witness to the events: *'Staff Captain Stewart caused no little discomfiture amongst the junior officers at the camp by finding*

Kinmel Park Camp main entrance c. 1916

fault with just about everything and everybody on his camp inspection'. However, on his way back to Wrexham from Kinmel Park Camp, his 'staff car' collided with a tramway car and was too badly damaged to be driven. So, 'Staff Captain Stewart' firstly commandeered two lamps from the tramway car, and then ordered some soldiers who were passengers on the tramway car to guard his 'staff car' all night by standing by it, assuring them that he would make things right with their own officers.

'Staff Captain Stewart' then stayed in the nearby town of Rhyl for a couple of days, and even made good his promise 'to make things right' with the soldiers' officers, who had kept a guard on his damaged 'staff car'. This aroused the suspicion of the authorities, and together with some leads from Wrexham, the net was closing in on Chamberlain. Two days after the Kinmel Park Camp bogus inspection, whilst in the company of genuine army officers in the coastal town of Rhyl, 'Staff Captain Stewart' alias Henry Alexander Chamberlain was arrested by the military authorities, and subsequently handed over to the police. The game was now well and truly up for Chamberlain.

Now in police custody, Chamberlain's past and his more recent misdemeanours caught up with him in a big way. Chamberlain gave his age as forty-nine (he was actually fifty-four or approaching it), and was said to be of a good physique, quite well spoken, and was found to have over the years served a number of prison sentences, including one stretch of seven years that he had not long been released from. It was found that Chamberlain as soon as he had left prison after his 'last stretch inside' as it was put, had again begun hoodwinking civilians and army officers alike, falsely obtaining monies, food and hotel accommodation. Three English warrants for criminal offences were out for him, one from the county of Gloucester, one from the county of

Suffolk and one from the county of Devon. But it was the offences at Llanbrynmair that took precedence.

He firstly appeared at Machynlleth Magistrates Court on Thursday, 22 July 1915, charged with three criminal offences relating to his time as Head Gamekeeper at the Llanbrynmair Estate. One local newspaper remarked: '*He was dressed in civilian clothes, and being well set-up and smart of carriage, had the appearance of a flourishing gentleman farmer*'.

A number of witnesses were called to give evidence against Chamberlain including William Laycock, agent for Sir Watkin William Wynn's, Montgomeryshire estates and John Morris, Llanbrynmair; Llewelyn Morris, Nantsaeson, Mallwyd and William James, Dolwen, Llanerfyl, who were all under-keepers.

Superintendent W. R. Williams then gave evidence to the court that the accused Chamberlain had been arrested by the military authorities at Rhyl on 7 July 1915, who did so as they had found him to be masquerading as an army staff captain, under the name of Captain Stewart (some accounts spell it as Stuart).

Others then gave evidence to the court, including Major Richard Alexander Scott, who had interviewed Chamberlain for the Head Gamekeepers position, and unwittingly accepted the bogus reference, which enabled Chamberlain to obtain the position. The defendant did speak in the court, but refused to repudiate the offences put to him, under oath. Neither did he wish to call any witnesses himself.

The Magistrates finding there was indeed a prima facie case against Henry Alexander Chamberlain committed him for trial at the Assizes on the three charges, until when he would remain in police custody.

In late October 1915, Henry Alexander Chamberlain appeared at the Ruthin Assizes, where he was described by the prosecution as being an audacious fraudster, and it was stated that he had now admitted to all of the charges put to him, including a new one, that of bigamy. The prosecuting barrister was the Denbigh born, Mr Artemus Jones.

Before the Judge at Ruthin Assizes evidence was given by Superintendent W. R. Williams, the Deputy Chief Constable of Montgomeryshire, who had made extensive antecedent enquiries into the prisoner, Chamberlain. Whilst the Head Gamekeeper at the Llanbrynmair Estate, Chamberlain had fraudulently converted (the term used in those days) to his own use, three cheques in the sums of £34, £31 and £14, received by him and drawn by Major Scott, and Mr Laycock, under-agent for the estate. Chamberlain had gone to the bank and 'converted' them to be paid to him and received cash from the bank.

A new indictment for bigamy was added to the charges against him. Bigamy by Chamberlain, for whilst his lawful wife was still alive, and no form of divorce had taken place, he had on 18 June 1915, married Mary Rodgers of Liverpool. Evidence was produced that only weeks before this bigamous marriage, Chamberlain had seen his lawful wife, Lilian Chamberlain, who was living with their daughter.

A number of witnesses were then called to give evidence. Superintendent W. R. Williams then gave further details of Chamberlain's recent criminal exploits, and they must have made the jaws drop of many in the court at Ruthin. For before going to Llanbrynmair, Chamberlain had been in Manchester posing as an army officer. Here it was said: *'he had caused a highly respected Gentleman, a Magistrate and Alderman of the city, to be arrested after telling the authorities that he had seen the man in the company of a Spy'.*

Then Chamberlain had moved on to Ashton-under-Lyne, and told the Mayor of that town that he was the Aide-de-Camp (ADC) at Chester to Sir Henry Mackinnon, a very senior military figure, and that, 'he was well done to there', no doubt trying to impress the Mayor with his boastful lies. The Mayor became suspicious and wrote to the army headquarters at Chester, and they were now on the lookout for Chamberlain, but he had by then moved into Wales – Llanbrynmair.

Mr Owen Roberts defending gave on behalf of the prisoner several lame excuses as to why his client had embezzled the monies when at the Llanbrynmair Estate. Mr Owen Roberts even claimed that he had recently received a letter from Major Scott, despite Chamberlain having stolen the monies from him, offering employment to Chamberlain when he came out of prison!

This was most likely to be true, such is the way with conmen, liars and fantasists like Henry Alexander Chamberlain, who have a way of making many of their kind hearted victims actually feel sorry for them, though they themselves are heartless thieves.

His Lordship the Judge however, was not as magnanimous in his view of the prisoner Chamberlain, and stated his surprise that a man of Chamberlain's highly criminal antecedents should so easily have gained such a position as the Head Gamekeeper at a noted country estate. Though this opinion was a little modified when he discovered the prisoner had obtained the position using the false reference.

The Judge before passing sentence had this to say: '*You posed as an officer in the Army and you wrote what is the easiest thing to write – a recommendation of your own merits. You say in this reference of yourself, that you were so anxious to work that you had not had a holiday for a long while. For seven years you were in penal servitude and I am glad you did not consider that to be a holiday. You were entrusted with large sums of money which you misappropriated. You bolted and since then you have been carrying on a career of crime. You are just the sort of man you know, who might have honestly attempted to do something considering the physique which you tell us you have, in helping defend your country, instead of purloining from others.'*

The judge then passed the sentence upon Chamberlain of five years penal servitude, this being the punishment for all the various charges that had been laid against him, and all of which he had pleaded guilty to.

When Chamberlain came out of prison after this 'prison stretch' he would have been aged about fifty-nine. Would he then go straight or would he resume his longstanding criminal ways? For my research revealed that Henry Alexander Chamberlain's criminal record went way back to at least his early twenties. For on Monday, 4 July 1884, in the County of Suffolk he was convicted of larceny (theft) when he posed as John Fenton, this was after he had an earlier conviction for an 'indictable misdemeanour' at Bury St Edmunds. For this latest offence he received six calendar months imprisonment with hard labour.

Then on 9 April 1885, again having posed as John Fenton, he was convicted at Ipswich for 'simple larceny' for which offence he this time received a prison sentence of twelve calendar months with hard labour.

In October 1893, at the Hampshire Assizes held at Winchester, the then thirty-two year old Henry Alexander Chamberlain was convicted, as the local newspaper put it of being, *'The Daring Swindler'*. For in the county of Hampshire, including at Bournemouth, he had posed as the military man, Captain Hugh D'Arcy Commerell, also as the Earl of Elgin, and as the Earl of Airlie, in order to swindle numerous people out of monies. The court heard that Chamberlain, who strangely gave his address at this time as being The Grange, Kilkenny, Ireland, was in reality a laundryman, and sometime painter and decorator. Swindle being an old term for basically cheating and defrauding.

Did Henry Alexander Chamberlain carry on with his criminal ways into old age? The answer is yes, as in June of 1930, now aged sixty-nine, he came before a judge at the Hereford Assizes for a number of 'swindles', mainly for obtaining food and lodgings whilst posing as the Earl of Elgin, a Scottish Earl. The judge told him that he had '*a perfectly appalling criminal record*' and sentenced him to twelve months' imprisonment.

Henry Alexander Chamberlain died in Staffordshire, England, in 1941, aged eighty.

10

Brothers in Arms and in Death – The Skillicorn Brothers of Llanrwst

To lose one son in war must be terrible. To lose two must be shocking. But to lose three one can only think in terms of words like horrific and unimaginable. But that is what happened to one particular family in the First World War – the Skillicorn Family of Llanrwst, in the Conwy Valley, North Wales.

The Skillicorn family was a most patriotic one, albeit for Britain and its Allies, rather than just for Britain. For three of their sons, George, Douglas and Conway were killed in action fighting in the armed forces of three different nations – Britain, Canada and the United States. A fourth son fighting with the British Army managed to survive the First World War and return home to what must have been a devastated family.

This Skillicorn family story begins with Henry William Leece Skillicorn, known as Henry, who was born in 1857 at Onchan, Douglas, Isle of Man. By the late 1870's Henry had found his way to live and work in the North Wales market town of Llanrwst (then in Denbighshire), in the Conwy Valley. Henry Skillicorn in 1880 married a local girl, Jane Evans, and they took over the running of a long standing bakery business in Denbigh Street, Llanrwst. Together they had a total of twelve children, sadly three of whom had died aged 0, 0 and 8, by late 1911.

Though some of their children, particularly their daughters stayed with them in Llanrwst, some chose to go farther afield, and to forge out new lives for themselves.

Douglas Skillicorn chose to emigrate to Canada and Conway Skillicorn to the United States.

George Edward Skillicorn, born in 1895 at Llanrwst, was the second Skillicorn son to enlist after war had broken out, and he was the first to be killed. In civilian life he was a driver of horse drawn delivery vehicles in the Llanrwst area, and when he enlisted in the Army Service Corps (ASC), not surprisingly he was made an army driver, service number T.3/028759. Enlisting aged nineteen on 17 November 1914, and described as being five feet, ten inches tall, he received a railway warrant and a total of 1s 6d, which enabled him on 19 November 1914, to arrive at the Army Service Corps Depot at Woolwich, London. George Skillicorn received his military training in the South of England, and he arrived at Le Havre, France, on a troopship to join the British Expeditionary Force (the BEF) on 28 March 1915. In France he was placed as a driver and attached to 58th Vaughan's Rifles, a British Indian Army Frontier Force, part of the Bareilly Brigade, 7th Meerut Division. George Skillicorn was involved in the Battle of Hill 60, near Ypres in Flanders which took place between 17 April 1915 and 7 May 1915. On 8 July 1915, George Skillicorn was killed in action by shellfire, and his parents were promptly informed of this, their first son to be killed.

George Skillicorn's parents subsequently received another official notification, this time from the Army Service Corps Record Office, Woolwich Dockyard, London, confirming that he had been killed in action, and had been buried in the Military Cemetery, Vielle Chapelle, Row 'A', Grave 18. This letter concluded with the usual expressions of sympathy and regret for their loss. After the Armistice, the body of George Skillicorn was removed from the above named cemetery and grave, and reinterred in the Cabaret-

Rouge British Cemetery, Souchez, near Arras, France, Grave Reference XV11.E.18. A total of some 7,000 bodies of British servicemen were removed from over one hundred other cemeteries in the area and placed here. Over half of these, unlike George Skillicorn's body, are unidentified ones.

Douglas Skillicorn, born on 7 December 1888, at Llanrwst, emigrated to Canada sometime after early April of 1911, as he appears on the 1911 Census, residing in the family home at Llanrwst, assisting his father in the bakery business. In Canada he lived in the Winnipeg area, was unmarried, and in the occupation of driver, until on 23 September 1914 he enlisted for war service at Valcartier, near Quebec. The Valcartier Military Base Camp was the main Canadian base for the equipping and training of the hastily gathered together Canadian Expeditionary Force (the CEF). Douglas Skillicorn underwent his basic training and speedy equipping here at a time when the base was in its infancy, consisting of row upon row of bell tents as the sleeping quarters for the recruits. On his attestation papers marked Canadian Over-seas Expeditionary Force Douglas Skillicorn signed his name and stated that he was or had been a member of the 100th Winnipeg Grenadiers – a Canadian Militia Regiment. On the reverse of the form are some of his personal details. He was stated to be of fair complexion, grey eyes, fair hair and five feet, eight inches tall. His religious denomination was given as Wesleyan.

On 1 October 1914, Douglas Skillicorn embarked for Britain on a troopship with thousands of other Canadian volunteers, many of them like him of British birth or of British parentage. Arriving in Britain, Douglas and his fellow soldiers underwent further military training. Douglas Skillicorn, Private 21423, was placed with 4th Company,

8th Battalion (90th Winnipeg Rifles), the Canadian Expeditionary Force. On 13 February 1915, they disembarked in France with 8th Battalion being made up of men recruited in Brandon, Winnipeg, Manitoba, Kenora and Port Arthur, and fought as part of 2nd Infantry Brigade, 1st Canadian Division.

Douglas Skillicorn was soon to be killed in action on 24 April 1915 – a very significant date for the Canadian Expeditionary Force, and indeed for the country of Canada and its people. For this was the first action of the war by an 'untried and unknown' Canadian force. They were greatly tested but were not found wanting, though suffered heavy casualties.

The 1st Canadian Division of the Canadian Expeditionary Force had moved to the Ypres Salient, Flanders, in April 1915, and was to face its first real test during the defence of St Julien – The Battle of St Julien taking place between 22 April 1915 and 5 May 1915, one of the battles that make up what is called The Second Battle of Ypres.

If glamour, glory or chivalry had existed in the First World War until then, on 22 April 1915 in the area of St Julien, France, all traces of them died a choking, blood vomiting death, when the German Army unleashed its new weapon, firstly upon French troops – thousands of tons of chlorine poison gas. It caused the victims of this vile new weapon of war to tear at their own throats in an attempt to be able to breathe, causing many to vomit blood as they were drowning from inside – their lungs filling up with a foamy substance.

This very first use in the First World War of poison gas by the Germans was the brainchild of the talented German chemist, Fritz Haber, who offered his services to the German Army, and began experiments in the use of a chlorine gas for attacks upon enemy trenches. Fritz Haber is 'credited' with having been the 'father of the poison gas cloud'. His own wife, Clara Haber, opposed this 'barbaric perversion of his abilities' as she put it, and later committed suicide, apparently in a protest against his work. Clara Haber (nee Immerwahr), was herself a chemist, and the first woman in Germany to earn a PhD. She was also a pacifist and women's rights activist. On 2 May 1915, at the age of forty-four, she took her own life by shooting herself in the chest with her husband's military revolver, dying in the arms of her son.

The Germans had waited for the wind to be favourable, and then in front of their own trenches, facing towards the enemy, they set fire to a sulphur chloride chemical that then drifted towards the enemy lines of French and some Belgian soldiers. The greenish-yellow cloud of poisonous gas took the soldiers by surprise. Some began to collapse, others who could run did so, and who could blame them. Until 22 April 1915, the village of St Julien (today called Sint-Juliaan) had been to the rear of the 1st Canadian Division, but now it was the front line.

On the morning of 24 April 1915, the Germans again released poison gas, chlorine gas, towards the re-formed Canadian lines, west of St Julien. Learning to some extent from the poison gas attack of two days earlier, the Canadians were told to put water, or better still to urinate on handkerchiefs or cloths, and place them over their noses and mouths. This worked to some extent, but obviously made fighting off attacks more difficult. The Canadians tried to hold firm, but had to withdraw under sustained German attack. The Canadians, including Private Douglas Skillicorn, and his 2nd Engineers laid low to the ground in an effort to escape the pervasive cloud of drifting poison gas, and then they dug in. The gas cloud and the withdrawal of their

Canadian enemies, made it difficult for German observers to work out distances, and exact locations for their artillery to fire upon the new Canadian positions, for such a barrage to be then followed up by a full scale German infantry attack.

The German infantry had to advance without artillery support, and when they reached the trenches that the Canadians had earlier occupied, from about 100 yards further back the Canadians opened fire, cutting down many of the German attackers. It was not the cakewalk the Germans had envisaged after their second use of poison gas. The Canadians fought like tigers, beating off many attacks upon them and inflicting heavy casualties amongst the enemy. Though, in other sections along the British and Allies lines, things did not go as well.

But the Canadians had held the line gallantly in their first major battle of the war, despite the use of poison gas against them, and being outnumbered by their determined enemy. Their own casualties were high, and in this and a few following battles that the Canadians took part in, proved that their Canadian Army issue Ross Rifle MK III was not up to the task – being long and heavy, had a tendency to jam under rapid fire use, and performed poorly in wet and muddy conditions. It was soon abandoned and used only for training purposes. The Canadians choosing instead the British Army issue stalwart, the Lee-Enfield, bolt action, magazine fed, repeating rifle. In these early battles for the Canadians, other items of their equipment including webbing proved unsatisfactory, and they favoured British Army issue kit.

The body of Douglas Skillicorn was never recovered, and he is remembered on the Ypres (Menin Gate) Memorial, Belgium, Panels 24 to 30. Ypres, the French name for the city is now known by its Flemish name of Ieper and it is in the Province of West Flanders. But Douglas Skillicorn and the Canadian soldiers who died alongside him have their own fine memorial – The St Julien Memorial is the stunning Canadian War Memorial set in a commemorative park on the outskirts of the village of St Julien, Langemark, Belgium, beside the main road from Ieper (then Ypres) to Bruges. This memorial column designed by Frederick Chapman Clemesha, himself a Canadian soldier in the First World War who was wounded in action, solely commemorates the 'Canadian fallen' in The Second Battle of Ypres, which included the first two shocking German poison gas attacks of the First World War, on 22 April 1915 and on 24 April 1915. The Battle of Gravenstafel Ridge 22 April 1915 to 23 April 1915; and 24 April 1915, the first day of The Battle of St Julien (24 April 1915 to 5 May 1915).The latter battle being the one during which Douglas Skillicorn was Killed in Action.

The German Army deployed some 168 tons of chlorine gas contained in over 5,700 cylinders buried immediately in front of their own trenches, ready for deployment. In that 48 hours in April 1915, 6,035 Canadians, one in every three of them became casualties, with approximately 2,000 of them, a figure of one in nine, being killed.

The memorial to them at St Julien was unveiled on 8 July 1923, and is called 'The Brooding Soldier'. The plaque on the memorial has written upon it these words:-

THIS COLUMN MARKS THE BATTLEFIELD
WHERE 18,000 CANADIAN
ON THE BRITISH LEFT WITHSTOOD THE
FIRST GERMAN GAS ATTACKS
THE 22ND – 24TH OF APRIL 1915.
2,000 FELL AND LIE BURIED NEARBY.

The column constructed from a single shaft of granite is a most imposing 35 feet high, and can be seen from miles around. It rises from a low flagstone terrace to a beautifully

The Canadian 'Brooding Soldier' War Memorial

sculpted in stone, head and shoulders, with the head slightly bowed sentinel figure of a steel helmeted Canadian soldier. His hands resting on a rifle butt, with rifle pointing downwards – in a 'knightly sort of pose'. The posture being in allusion to the ceremonial military custom of the reversing of arms by military personnel at a military funeral. It is surrounded by no ordinary gardens, for here the tall cedar trees are neatly trimmed into the shape of artillery shells and the smaller cedars are trimmed outwards, frond like to appear as if exploding shells. Back in 1923, at the time of construction, soil was especially brought here from Canada to be used in the gardens – a fitting addition for those Canadians who quite literally 'fell on foreign soil'.

A replica of this quite stunning, column monument by Clemesha, was in 1926 incorporated into R. W. G. Heughan's designed cenotaph at Victoria Park, Regina, Saskatchewan, Canada.

Conway Skillicorn, born at Llanrwst, on 24 April 1890, emigrated to the United States, arriving on 12 September 1910 at Ellis Island, Upper New York Bay, New York – 'the gateway for millions of immigrants into the United States'. He went to live in Chicago, Illinois, and on 27 January 1916, aged twenty-five, Conway Skillicorn became a naturalised citizen of the United States – his place of residence then being 2251, Park Avenue, Chicago.

In May of 1917, with the United States no longer neutral but 'officially' on the side of Britain and its Allies, Conway Skillicorn joined the United States Army. At the time of his enlistment he was boarding at 1418, North Central Park Avenue, Chicago. He underwent his initial military training in the United States, and was placed with 2nd Regiment of Engineers, which was sent over to Europe as part of the American Expeditionary Force (the AEF).

On page five of the 17 July 1918 edition of the *Chicago Tribune* newspaper under the heading of 'More Stars in Heroes Flag' was a photograph of Conway Skillicorn in his U.S. Army uniform, and below it was written this:-

Private Conway Skillicorn, missing in action, came to Chicago eight years ago from Llanrwst, Wales, where his parents live. He was boarding at 1418, North Central Park Avenue when he enlisted in the regular army in May 1917. He has suffered much at the hands of the Hun. A brother in the Canadian army died at Ypres; another fell in the Marne drive with the British; and a third is with the British territorials seeking vengeance. Conway was with the Second Engineers.

Memorial at Llanrwst to the Skillicorn Brothers

On his arrival in France in the Spring of 1918, Private Conway Skillicorn as a member of 'B' Company helped construct the divisional headquarters in the hill East of Boucq; operated sawmills at Marbache and near to Commercy; assisted in the construction of the U.S. Army dump at Leonval, and repaired the road camouflage leading to the Front. Until as part of 'B' Company he was on 30 May 1918 called upon to march to the area of Chateau Thierry to act not as an engineer, but as an infantry soldier.

Private Conway Skillicorn of 'B' Company, 2nd Engineers was posted as missing after an attack upon the German lines during the 31 May 1918 to 16 July 1918, Chateau Thierry offensive. The 2nd Engineers was not a fully trained engineers regiment when it went into battle at Chateau Thierry, it was also grossly underequipped. During this period, the 2nd Engineers were as often used as infantry, as they were engineers.

It was during The Battle for Belleau Wood, that took place between 1 June 1918 and 26 June 1918, that Private Conway Skillicorn was Killed in Action, with his body never being recovered, though officially at the time he was posted as Missing in Action. In this Battle for Belleau Wood, it was the first battle that the American Expeditionary Force experienced heavy casualties in the war. The actions of its soldiers showed here that the United States was on the Western Front to fight, and to do so with dedication, determination and pride. They were attacked, they made attacks themselves, and they were regularly shelled by the Germans, including with poison gas.

Private Conway Skillicorn is proudly listed on the 'Roll of Honor (U.S. spelling) of the 2nd Regiment of Engineers' and his name appears in the fallen in the official history of 2nd Regiment of Engineers.

There is a fine, special monument at Belleau Wood, France, in Honour of 2nd Engineers who fell there, one of whom was of course Private Conway Skillicorn, born and bred in Llanrwst, North Wales.

The Belleau Wood Memorial Association, using the official records wrote this in June of 1927:-

May 30, 1918

After various experiences with French Units, the 2nd Division is ordered by General Foch to the Belleau Wood sector, and takes up its position in front of Lucy-le-Bocage on the evening of June 1st, covering a front extending six miles, from east to west. Division Headquarters were in the vicinity of Montreuil-aux-Lions. After continuous fighting for 21 days, and a final bombardment by French and American artillery from the west, when 33,000 shells of every calibre were thrown into the Wood, the enemy was driven out by the 4th Marine Brigade, comprising the 5th, and 6th Infantry Regiments, and the 2nd Engineers of the U.S. Army, on the 25th June. During these 21 days the 2nd Division lost 1,811 officers and men killed, and 7,252 wounded. After the 9th and 23rd Infantry Regiments had driven the Germans out of the village of Vaux, the Division is sent back of the line for a period of repose, but almost immediately is ordered to take position on the front line in the Soissons sector.

The father of the three fallen brothers, baker and confectioner, Henry William Leece Skillicorn, still of 44, Denbigh Street, Llanrwst, died at Llanrwst on 10 August 1921, at the age of sixty-three. His widow, Jane Skillicorn, mother of the three, died on 30 April 1940, aged eighty, also when still residing at the same Llanrwst address the family had lived at, and worked from, for so many years.

The three Skillicorn Brothers, George, Douglas and Conway are also remembered with their names upon the Llanrwst War Memorial, Denbigh Street, Llanrwst, and on a fine white marble tablet to be found inside St Grwst Church, Llanrwst.

11

Welsh Victims of the Sinking of the Lusitania

The many terrible 'incidents' of the First World War to directly touch the people of North Wales included the sinking of the RMS *Lusitania* – one of the perceived 'German atrocities of the war'. Recriminations over this sinking continue even today.

The RMS *Lusitania*, a British, Cunard Company, ocean going passenger liner, was on the afternoon of Friday, 7 May 1915, sunk as a result of a torpedo fired on her by the German U-Boat, the U-20, under the command of Kapitanleutnant Walther Schwieger.

It should be remembered that only three years earlier in 1912, the sinking of the 'unsinkable' *Titanic* had taken place – a shocking event. But that was an accidental catastrophe, whilst the sinking of the RMS *Lusitania* with the loss of 1,198 civilian lives (plus three suspected German spies in holding cells in the ship), many of them being women and children, was truly shocking. To many then and even today, it was nothing more than 'cold blooded murder'.

Among those 'lost' on the RMS *Lusitania* were a Welsh born couple and their two young children – a tragically poignant story amidst the horror and gore of the First World War. When one looks beyond the bare statistics for those who perished, instead considering them as individuals and as members of families, the viewing today of photographs, especially of some of the children who were lost, a number whose bodies were never recovered, is still a truly sad experience even a century later.

Depiction of Ailsa Georgina Booth-Jones on the deck of RMS Lusitania

Edward Booth-Jones was born in 1875, at Llandudno, North Wales, the second son of John Jones, farmer, grazier and butcher of Dinarth Hall, Rhos-on-Sea, and of Central Buildings, Llandudno. Edward Booth-Jones went into the antiques business and in 1902, at Newtown, then in Montgomeryshire, he married Millichamp Letton Percival, who was born in 1877, at Newtown. Millichamp was a daughter of London born, book keepers clerk, Henry Letton Percival, and his Liverpool born wife, Charlotte Amelia Percival (nee Jones).

In 1911, Edward, Millichamp and their two children, Ailsa Georgina and John Percival (known as Percival) resided at Old Cottage, Bowdon, Cheshire. Edward Booth-Jones described himself as being a dealer in antiquities and works of art in the furnishing industry. The family were wealthy enough to employ a domestic servant cook and a children's nurse.

This Booth-Jones family then resided for a time in London for Edward's business reasons, and in the autumn of 1914, the family sailed to New York for Edward to pursue further business opportunities. They decided to return home to Britain in order to attend the wedding a few weeks hence of one of Edward Booth-Jones' sisters. The Booth-Jones family boarded the RMS *Lusitania* at New York as Second Class Passengers. This luxury passenger liner was on her return trip to the port of Liverpool, England, and departed Pier 54 at New York, on Saturday, 1 May 1915. The RMS *Lusitania* was under the command of the highly experienced and well respected Captain William Thomas Turner.

During the voyage Ailsa was said to have enchanted a number of the other passengers, with her excelling in the sports and games organised on board ship for the entertainment and amusement of the children aboard.

At 2.10 p.m. (but 2.15 p.m. according to the later testimony of Captain Turner), on Friday, 7 May 1915, the German U-Boat, the U-20 fired one standard G6 torpedo, with a running depth of about ten feet which hit the RMS *Lusitania* on the starboard side, then moments later a second explosion occurred, causing the passenger liner to sink within a mere eighteen minutes. The exact cause of the second explosion remains even today an unsolved mystery, which has been much speculated upon over the ensuing years. The theories as to the cause of this second and catastrophic explosion include: an aluminium powder explosion; piles of 'contraband' ammunition on the liner had been hit, or coal dust having ignited. However recent surveys of the wreck of the RMS *Lusitania* and further studies, have put forward the strong argument that the second and catastrophic explosion was caused by a boiler explosion. The RMS *Lusitania* had twenty-five boilers, known as scotch or scotch marine boilers. It had initially only three funnels, but when more boilers were added to the ship in 1904, it had a fourth funnel added for exhaust. It had at the time of its sinking, twenty-three double ended boilers and two single ended boilers.

After the torpedo had struck the RMS *Lusitania*, and then the second explosion occurred, it suffered serious mechanical failure, and as a result continued forward at full speed, causing the ship to list even more. The RMS *Lusitania* went down eyewitnesses later stated, bow first, falling onto the starboard side. The location was some eleven miles off the Old Head of Kinsale (in Irish: An Seancheann), a headland near Cork, County Cork. This was the nearest land to where the RMS *Lusitania* sank.

As usual after such a terrible event at sea, confusion abounded as to who exactly had survived, whose bodies had been recovered, and who was missing presumed drowned.

Learning that a large number of the passengers had miraculously survived the sinking, an anxious close relative of the Booth-Jones', Edward Booth-Jones' brother, Griffith, had travelled to Ireland, and staying at the Imperial Hotel, Cork, decided to place this advertisement in the local newspaper the Cork Examiner: *Wanted, any information regarding a girl of eight years, light-golden hair, blue eyes, nice complexion, very pretty, named Ailsa Booth-Jones.*

Sadly however, Ailsa had not survived, and her body was recovered from the sea wearing a green velvet dress, lace-up boots and a blue jersey. The miniature mock-gold brooch, in the shape of the RMS *Lusitania* that she had won in a competition whilst on board ship, was still pinned to her jersey. This aided the recognition of her body, after the time it had spent in the sea had taken its toll upon it. Ailsa Georgina Booth-Jones was buried in a private grave in the Old Church Cemetery at Queenstown (now called Cobh), along with the body of her mother, Millichamp Booth-Jones, which was also recovered and was able to be identified. The bodies of the father, Edward Booth-Jones, and young son Percival, were never recovered. Cobh was known as Queenstown from 1850, until the late 1920's, when unsurprisingly it was changed from its English Royal name to an Irish one, after it had become the Irish Free State.

Reference is made to young Ailsa Georgina Booth-Jones during the *Lusitania*'s fateful voyage from New York, in the book, *Lusitania: An Epic Tragedy*, by Diana Preston:-

Avis Dolphin had taken another enjoyable walk with Professor Holbourn, who pointed out the coast of Ireland to her. Like many children on board, she understood why so many of the adults seemed anxious and preoccupied. One small boy had even got into the habit of adding to his nightly prayers an additional plea:

'Please God, do keep the nasty submarines away'. Holbourn reflected how a little girl of eight, Ailsa Booth-Jones had proudly shown him and Avis the four prizes she had won in the various sports and games organised for their amusement. They included a small, mock-gold brooch in the shape of the ship.

Avis Dolphin was Avis Gertrude Dolphin, a twelve year old British Citizen, from St Thomas, Ontario, Canada, who was travelling second class with two nurse guardians, Hilda Ellis and Sarah Smith, who were escorting her to school in England, and then for themselves to enjoy a holiday in England. Avis was placed in Lifeboat 17, launched by First Officer Arthur Rowland Jones of Prestatyn, North Wales. But as Lifeboat 17 was being lowered from the side of the sinking *Lusitania*, it overturned, spilling many of its occupants to their deaths, including Hilda Ellis and Sarah Smith, but miraculously Avis Gertrude Dolphin survived. Professor Holbourn was Professor John Bernard Holbourn, known as Ian, a British Citizen living in Edinburgh, Scotland. Aged forty-three, a mathematician, lecturer and teacher, he managed to scramble into Lifeboat 15, which was under the command of First Officer Arthur Rowland Jones, who emerged from the sinking as something of a hero. Professor 'Ian' Holbourn had befriended young Avis and her two nurse guardians, as Avis was constantly seasick and this kindly man would tell her adventure stories set in his native Scotland to try to take her mind of her malady.

It was no doubt the witness recollections of Professor 'Ian' Holbourn and Avis Gertrude Dolphin that had enabled the positive identification of the body of Ailsa Georgina Booth-Jones, with regard to her clothing, and especially that small, mock-gold brooch of the *Lusitania* that she had worn.

The *Denbighshire Free Press* of Saturday, 15 May 1915, had the story of the loss of the Booth-Jones family with Dinarth Hall being given as in Colwyn Bay, when it was actually in nearby Rhos-on-Sea. At Dinarth Hall, Messrs John Jones & Sons the title of the family business, ran a quite famous pony stud farm and sheep breeding farming enterprise:-

COLWYN BAY PASSENGERS LOST ON LUSITANIA

Among the passengers on the Lusitania and not reported among the saved were Mr and Mrs E. Booth-Jones and their two young children. Mr Booth-Jones was the second son of the late Mr John Jones, of Central Buildings, Llandudno, and Mrs Jones, Dinarth Hall, Colwyn Bay. The late Mr John Jones was well known in the Vale of Clwyd, as in other parts of Wales, for a quarter of a century one of the best known agriculturists and breeders in North Wales, and he was one of the men who built up the modern Llandudno.

Mr Booth-Jones was in business in Manchester for a number of years as a dealer in curios and antiques, but he sold the business some years ago, and six months since he went with his wife and family to the United States, in connection with some business interests. They returned in the ill fated ship, and have apparently been lost, the whole family perishing together. Much sympathy is felt for the bereaved mother, brothers and sisters of the late Mr Booth-Jones and with the other relatives of himself and his wife. Mr J. T. Jones, the eldest brother, and the present head of the Dinarth Hall Stud Farm, who is a member of the Llandudno Council and other authorities, has received many messages of condolence.

The *North Wales Chronicle* of Friday, 4 June 1915, had an

account of the harrowing time Griffith Jones, brother of Edward Booth-Jones, had in Queenstown (Cobh) in the aftermath of the *Lusitania*'s sinking:-

GENEROUS-HEARTED IRISH
LLANDUDNO MAN'S EXPERIENCE AFTER 'LUSITANIA' DISASTER
To the general public the tragedy of the sinking of the Cunard liner 'Lusitania' seems now little more than a bad dream when viewed as a part of the terrible conflict between the great European Powers, but to the relatives of passengers on the ill-fated liner, mention of the disaster brings a pang which only time can soften. Something of the terrible nature of the heartrending scenes witnessed on the Quayside at Queenstown Harbour during the awful days following the sinking of the liner was brought home to our representative in a brief interview with Mr Griffith Jones, of Dinarth Hall, who made the journey to Ireland to ascertain the fate of his brother, Mr E. Booth-Jones, and family. It was Mr Jones' melancholy duty to examine the bodies as they were brought ashore. His quest was partially successful, for, as already reported, he was only able to identify the bodies of Mrs E. Booth-Jones and her little daughter Ailsa, both of whom were buried privately in Queenstown Cemetery.

Mr Jones dwelt particularly on the kindness and courtesy of the officials of the Cunard Company and of the residents of Queenstown generally. He said the officials worked unceasingly night and day, and not only did everything in their power for the survivors, but assisted in every possible way for those who were involved in the gruesome task of identifying their dead relatives. Of the assistance rendered by the people of Queenstown, it was impossible to speak too highly.

They rendered assistance in the most unostentatious manner, and earned the sincere thanks of all who were so closely affected by the disaster. Mr Jones referred especially to the services of Mr Ruby Robinson, son of Mr Wm. Robinson of East Beach, Queenstown, who voluntarily joined the crew of the trawler, 'Flying Fish', engaged in the search for bodies. On one occasion he was out in the worst possible weather for three days and nights.

The 'Flying Fish' was actually an admiralty tug, an old side-wheeled paddle steamer, under the command of Captain Thomas Brierley. The 'Flying Fish' was instrumental in the rescuing of a large number of survivors of the RMS *Lusitania*, but also assisted in the grim task of recovering bodies from the sea. Of the 1,198 who 'officially' perished that fateful day, only 289 bodies were ever recovered. About 149 bodies that could not be identified were buried in three mass graves at the Old Church Cemetery, some two miles outside of Queenstown (Cobh). These three large graves for the unidentified had been dug the previous day by soldiers. Some bodies were found in searches made of the area where she sank, but many washed ashore over a period of days and weeks, especially in the Cobh area due to the tidal system. Some bodies though floated into Ballycotton Bay, Courtmacsherry Bay, and to Garretstown Strand. Eventually bodies were washed ashore as far west as Barry, South Wales, and as far to the east as the Arran Islands, off Galway.

The recovered corpses were bloated from their time in the sea, many mutilated beyond recognition by fish or birds as they floated in the sea for many days. Some of the identifiable bodies were quickly embalmed or the ones who were American citizens were sealed in lead caskets, for they were to be repatriated to the United States.

When rescued by the trawler *Bluebell*, after having being in the sea for between two and three hours after the sinking, Captain Turner stated that he had seen seagulls massing and diving on helpless people in the water, and were pecking their eyes out. He was lucky to have been seen by his rescuers who said that the gold braid on the arm of his captain's uniform had attracted their attention.

There was a rapid need for many coffins, and the local undertakers in Queenstown and Cork could not provide enough, so more were hurriedly brought in by train from Dublin and Kildare. For a time many of the coffins were laid out on the Cunard Wharf, on the quayside at Queenstown Harbour, in order for relatives to try to identify loved ones.

Many years later, the sculptor Jerome Connor designed a special memorial to the victims of the RMS *Lusitania*, with the stone carvings by Seamus Murphy. This striking, large, and rather imposing memorial called simply, 'The Lusitania Memorial' stands in the centre of Cobh. The memorial has the effigy of 'The Angel of Peace' and below to emphasise the fine assistance given by local fishermen in the rescue of the survivors and later the recovery of bodies – the figures of two fishermen.

Cobh, formerly Queenstown, has a fine museum, located overlooking Cork Harbour, much of which not surprisingly is devoted 'to the sea'. In its varied and interesting collections it has a photograph of Captain Thomas Brierley, Master of the 'Flying Fish', and two of his smoking pipes.

Captain William Thomas Turner, OBE, who had first gone to sea as an eight year old cabin boy in 1864, became something of a recluse, and was said to have been haunted by the sinking of his ship, the RMS *Lusitania*, with the loss of so many lives. He died of cancer on 23 June 1933, aged seventy-six. He was buried with a fine headstone placed upon his grave at Rake Lane Cemetery, Wallasey.

As for Kapitanleutnant Walther Schwieger, the commander of the U-20, well he did not survive the First World War. After having received four lower military decorations for being a 'U-Boat Ace', he was on 30 July 1917, decorated with Prussia's highest military award, the Pour le Merite, better known to us today as the 'Blue Max'. On 5 September 1917, now the commander of the large and powerful German U-Boat, the U-88, Kapitanleutnant Walther Schwieger, and his crew were being chased by the British Q-Ship, HMS Stonecrop. When off the West Frisian Island of Terschelling in the North Sea, the U-88 struck a British mine, and blew up with no survivors. The bodies of the Kapitanleutnant and his forty-two crew are entombed in the wreck at the bottom of the sea. After his torpedoing and sinking of the RMS *Lusitania*, Schwieger had been given the infamous nickname by the British – 'The Baby Killer'.

In August of 1915, Karl Goetz a German medal and medallion producer decided to design, privately make and distribute bronze 'Lusitania Medallions', which were a 'celebration' of the sinking of the RMS *Lusitania* and mocked the British, and foolishly also the then still 'neutral' United States, who had of course lost 124 (some record other figures, ranging between 120 and 132) of its citizens from the ship. But Karl Goetz made a serious error, for he mistakenly had the date of the sinking of the RMS *Lusitania* as 5 May 1915, instead of the correct 7 May 1915. As a result, the British seized upon this and made it a propaganda coup for them. For the British claimed that the date on the German Lusitania Medallions 'proved' that they had planned the sinking in advance and that it was a premeditated action. On the instructions of Captain Reginald Hall, RN, Director of British Naval Intelligence, some 300,000 British copies of the German version were issued. The British copies can easily be distinguished from the German originals due to a number of minor differences. The British copies were sold for one shilling each, came in a hinged cardboard box and the proceeds of sales went to the St Dunstan's Blinded Soldiers and Sailors Hostels, and to the Red Cross.

The original German Lusitania Medallions were never officially sanctioned and Karl Goetz came under pressure over his incorrect date of the sinking then produced a second issue showing the correct date. But it was too little and too late! By January 1917, the Bavarian War Office forbade the manufacture of this original German Lusitania Medallion and made attempts to confiscate and destroy ones already in circulation.

But this was not the first occasion on which the Germans had made such a faux-pas, for back in early September of 1914, they had been so supremely confident of reaching (conquering) Paris, that a German Commemorative

German postcard issued to 'celebrate' the sinking of RMS Lusitania by a German U-Boat

Medallion was struck to celebrate 'The Capture of Paris' (The German Troops into Paris). However, the medallions were quickly recalled or scrapped after the vast German Army hitherto appearing peerless, had been stopped in their tracks by the Allies at the First Battle of the Marne (fought 5 September 1914 to 12 September 1914).

German postcard makers issued a number of propaganda postcards that coldly celebrated the sinking of RMS *Lusitania*, with the vast loss of life – including of course many women and children. One such postcard has the ship depicted being struck by the torpedo, and a small photograph above it of the then Secretary of State for the German Imperial Navy, Grand Admiral Alfred von Tirpitz.

12

The Anti-German Riot at Rhyl, in May 1915

The sinking of the RMS *Lusitania* and the early Zeppelin Raids on parts of Britain greatly fermented the anti-German agitation in Britain, and this agitation was to seriously manifest itself in the North Wales Coastal town of Rhyl in late May of 1915.

It was on the evening of Friday, 21 May 1915, that a drunken man, or a man who was certainly acting in a peculiar manner, Arthur Robert Brougham, a piano tuner, lodging at Pier Cottage, Foryd, Rhyl, was on the Foryd Bridge on the outskirts of Rhyl. He was overheard by a local woman to be spouting anti-British and pro-German sentiments. As a result of this a number of local civilian men together with a group of locally billeted soldiers decided to seek out anyone in the Rhyl town centre area they believed to be of German nationality. They made their way to Queen Street, Rhyl, to outside number 35, Queen Street. This was the home and hairdressing premises of one Robert Fassy whom it transpired, though apparently not German born, had served in the German Army for twelve months some years earlier in order to comply with certain regulations relating to property owned by his mother on the German/Swiss frontier. On 14 February 1912, at the English Wesleyan Methodist Chapel, Rhyl, Robert Fassy, aged twenty-seven, giving his residence as 21, Bodfor Street, Rhyl, had married Edith Gunner, a twenty-seven year old spinster of Irvinedale, Elwy Street, Rhyl, whose family had a longstanding boot and shoemaking business in Rhyl. On the marriage certificate is written that Robert Fassy was a hairdresser by occupation, and that his father was Gustave Fassy, a hotel proprietor.

Robert Fassy claimed he was actually a Swiss subject having been born in Switzerland, of a German father and a Swiss mother, but not being a Naturalised British Citizen had been interned as an alien from 23 October 1914, until 25 October 1914, at the temporary German Prisoner of War and Internment Camp at Queensferry, North East Wales. However, he was released from there on a form of bail, due to sureties that had been provided by some Rhyl business people. Robert Fassy returned to his family and continued as a hairdresser quite undisturbed until the fateful evening of Friday, 21 May 1915. The couple by this date had two young children, Jean aged two years, born in 1913, and Donald aged only six weeks.

By about 9.15 p.m. on this Friday evening, a 'mob of men', many being soldiers from Kinmel Park Military Training Camp, together with some civilians, most of them the worse for drink found themselves outside number 35, Queen Street. A 'mob' needs a target for their ire and one had been selected, Robert Fassy and his family. Arthur Robert Brougham the instigator of all this had already been taken into custody at the local Rhyl Police Station, so he could not easily be got at. The 'mob of men', ostensibly led by the soldiers present, began smashing the plate glass front windows of the premises, which were double fronted. They then carried away all the items which became exposed in the windows. Amongst the items stolen were walking sticks, artificial wigs, hairbrushes, combs, tobacco pouches, cigarette cases, cigars and tobacco. It was said that there was a *feeling amongst the soldiers* (rioters) *present, that it would not be long before Kinmel Camp would be blown up*. The four members of the Fassy family were all inside the premises at this time and quite naturally were absolutely petrified by the events taking place. The police had to force their way through the assembled mob to enter the premises. They escorted the Fassy family out of their home and business premises, then away to the 'relative safety' of the local police station. The police officers were jostled and manhandled with much abuse and jeering being aimed at the Fassy family by the mob gathered outside, despite their having the two small children with them. The mob, who could by now fairly be described as rioters then followed, and tried to break into the police station in a concerted effort to get at the Fassy family. They were totally out of control, caused damage to the outside of the police station and were refusing to disperse. Brigadier General Dunn, Commanding at Kinmel Park Camp was informed of the serious situation by telephone and he promptly attended the scene. Outside the police station he spoke to the soldiers amongst the rioting mob and ordered them to fall-in, in nearby Bodfor Street. They were then marched to the promenade and to their billets. The official report of Police Superintendent Richard Davies stated that the police officers and special constables protecting the police station were roughly handled and assaulted by the soldiers. It was assessed that some £46 of damage had been caused to the Fassy's Hairdressing premises, and some £6 worth of damage to the Police Station, where five large panes of glass had been broken.

The knee-jerk reaction to this riot by the local police, together with the Chief Constable and local magistrates, was for the immediate curtailing of the licensing hours in the Rhyl area. The suggestion being that the public houses close at 6.00 p.m. each day, and to be closed on the whole of Sundays, commencing on 23 May 1915. These greatly reduced 'drinking hours' obviously did not go down well with the local publicans, or with the soldiers who openly refused to accept the measures. The soldiers were indeed soon to win 'their case' and the licensing hours remained as before the riot of Friday, 21 May 1915.

The Fassy's lives however changed dramatically from then on. No doubt in deep shock after their ordeal, and fearing for their future safety, they abandoned their home and business premises for good. After being smuggled out of Rhyl Police Station, the Fassy's spent the next two days at 6, Victoria Avenue, Rhyl, the home of Edith's brother, George William Gunner and his wife, Ellen, known as Nellie. On the following Monday, 24 May 1915, the Fassy's left Rhyl for Birmingham, to stay with other relatives. Robert Fassy was very soon to again find himself interned in Britain as an alien enemy.

Some time later, Robert Fassy, through his solicitors, Messrs Williams and Williams of Water Street, Rhyl, made a compensation claim for a total of £110 12s. 6d. This figure was for the damaged windows, the stolen items and for the subsequent boarding up of the premises, being a claim made for some reason as far as I can gather against the local county council. A great deal of correspondence took place in this matter until on 11 July 1917 the case came up at the Chester Summer Assizes before Mr Justice Sankey. His was a definite and I suggest rather harsh ruling that no compensation was to be paid to the Fassy's as a result of that horrific evening for them of 21 May 1915. Apparently the claim had not been made during the required time period. Justice Sankey was recorded in the press as stating the following: '*The man Fassy is a Swiss, German or whatever he is. But his wife is one of our own fellow countrymen*'. But no compensation was forthcoming from any source, and with Robert Fassy interned and the Fassy's having lost their home and business premises at 35, Queen Street, Rhyl, it was a terribly trying situation, not of their making.

The above account has been gleaned from a variety of sources, but the account below of the attack on the Fassy's hairdressing shop and the subsequent problems at the Rhyl

Police Station is one given in a report from the Deputy Chief Constable in Rhyl, to the Chief Constable in Mold. It is of course from the perspective of the police. Taken from the Flintshire Historical Society Journal – Volume 26 of 1973-74:

FLINTSHIRE CONSTABULARY
Deputy Chief Constable's Office,
Rhyl.
23rd May 1915.
Sir,
I beg to report that at 7.45 p.m. on Friday the 21st instant, a man named Arthur Robert Brougham, Piano Tuner, lodging at Pier Cottage, Foryd, Rhyl, and employed by Mr Wadsworth, Pianoforte Warehouse, Queen Street, Rhyl, was brought to the Police Station by a Military Picquet, No. 19891 Sergeant James Fielding, 15th (Service) Battalion, Welsh Regiment, Rhyl, being in charge. No. 19115 Private Thomas Howard Evans, 'B' Coy. 15th (Service) Battalion, Welsh Regiment, stated that Ada Rayner, Toll Bridge House, Foryd, Rhyl, informed him that Arthur Robert Brougham said, ' It will not be long before Kinmel Park Camp will be blown up'. The man Brougham was then proceeding in the direction of Rhyl. The Sergeant in charge of the Picquet followed him and questioned him respecting his nationality, and asked him for his name and address. He refused to answer, whereupon he was taken into custody by the Picquet as a suspected person. Brig-General R. H. Dunn, Commanding the 129th Infantry Brigade, Rhyl, was informed per telephone that the man Brougham had been brought to the Police Station by the Military Picquet. He ordered him to be detained and examined by a Doctor.

Dr A. Eyton Lloyd, JP, Rhyl, examined the prisoner. The Doctor certified that the prisoner was not insane, but peculiar.

A large crowd followed the prisoner when he was brought to the Police Station.

The crowd was composed chiefly of soldiers who remained opposite the Police Station until about 9.15 p.m., when they moved in the direction of Queen Street and raided a shop, No. 35 Queen Street, in the occupation of Robert Fassy (German), Alien Register Serial No. 37. The plate glass windows, which were double-fronted, were broken by the soldiers, who carried away all the articles which were exposed in the windows. The articles comprised chiefly of walking sticks, artificial wigs, hairbrushes, combs, tobacco pouches, cigarette cases, cigars, tobacco, etc., the amount of damage being estimated at about £ 45. Robert Fassy, together with his wife Edith, and two children age 2 years and 6 weeks respectively, were removed to the Police Station for their safety. The soldiers raided the Police Station and broke five large panes of glass in the windows, and damaged private property belonging to myself, also property belonging to Acting Sergeant Foulkes, comprising of window curtains, crockery, etc. The amount of damage is estimated at about £ 6. Several attempts were made by the soldiers to break into the Police Station through the windows, but they were prevented by the Police and Special Constables. All the Police and Special Constables on duty, from myself downwards, whilst protecting the Police Station, were roughly handled and assaulted by the soldiers. An armed guard in charge of officers arrived at the Police Station, but they were of no use, being powerless. Brig. General Dunn was informed per telephone, and he arrived at the Police Station about

10.30 p.m. He spoke to the soldiers and ordered them to fall-in in Bodfor Street, after which they were marched to the Promenade and subsequently to their billets. Robert Fassy and his wife and children proceeded to Victoria Avenue, Rhyl, the same night, to stay with relatives. They are leaving Rhyl for Birmingham tomorrow (Monday). Arthur Robert Brougham was detained at the Police Station until 5 p.m. on Saturday, 22nd instant, when he was served with an order from the Competent Military Authority (General Phillips), Colwyn Bay, informing him that he was not to reside in the following Counties, viz: Carnarvonshire, Denbighshire, Flintshire. He was released from custody and escorted to the Railway Station. He left Rhyl by the 5.30 p.m. train, and booked to London. On Saturday, the 22nd instant, the Magistrates at Rhyl held a Special Meeting at 4 p.m. at the Town Hall, Rhyl. Brig General Dunn was present. Owing to a large number of the soldiers who took part in the raid on the previous night being drunk at the time, I suggested to the Magistrates on the recommendation of the Chief Constable that the licensed houses at Rhyl be closed at 6 p.m. each day, and the whole of Sundays, commencing on the 22nd instant. Brig General Dunn approved of the recommendation.

The Magistrates made an order for the closing of all licensed houses at Rhyl from 6 p.m. each day and all day Sunday's, commencing from 22nd instant. The license holders were informed, and the houses were closed at 6 p.m. Shortly after the licensed houses were closed, a large number of soldiers assembled in front of the Police Station and threatened to use violence if the licensed houses were not opened. There were no Military Picquets or Military Police near at the time. Brig General Dunn was informed and he arrived about 7 p.m. and spoke to the soldiers, after which he proceeded to confer with the Magistrates' Clerk (F. J. Gamlin, Esq.) and S. Perks, Esq., JP. Brig-General Dunn arrived at the Police Station at 8 p.m. and announced that on the authority of the Magistrates and himself, the licensed houses would be opened at once until 9 o'clock.

Everything has gone on smoothly since.

I am, Sir,

J. Ivor Davies, Esq., Your obedient Servant,

Chief Constable, RICHARD DAVIES. Supt & D.C.C. MOLD.

This short account is from an unnamed Rhyl source, written just after the end of the First World War:-

Here in Queen Street, Rhyl, a German, Robert Fassy ran a Tobacconist and Barbers Shop. He had lived in the town for over ten years before the war. But that did not save him when the mob came to his shop one night in May 1915. Three or four Germans lived in Rhyl at this time – known ones.

Between 1851 and 1910, over four million people migrated from Germany. The vast majority of these made their way to America, but a considerable number came to Britain, particularly to the large towns and cities of England. In 1861, the Census of that year reveals that the German population in England was 28,644. But by the 1891 Census it had risen to 50,599, though it did fall back slightly over the next ten years. By the 1911 Census it was at its peak at 53,324 men, women and children. Many of the German born men being in such trades as the hotel trade, hairdressing and in the many German Bands (Music) that where so popular in Britain. Popular that is until the First World War began! A number of Germans had also come to

Wales to settle permanently or temporarily, especially in the coastal towns such as Rhyl and Llandudno, with their many hotels and being places popular with holidaymakers.

Arthur Robert Brougham the catalyst for this anti-German Riot in Rhyl was a most strange character, born in the London area in 1884, to London born parents, Edward C. Brougham, a printer's manager and his wife, Elizabeth C. Brougham. Arthur Robert Brougham resided for a number of years with his family in Kilburn, London, and later at 48, Mazenod Avenue, West Hampstead, London. As a pianoforte tuner he found his way to Rhyl, and 'perhaps' unwittingly was the catalyst for the events of that Friday evening, 21 May 1915.

After medical examination by local Rhyl GP, Dr Albert Eyton Lloyd, of 'Eytonhurst', East Parade, Rhyl, the doctor had this to say of Arthur Robert Brougham: *'the prisoner was not insane, but was peculiar'*. After his release from Police Custody in Rhyl, and his being sent away from the area, Brougham next reappeared on 9 June 1916, when he attested and six days later enlisted at the Central London Recruiting Department, Whitehall, London, joining 15th Battalion, the Northumberland Fusiliers. Two months later on 15 August 1916, he was discharged from military service 'permanently' under King's Regulations, on the grounds that he was not likely to have become an efficient soldier. This was almost certainly a big understatement as Brougham was a complete disaster as a soldier, as his Army Service Record clearly shows when undergoing his military training at Rugeley Camp. In the short period of his army service his offences included: 1) Not complying with an order. 2) Attempting to strike an NCO and 3) Threatening an NCO. His military character was described as 'Bad' and Lieutenant Dr S. R. H. Walker of the Royal Army Medical Corps who examined him prior to his being discharged wrote: '*His mental condition is not normal*'. Brougham I have found had been an inmate of the Middlesex County Lunatic Asylum (as it was so cruelly called in those times) from 19 April 1904 until 28 October 1905. He was also said to be prone to sudden fainting. The Army paid him off for the two months he had 'served' undergoing military training. Brougham had given his next of kin as an elder sister, Amy Florence Brougham of 48, Mazenod Avenue, this being the family home.

Arthur Robert Brougham of home address 67, Winchester Street, Salisbury, died on 16 August 1945, aged sixty-one whilst an in-patient at The Wiltshire County Asylum – Roundhay Hospital, near Devizes, Wiltshire. This asylum previously referred to as a lunatic asylum, was an imposing Victorian building built in 1851, which finally closed in 1995. His sister, Amy Florence Brougham born on 7 January 1883, never married and died in 1971, aged eighty-eight.

Research shows that Arthur Robert Brougham had at least one brother in the military during the First World War. He was a younger brother, Harold James Brougham, born in 1891, a dental mechanic by profession. Harold enlisted in the Royal Army Medical Corps on 20 August 1918, Service Number 155963, and did Home Service until the end of the First World War. Though between 22 October 1918 and 15 November 1918, he was hospitalized with influenza and was lucky, unlike so many others, to survive 'the Spanish Flu' epidemic as it was called. He remained in the Royal Army Medical Corps and was promoted to acting sergeant, when on 12 May 1919 he left the Cambridge Military Hospital, Aldershot, for duty in Egypt at the RAMC Base Depot, No. 3, Egyptian Stationary Hospital at Kantara. Harold was discharged or demobilised from military service on 16 May 1920. In 1924 he applied to be sent the Victory and British, War Medals, to which he was entitled.

13

Letters and postcards from the Front in the Welsh Language

This article from the *Flintshire Observer* of Thursday, 8 April 1915, was written concerning the 'difficulties' being experienced by Welsh Soldiers writing their letters and postcards home in the Welsh Language from overseas:-

WELSH-SPEAKING GERMANS

The Censor at the front is taking no chances. What he cannot read he will not pass, with the result that Welsh soldiers can neither send nor receive letters as usual, unless they and their people are coast or border folk well used to English.

It is of course, well within the bounds of possibility for German Headquarters to gain useful information through the medium of a letter in Welsh found on a prisoner of war (remarks a 'Manchester Guardian' correspondent). Plenty of German reservists who after years of familiarity have become acquainted with the language left Wales at the outbreak of war – was it not in a German trench at Neuve Chapelle that an Anglesey Sergeant of Engineers found a razor inscribed with the name of a Bangor hairdresser?

There are several German students of philology and university teachers also who are familiar at least with literary Welsh. In fact, quite a translation bureau might be set up formed of scholars like Dr Kuno Meyer and others who have spent their summers in Snowdonian Villages picking up the language, and who have 'kept it up' after their return to Germany by subscribing to Welsh weekly newspapers and magazines.

Disquiet was now slowly fermenting in parts of Wales in relation to the difficulties Welsh Soldiers were having in sending letters and postcards home to loved ones and friends in their native language – Welsh (Cymraeg). Attempts were made by the War Office and Army Council to refute that any such problems existed – but they did! This 'cause' was taken up by a number of 'bodies' in Wales and by several individuals.

The *Flintshire Observer* of Thursday, 6 May 1915, provided readers with the 'official Army Council' view on this most sensitive of matters, though 'on the ground' different practices were actually taking place:-

SOLDIERS' LETTERS IN WELSH

Complaints by Welshmen on active service that they were refused permission to write home in the Welsh language formed the subject of correspondence between Mr Huw T. Richards (Chairman of the Pontypridd Cymmrodorion Society) and the Army Council. He communicated a few days ago with Lord Kitchener, stating that his son, who is 'somewhere in France', wrote a postcard in Welsh, but was called before his regimental censor, and told to write in English, otherwise it could not be passed. He was further informed that Welsh was not allowed to be written, as they had no one who understood the language to censor it.

Mr Richards received the following reply from the War Office:-

'I am commanded by the Army Council to acknowledge the receipt of your letter of 22nd April, in which you state that you have heard from your son that in future he will not be permitted to send home any

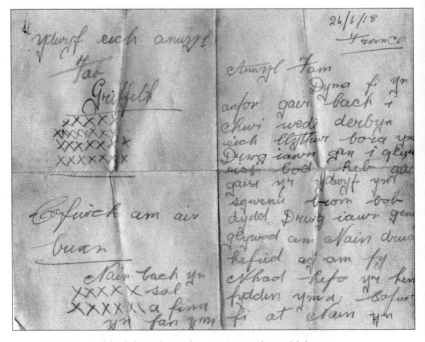

A soldier's letter home from France in the Welsh language

further letters or postcards in Welsh. I am to inform you that your son must be under a misapprehension in the matter, and that he is at liberty to conduct his correspondence in Welsh if he desires to do so. Sir Jesse Herbert, Secretary of the Parliamentary Recruiting Committee states that proper arrangements have been made for dealing with all such communications.'

The *Barry Dock News* of Friday, 28 May 1915, reported upon further developments with regard to this matter:-

WELSH SOLDIERS ON ACTIVE SERVICE
LETTERS FOR HOME IN THEIR OWN LANGUAGE
Following a resolution passed by the Barry

Cymmrodorion Society some time ago, and sent to the War Office on the instructions of the Union of Welsh Societies, the following reply has been received from the War Office:

'I am desired by the Army Council to inform you that they see no objection to the publication in the Welsh Press of a notice to the effect that letters from soldiers on active service may be written in the Welsh Language'.

This will be useful information for soldiers whose parents or friends are unable to read or speak English.

This sensitive matter was debated in the House of Commons and with David Lloyd George a fluent Welsh speaker so prominent in the Government at this time (not yet Prime Minister, but Minister of Munitions) and recruitment from Wales being high in relation to its population, 'the military authorities' were keen to handle the matter with kid gloves. The *Herald of Wales* of Saturday, 27 November 1915, had this:-

SOLDIERS' LETTERS IN WELSH
In the House of Commons on Monday, Mr Llewelyn Williams (R. Camarthen District) asked the Under-Secretary for War, whether soldiers at the front were allowed to write letters home in the Welsh Language; If so, whether these letters were censored by an official conversant with the Welsh Language; Whether he was aware that many letters written by soldiers at the front in Welsh had never reached their destination; And, whether, having regard to the response from Welsh-speaking Welshmen to the Country's call, he would expedite in every possible way the passage of Welsh letters to and from the front in France and Flanders, and the Gallipoli Peninsula.

Mr Tennant: I described the arrangements in force in reference to this matter in an answer I gave to the Hon. Member for Carnarvonshire South on October 28, and I may state that these arrangements were acknowledged in a cordial letter of thanks forwarded by the General Secretary on behalf of Undeb y Cymdeithasau Cymraeg. No complaints that letters written in Welsh do not reach their destinations have been received at the War Office since the arrangements mentioned were brought into force. I am, of course, aware of, and appreciate the response which Welshmen have made to the Country's call, and I think that every proper step has been taken in order to expedite the transmission of their correspondence.

This sensitive matter and its resolution rolled on into 1916, as reported in the *Herald of Wales* of 11 March 1916:-

WELSH SOLDIERS' LETTERS
The Carnarvon Town Council on Tuesday night resolved to address a complaint to the Prime Minister, Mr Lloyd George, and others, with reference to the attitude of Censors to Welsh Soldiers' letters, and to ask the Government to appoint Welsh Censors in connection with the Mediterranean Expeditionary Force, as has been done in France.

Mr Abbott, who moved the resolution, quoted from the letters of two men, who said the Censors had declined to accept their letters, and that it was afterwards put in divisional orders that letters must be written in English.

The *Herald of Wales*, Saturday, 27 May 1916, with a further response from the Under-Secretary for War, Mr Harold John 'Jack' Tennant:-

LETTERS IN WELSH

Mr Tennant told Mr Herbert Roberts on Tuesday that letters written in Welsh at the front are not exempt from censorship, but it was certainly not the case that there is a prohibition against letters written in Welsh.

Further Reading

1. Robert Graves, *Goodbye To All That* (London, revised edition 1957).

2. Major C. H. Dudley Ward, DSO, MC, *History Of The Welsh Guards* (1920).

3. Diana Preston, *Lusitania: An Epic Tragedy* (Walker & Company, 435, Hudson Street, New York, 2002).

4. C. P. Clayton, *The Hungry One*, edited by Michael Clayton (Gomer Press, Llandysul, 1978)

5. Suzie Grogan, *Shell Shocked Britain: The First World War's Legacy for Britain's Mental Health* (Pen & Sword Books Ltd, Barnsley, South Yorkshire, 2014).

6. John H. Morrow Jnr: *The Great War: An Imperial History* (Routledge, 2005)

7. David Castleton, *In The Mind's Eye: The Blinded Veterans of St Dunstan's* (Pen & Sword Books Ltd, Barnsley, Yorkshire, 2013)

8. Alan Llwyd, *Out Of The Fire Of Hell: Welsh Experience of the Great War 1914-1918 in prose and verse* (Gomer Press, Llandysul, Ceredigion, 2008)

9. Phil Carradice, *an illustrated introduction to The First World War* (Amberley Publishing, Stroud, Gloucestershire, 2014).

Acknowledgements

1. My sister-in-law and friend, Sarah Jones of Denbigh, a talented artist – for the sketch of Ailsa Georgina Booth-Jones depicted on the deck of RMS *Lusitania*.

2. Martin Pritchard from Porthmadog, who kindly works to preserve the local history of his area in photographic form – for the photographs of the Boston Lodge Munitions Factory workers.

3. Greater Manchester Police, Museum and Archives, 57A, Newton Street, Manchester, M1 1ET – for the photograph of the police group which includes Moses Idwal Valentine.

4. The War Graves Photographic Project (TWGPP) – for the photographs of the headstones on the graves of Llewelyn Jones-Bateman and Francis Jones-Bateman.

5. The Denbighshire Records Office/Archives, Ruthin Gaol, 46, Clwyd Street, Ruthin.

6. The Flintshire Records Office, The Old Rectory, Rectory Lane, Hawarden.

7. The National Library of Wales, Penglais Road, Aberystwyth, Ceredigion.

8. The Commonwealth War Graves Commission (the CWGC).

9. The Imperial War Museum.

And: To Myrddin ap Dafydd, for believing in me and the First World War related books, with a North Wales emphasis, that I write.

Other WW1 titles from
Gwasg Carreg Gwalch

The Story of Kinmel
Park Military Training
Camp 1914-1918

by Robert H. Griffiths

£8

'Arm to save your
Native Land!'
Army Recruiting in
North-west Wales
1914-1918

by Clive Hughes

£8.50

www.carreg-gwalch.com